Eighteen Woody Allen Films Analyzed

ALSO BY SANDER H. LEE

Woody Allen's Angst:
Philosophical Commentaries on His Serious Films
(McFarland, 1996)

Eighteen Woody Allen Films Analyzed

Anguish, God and Existentialism

by
Sander H. Lee

McFarland & Company, Inc., Publishers
Jefferson, North Carolina, and London

Library of Congress Cataloguing-in-Publication Data

Lee, Sander H.
    [Woody Allen's angst.]
    Eighteen Woody Allen films analyzed : anguish, God and
existentialism / Sander H. Lee.
       p.   cm.
    Abridged [and revised] ed. of: Woody Allen's angst.
    Includes bibliographical references and index.
    ISBN 0-7864-1319-0 (softcover : 50# alkaline paper) ∞
    1. Allen, Woody — Criticism and interpretation. I. Title: 18
Woody Allen films analyzed. II. Title.
PN1998.3.A45L44   2002
791.43'092 — dc21   2001008619

British Library cataloguing data are available

Manufactured in the United States of America

*McFarland & Company, Inc., Publishers
  Box 611, Jefferson, North Carolina 28640
    www.mcfarlandpub.com*

To my wife Wendy and my daughter Catherine.
Your support and encouragement made this book a reality.
I cherish you. Thanks for all the eggs!

ACKNOWLEDGMENTS

I wish to thank Keene State College for supporting me in countless ways during my work on this book. My thanks also to the following programs, institutions, and societies for their support of my work on this project: the American and International Societies for Value Inquiry, the Bergen Community College Philosophy Club, the Elderhostel program, the Keene Public Library, the Jasper and Marion Whiting Foundation, *The Journal of Value Inquiry*, the Mason Library of Keene State College, the New Hampshire Humanities Council, the Northern New England Philosophical Association, P. M. K. Publicists, the Society for the Philosophical Study of the Contemporary Visual Arts and its journal *Film and Philosophy*.

For their support, encouragement and suggestions, I am grateful to the following individuals and organizations: Woody Allen, Anne Ames, Suzy Berkowitz, Laura Castro, Jane Cullen, Debra Daigle, Leslee Dart, Kendall D'Andrade, Nona Feinberg, Robert Ginsberg, Joram Haber, Nancy Haggarty, Mike Haines, Marion Koltie-Levine, Paul Laliberté, Mike Lee, Tony Lee, Tom Magnell, Anne-Marie Mallon, Rita Miller, Mary Nichols, Nancy Pogel, Chris Pratt, Keith Regan, Mark Roche, Alan Rosenberg, Grace Smith, Sanford Smith, Jean Whitcomb, John Vitale, Maurice Yacowar, and all my students. Special thanks go to Joan Norcross for her help in creating the book's index.

I am grateful to Mike Lee, who created the art on the front cover.

Finally, thanks go again to my wife, Wendy, for her editing advice and for putting up with my *mishegoss* all these years.

TABLE OF CONTENTS

PREFACE TO THE PAPERBACK EDITION

Although Woody Allen's films differ dramatically in content and tone, there are recurring themes that permeate his work. These themes reappear again and again, yet each time they are handled somewhat differently. It's as though Allen has engaged in a decades-long debate with himself, an ongoing dialectic in which he presents all sides of the arguments concerning the most profound philosophical issues. This book is a systematic analysis of these themes as they appear in a representative selection of Allen's films including those that I consider to be his most influential.

The reader might wonder why I don't analyze all of Allen's films rather than a mere eighteen. The answer is that I already have. In 1997, in the hardback book *Woody Allen's Angst: Philosophical Commentaries on his Serious Films*, I presented detailed analyses of all thirty of Allen's films to that date, from *What's New Pussycat?* (1965) to *Mighty Aphrodite* (1995). Running to more than four hundred pages, that book examined Allen's films in exhaustive detail, often engaging in scene by scene analyses of Allen's most important films.

This book explores those same themes in a shorter format both in terms of the number of films examined and the degree of detail presented. It has two intended audiences: students in undergraduate courses and lay readers interested in Allen's films who do not desire to immerse themselves in the comprehensive approach of the hardback. As a textbook, this edition might be used in a variety of contexts, including film courses that take a more theoretical approach and philosophy courses that use film to illustrate their content. Although the philosophers discussed in this volume range from Plato and Aristotle to Buber and Sartre, the emphasis here, as in Allen's films, is on those philosophers usually associated with the movement known as existentialism.

I. What Is Existentialism?

Philosophers argue about everything, including labels like "existentialism." Existentialism is a name given to a philosophical movement that became popular in the decades following World War II. The philosopher most associated with this movement was the Frenchman Jean-Paul Sartre. While Sartre may not have coined the term, he was well known for his willingness to describe himself as an "existentialist."

In fact, in France and much of Europe, Sartre became as recognizable as a movie star or a sports hero. In the United States, the image of the gloomy existentialist, dressed all in black with a beard or goatee, drinking wine in a smoke-filled jazz club, became a cliché on TV and in films. This image also became associated in people's minds with the Beatniks of the 1950s.

For a classic example of this popular stereotype, take a look at the 1957 film *Funny Face*, in which a sophisticated Fred Astaire transforms Audrey Hepburn from an unhappy beat existentialist into a glamorous fashion model. This story was a variation on a theme found in an earlier film, the wonderful 1939 *Ninotchka*, in which a sophisticated Melvyn Douglas transforms Greta Garbo from a dour Communist functionary into a glamorous woman of the world. Indeed, for many, the popular images of the existentialist and the revolutionary Marxist blur together, partially because Sartre himself attempted to combine the two.

But Sartre's atheistic approach is not the only philosophy that has been labeled as "existential." In the wake of its postwar popularity, a number of commentators, such as Walter Kaufmann and William Barrett, made the argument that existentialism comprised a set of themes or concerns; and that, perhaps, a number of philosophers who wrote before Sartre, and had never even heard the word "existentialism," could accurately be described as important influences on its development. Two of the philosophers often named in this connection are the nineteenth century theorists Søren Kierkegaard and Friedrich Nietzsche.

In addition, in their books on existentialism, these same commentators also included twentieth-century philosophers who may have heard of existentialism but either did not actively associate themselves with the movement or actually denied that their philosophy should be identified with it at all. For example, both Martin Heidegger and Albert Camus were very well aware of Sartre's philosophy and publicly disassociated themselves from it. Yet, in Kaufmann and Barrett's books on existentialism, and in many of those which followed, both Heidegger and Camus are discussed extensively in the context of existentialism, even though Kaufmann, for one, is careful to acknowledge that neither philosopher considered himself to actually be an "existentialist."

Further, there are those philosophers of the twentieth century who were willing, or even eager, to accept the label of "existentialist" despite the fact that their philosophies would appear, on the face of them, to differ significantly from Sartre on important issues such as religious faith. In this group could be placed such contemporary religious philosophers as Martin Buber, Gabriel Marcel, Paul Tillich, and Joseph B. Soloveitchik.

So, given all this, what does it mean to say that someone is an existentialist? According to Walter Kaufmann, "The refusal to belong to any school of thought, the repudiation of the adequacy of any body of beliefs whatever, and especially of systems, and a marked dissatisfaction with traditional philosophy as superficial, academic, and remote from life — that is the heart of existentialism" (Kaufmann, 1975, p. 12). He also says, "The existentialist has taken up the passionate concern with questions that arise from life, the moral pathos, and the firm belief that, to be serious, a philosophy has to be lived" (Kaufmann, 1975, p. 51).

From this, existentialism sounds like no more than an attitude, a rebellious and passionate commitment to living, but one with no particular beliefs. Yet it must be more than just that or all rebellious and passionate people would be existentialists, a group which could arguably include both Socrates and Adolf Hitler! No one who knows anything about the movement would seriously consider either of those two to be members, however, so we need to know more about what makes someone an existentialist.

In his 1996 book *Existentialist Philosophy: An Introduction*, L. Nathan Oaklander points out that:

> Books on existentialism often stress certain themes that are shared by a variety of philosophers who are called "existentialists." One common theme is the emphasis on human freedom and the related Sartrean slogan that "existence precedes essence," meaning that we have no prepackaged essence or nature, but that what we are is what we choose to be. Another theme stressed by existentialists is the contingency of the world, the fact that the universe has no meaning and is absurd. A third is that there are no objective values [Oaklander, 1996, p. 7].

This helps, but it still doesn't make entirely clear what most existentialists agree on and what they are most likely to disagree about among themselves.

I believe that one of the best sources for clarifying these two issues lies in an analysis of the themes found in the films of Woody Allen.

But before beginning this analysis, I must stop to answer an obvious question: why should we take Woody Allen seriously? This is precisely the issue with which I begin the next chapter, the Introduction.

II. What About the Allen Films Not Covered in This Book?

One of the hardest parts of preparing this abridged and revised paperback edition of my book was deciding which films would be covered and which would not. In limiting the number of films covered, I'm sure I've left out films that some consider Allen's best (e.g., *Stardust Memories* or *Zelig*) while including films which others may never have heard of (e.g., *Another Woman* or "Oedipus Wrecks") or which some consider to be of little interest (e.g., *Husbands and Wives* or *Deconstructing Harry*). While I did consult with many people in making my choices, ultimately I decided which Allen films to include or exclude based on my estimation of each film's contribution to the philosophical dialectic which I claim exists throughout Allen's work.

For example, even though *Another Woman* did not receive much attention when it was released in 1988, I consider it to be one of Allen's finest serious films, better than *Interiors* or *September* yet representative of the tone found in both. As in this case, I have often chosen to pick one film to stand in for a number of similar films while making references to elements from those other films in the course of my discussion. So, in the chapter on *Deconstructing Harry,* I make frequent references to *Stardust Memories,* a film I argue it resembles in many ways, almost to the point of being a remake.

Of the films which have appeared since the publication of the hardback, I have chosen to include only *Deconstructing Harry* as the rest seem to me to be so derivative (e.g., *Everybody Says I Love You, Celebrity*) or light (e.g., *Small Time Crooks*), that the issues they raise are already discussed sufficiently in the discussions of the earlier films. One possible exception is *Sweet and Lowdown,* which I did strongly consider including; however, I ultimately decided its similarities to other films such as *Bullets Over Broadway* and *Deconstructing Harry* were strong enough to make its inclusion redundant. Why exclude any films one might ask? Why not simply expand the earlier hardback to include all the films that have appeared since *Mighty Aphrodite?* The answer to this question is primarily practical: A number of colleagues, including Maurice Yacowar (author of the wonderful *Loser Take All: The Comic Art of Woody Allen*), have asked me for a lower-cost paperback edition of the book that would be appropriate for use as a textbook in their courses. Once I started the process, however, I decided that this revision was very beneficial. I believe that the book has benefited from this tightening of the chapters by paring them to their most essential elements.

On the other hand, if you should become interested in exploring the longer versions of the chapters or if you wish to see the chapters that cover films not included in this edition, you could of course refer to the earlier hardback.

Sander Lee
Keene, New Hampshire
January, 2002

INTRODUCTION:
WHY STUDY WOODY ALLEN?

Why should we take Woody Allen seriously? To many, Allen is unquestionably better known for his highly publicized personal life and for his early work as a comedian than for his serious exploration of philosophical themes in later films such as *Crimes and Misdemeanors*, *Another Woman*, and *Husbands and Wives*. While Allen is generally conceded to be an influential master of the comic genre in which he began, many look with disfavor on his efforts at creating more serious films.

Yet, in this book, I will contend that Allen has developed into one of the most important of America's film artists. From a philosophical standpoint, Allen's films are of enormous import in that they are obsessed with issues of contemporary metaphysical concern. While I will explore a broad variety of such issues, for the purpose of this introduction these themes may be reduced to the following five:

(1) Philosophically, perhaps the greatest tension in Allen's work is based on the desire of many of his characters to ground their lives in a set of traditional ethical values for which they simultaneously and sadly acknowledge the lack of an ontological foundation. This tension could be called "the existential dilemma," as it plays a vital role in the work of a variety of so-called existential philosophers such as Kierkegaard, Nietzsche, Buber, Heidegger, and Sartre.

I will investigate the role which such existential themes explicitly play in Allen's films, and his rejection of other philosophical approaches— for example, those presented by the so-called analytic philosophers such as Bertrand Russell, who have argued that the primary role for philosophy in the twentieth century is to act as a servant to the sciences.

(2) A second tension in the body of Allen's work relates to the first.

7

There appears to be a dialectical opposition between what might be called his more optimistic films (e.g., *Manhattan, Hannah and Her Sisters, Another Woman*) and his more pessimistic films (e.g., *The Purple Rose of Cairo, Husbands and Wives, Deconstructing Harry*). While some may find this characterization too simplistic (it has been suggested to me that there should be a third category for "ambiguous films"), it certainly raises the question of whether Allen will ever be able to resolve the conflict in his films between despair and a hope based on some sort of faith. An examination of this question will lead to an examination of Allen's love-hate relationship with God in which his intellectual tendency towards atheism combats his spiritual yearning for some form of salvation. As one way of portraying Allen's inner religious struggles in the course of his career, I will use some of the ideas presented by Rabbi Joseph B. Soloveitchik in his lengthy essay, "The Lonely Man of Faith," which was written in March 1965 for the journal *Tradition*, but which has recently been republished in book form for the first time.

(3) Allen's films present us with penetrating insights into gender issues relating to romantic love, sexual desire and the ongoing changes in our cultural expectations of both men and women. Throughout these films, many relationships are presented as being of the "Pygmalion-Galatea" variety; i.e., relationships between a mentor and an apprentice which always end in the emotional suffocation of the apprentice and the abandonment of the mentor. I will explore the significance of Allen's repeated use of this motif and the possibilities for successful love relationships as they are presented in his films.

(4) Throughout Allen's career, he has frequently been accused of narcissism and the advocacy of moral relativism, when in fact he has been, and continues to be, one of film's most forceful advocates of the importance of an awareness of moral values in any meaningful life. Indeed, the one theme which permeates all of his films derives from his contention that contemporary American society is rapidly descending into barbarism precisely because of our societal failure to maintain our sense of individual moral responsibility.

Ethically speaking, he clearly believes that things were much better for his parents' generation, for whom there existed an acceptance of a common set of societal values. I will examine what responsibility Allen believes artists have for creating this situation and what, if anything, he believes they can do to revitalize this sense of community, especially given the current emphasis on "diversity" within American society.

(5) Allen's films also explore our society's interest in, and suspicion of, the use of the techniques of psychoanalysis for understanding human

awareness and behavior. I will investigate Allen's attitudes towards analysis, his perception of its relationship to other aspects of our culture such as religion and the media, and his conclusions concerning its strengths and limitations.

I. Allen as Philosopher

In his serious films as in his earlier comedic work, Allen demonstrates an understanding of the history of Western philosophy which is quite extraordinary for a man whose formal education ended at the age of nineteen when he was ejected from New York University. His early parodies of traditional philosophical concerns (as in his essays "My Philosophy" and "Mr. Big" from his 1971 book, *Getting Even*) show that, even then, Allen had read and thought about philosophy. In the first five films he directed, ending with *Love and Death*, Allen continued to comedically explore such concerns, including, in the last film, parodies of both Tolstoy's musings in *War and Peace* and Ingmar Bergman's obsessions with human mortality in *The Seventh Seal*.

Starting with *Annie Hall* (1977), Allen's first really serious film, elements of his own philosophy appear in ways that are no longer primarily comedic. Structured in the form of a long therapy session, this film begins and ends with Allen's persona, Alvy Singer, telling us jokes which are more serious than funny. In this film Allen perfects his technique of using humor to genuinely explore philosophical issues, as opposed to his earlier practice of exploiting traditional philosophical arguments in order to be humorous.

Allen's distinctive wit is the thread running through all the characters he has played. Allen's humor imposes an existential running commentary on all the events in his films, a commentary which proclaims his unique identity and his rebellion against the traditional behavior of others. Whether tearing up his driver's license as he explains to a policeman that he has always had a problem with authority (*Annie Hall*) or portraying his employer, a successful television producer, as a clone of Mussolini (*Crimes and Misdemeanors*), Allen uses humor to distance himself from others and proclaim his ultimate autonomy.

Yet Allen never suggests that humor can fulfill his characters' goals or even uncover the truth. Alvy Singer can only get Annie to return to New York in his fictional play, not in the reality of the film. Alvy's obsession with his own mortality, his condemnation of the lax moral values of Los Angeles, and his attempt to create meaning for his life through his destructive relationship with Annie, are all vital elements of the philosophical themes which will haunt Allen's work throughout the rest of his career. It is also in this film that Allen first makes reference to a specific text, in this case Ernest Becker's *The Denial of Death*, as a source for his concerns. Becker's book, a serious study of philosophical and psychological issues from the perspective of such thinkers as Søren Kierkegaard and Otto Rank, sets the parameters of the treatise on mortality which Allen presents in his film.

From this point on, Allen's films continue to explore these and other serious philosophical themes in ways that are quite explicit. These films are filled with clues and frequent specific references to thinkers and their work. For example, *A Midsummer Night's Sex Comedy* (1982) begins with a lecture given by a pompous philosopher, Professor Leopold Sturgis (José Ferrer), on the impossibility of knowledge in all areas of metaphysics, including ethics, religion, social theory, and aesthetics. For those familiar with the history of philosophy, Allen clearly intends Sturgis's views to mirror those of contemporary analytic thinkers such as Bertrand Russell, and Sturgis's eventual transformation into a being of pure spirit may be read as Allen's critique of such views.

Similarly, in *September* (1987), Jack Warden plays a physicist who shares his professional frustrations at discovering that the universe appears scientifically to be a meaningless place, governed by arbitrary rules which appear indifferent to human concerns and values. Allen shows us how such conclusions lead this character, and those who hold similar views in Allen's other films, to abandon all responsibility for moral action in their cynical search for hedonistic pleasure.

On the other hand, in *Another Woman* (1988), Allen's primary protagonist is a professional philosopher named Marion Post (Gena Rowlands), who is initially identified as a critic of the views of the existential theorist Martin Heidegger. Yet, as the film progresses, we watch her transformation from a repressed intellectual into a caring, authentic individual as she personally discovers the truth of Heidegger's insights and her own spiritual beauty as symbolized in the poetry of Rainer Maria Rilke.

Allen's pessimism is portrayed most powerfully in *Crimes and Misdemeanors* (1989), perhaps his best film to date, in which the main character, Judah Rosenthal (Martin Landau), comes to "see" that in a world devoid of a divine presence, all acts are permissible, even murder. The apparent philosophical despair of this film, in which the most moral individual, a rabbi, is shown gradually going blind, refers us to the writings of such thinkers as Kierkegaard, Nietzsche, and Buber.

Husbands and Wives (1992) presents a pessimistic view of romantic love and marriage which clearly mirrors that of Jean-Paul Sartre in his existential writings. Once again, Allen peppers his audience with clues and references to help us identify the theories he is using. In this case, the first clue comes at the film's beginning when we see Judy Roth (Mia Farrow) holding a book with Sartre's name emblazoned on its cover. Later, Jack (Sydney Pollack) mentions Simone de Beauvoir, Sartre's lifelong companion and collaborator. And, at two points in the film, there is discussion of the desire of Allen's character, Gabe Roth, to move to Paris, where he would like to live in a small apartment and spend his days writing at a table in a cafe — precisely the lifestyle traditionally associated with Sartre. These clues by themselves seem trivial, but given the similarities in the apparent conclusions reached by Allen and Sartre on the issues of love and marriage, there can be no serious doubt that Allen intended to make the connection explicit.

II. What Makes a Film Study Philosophical?

What does it mean to say that my analyses of Allen's films in this book are philosophical? How does this book differ from others on the subject of Allen and his work? For the purposes of my study of film, and in my role as an officer of a scholarly society dedicated to the philosophical study of the visual arts, I have reflected a great deal on these issues, both on my own and in rigorous debates with my colleagues in philosophy.

In my view, philosophical writing about film plays a distinct role within the general field of film studies. Clearly, some approaches to film studies, such as those emphasizing the technical, psychological, or historical aspects of the filmmaking process, have little or nothing to do with philosophy. On the other hand, it is equally obvious that theoretical or aesthetic approaches may raise general questions that also apply to the realm of philosophy. This is especially obvious when theorists make specific references to the work of undisputed philosophers or relate their discussion to a more general debate of traditionally philosophical issues. But what about projects, such as this one, which also engage in examinations of specific films in order to reveal the philosophic themes contained within them?

The philosophical interpretation of a film is not simply a matter of uncovering themes obviously contained within the text. In my view, some of the most valuable contributions to the philosophical study of film are made when an author presents an unusual interpretation which may initially appear unlikely, but which, upon further examination, is found to be a credible reading that furthers our understanding and appreciation of the film's complexities. In these cases, the author must argue for an interpretation using the standard tools of philosophical debate in any area. When such innovative interpretations are successful, as in the work of such theorists as Raymond Bellour and Stanley Cavell, they deepen our appreciation of the work while stimulating fruitful philosophical debate.

Thus I would argue that a film's ability to elicit a wide range of interpretations deepens its philosophical significance. Of course, there are films which make sense only when viewed from a single philosophical perspective. While such films may have aesthetic worth, other films which are more ambiguous in their philosophical content are of particular interest to philosophers because they encourage us to explore their themes creatively. Any author who succeeds in arguing for a specific philosophic interpretation of a film, using the material presented in the text of the film in a manner consistent with all aspects of that text, has, in my view, made an important philosophic contribution to the understanding of that film, even if his or her interpretation differs from others that are better established.

It is of course essential that any serious analysis of a film give an accurate account of its text. Technological advances of the past twenty-five years, such as videocassette and DVD players, allow a level of accuracy previously impossible in scholarly examinations of film. They also allow the reader of film studies to obtain and examine copies of the films under discussion, a practice I recommend. In the first version of this book, to assure scholarly accuracy, I engaged in a detailed scene-by-scene analysis of each of Allen's films. In rewriting, I have removed a great deal of this sort of detail in order to make the work less cumbersome. Throughout the book, I assume that the reader not only has seen the films in question but is willing to examine them again in a detailed way in order to better understand the philosophical claims of this study.

Another issue which came up in the writing of this book has to do with its organization. One editor suggested that I arrange the book by idea or concept rather than film-by-film. This would avoid giving readers the impression that "there are no qualitative distinctions to be made among the films." In other words, in a film-by-film format where each work merits a separate discussion, *Mighty Aphrodite* (for example) may wrongly appear to be "the artistic and intellectual equivalent" of *Crimes and Misdemeanors*. Also, so this argument goes, it is strange to have such great disparity in chapter lengths. After all, the chapter on *Manhattan* is more than twice the length of the chapter on *Deconstructing Harry*.

I am extremely grateful to this editor, and to all the other colleagues whose constructive criticisms of the earlier drafts of this book helped me immensely in completing this project. Yet, in the final analysis, I decided, for a variety of reasons, to retain the film-by-film approach. First, I believe each of Allen's serious films deserves to be viewed initially as a complete and independent work of art rather than merely as a small part of his overall aesthetic project. While I obviously agree that the meaning of each of Allen's films is enhanced by an understanding of its relationships to his other works, it seems to me that something of great value is lost if one merely skips from film to film to examine similar themes without also analyzing each film in its entirety.

Furthermore, I trust the reader to recognize that the arrangement of this book is not meant to imply that all of the films under discussion are equally valuable or thought-provoking. Indeed, by allowing the analyses of some films to grow much larger than those of others, I believe that I am making clear my views on the qualitative differences between these films.

III. Allen as "Auteur"?

In exploring the philosophical themes which pervade Allen's films, I will speak of Allen as the primary artist responsible for those themes. In doing so, I confess that I am relying somewhat on an approach to film interpretation usually referred to as the "auteur theory." Since this theory was first introduced in the French film journal *Cahiers du Cinéma* in the 1950s, many have attacked and rejected it. Perhaps the most famous American battle over this theory took place in the early 1960s between Andrew Sarris and Pauline Kael, two noted film critics.

In his "Notes on the Auteur Theory in 1962," Sarris discussed what he called the three circles of the theory. The first, according to Sarris,

> is the technical competence of the director as a criterion of value.... The second premise of the auteur theory is the distinguishable personality of the director as a criterion of value.... The third and ultimate premise of the auteur theory is concerned with interior meaning, the ultimate glory of the cinema as an art. Interior meaning is extrapolated from the tension between a director's personality and his material [1985, pp. 537–538].

Kael, in her 1963 article "Circles and Squares," vehemently attacked Sarris's interpretation of the theory in ways that are unquestionably justified; yet, rather than destroying the theory, this interchange deepened American critics' understanding of it by pointing out Sarris's misreading and allowing each critic to interpret the theory in a way that seemed appropriate. One could even make the case that Kael herself utilizes an interpretation of this theory. Thus, without going into all of the details of the dispute between Sarris and Kael and the many others who have followed them, I will now briefly explain how I am using the theory when I claim that Allen is one of the clearest examples of an American film auteur in this century.

François Truffaut, the noted French film director and film critic, is generally conceded to be the originator of the notion that the relationship between certain directors and their films should be regarded as equivalent to the relationship between other artists and their works. Truffaut's presentation of the theory subordinates the importance of the contributions of others involved in creating a film — for example, the screenwriter, the producer, the cast, the technical crew, and the film editor. Truffaut would acknowledge that the auteur theory does not apply to the works of directors whose films are strongly influenced by others involved in their production. Yet the auteur theory is convincing when applied to directors, such as Allen, who exert complete control over all facets of their films.

As Kael has pointed out, not all directors are auteurs, and films made by auteurs are not necessarily better than any other films. An auteur does not necessarily have any greater technical competence, nor need there be, as Sarris mistakenly states, any tension between the director's personality and the material. Many filmmakers who are not auteurs are more technically competent than many of those who are, and most auteurs are in no conflict with their material because they are the ones who have chosen or written that material. To say that a director is an auteur is to imply a control so complete that his or her films may reasonably be regarded as the works of a single artist. Not all auteurs are great filmmakers. Some never rise much above competence, and some use their complete control to churn out endless rubbish. To say that a film was or was not made by an auteur tells us nothing about the quality of the film in question. Some of the best films ever made — *Gone with the Wind*, *The Wizard of Oz*, or *Casablanca*, for example — were the work of many people, none of whom had anything like total control. There are other magnificent films, for example *Rebecca*, where control was split between two powerful individuals (in this case Selznick and Hitchcock) who were at odds with one another throughout the creative process, yet were able to create a masterpiece.

One advantage of the auteur theory is that it offers a structure within which a film may be critically analyzed and profitably discussed. Yet this approach has been seriously, and often successfully, criticized over the past three decades by a succession of important theorists, including semiotic structuralists, Marxists, Freudians, feminists, and deconstructionists. This is not the place to engage in the kind of detailed and careful analysis which these criticisms deserve. However, given the overall existential perspective of this book, and of its author, one obvious disagreement between these perspectives and my own bears consideration here.

A major theme of this book, and of Allen's films, is that although we are affected by our genetic makeup and environment, ultimately each of us is free to choose the fundamental meaning of his or her life; and, furthermore, each of us is responsible for the consequences of that choice. Thus while I accept many of the claims made by the theorists just mentioned (particularly those of the feminists), I reject any views which deterministically attempt to separate the creative activities of the artist from the ultimate meaning of his or her work. I acknowledge that the themes in an artist's work might be better understood if one engaged in a systematic examination of the artist's economic, cultural, and psychosexual history, but I do not attempt to engage in such an investigation in this book.

Obviously, not every film in which Allen has been involved has been the result of his work alone. Other important artists—Marshall Brickman, Diane Keaton, and Gordon Willis, for example—have made important contributions to the success of parts of his work. Yet it is clear in all of these films that the hand of Allen has been the determining factor of their overall worth. In addition, Allen has contributed to film projects on which he is not the sole auteur. While this fact must be kept in mind while analyzing such films as *What's New, Pussycat?* or *Play It Again, Sam*, it does not mean that these films may not be studied for interesting indications of the themes we find in later films which are solely Allen's own.

Although Allen does not produce his films, all of those which he has written and directed, starting with *Take the Money and Run*, have been produced by individuals who have unquestionably given Allen control over all their artistically interesting aspects. For each such film, he has either written or co-written the screenplay; chosen the cast, crews and locations; had the final say on all of the technical aspects of the filming process; done the final editing; and participated in the marketing and distribution process. On the American scene, in fact, very few individuals have ever had such complete control over their work as has Allen. (Alfred Hitchcock, in the latter half of his career, comes to mind as one of the few other examples.) Thus there can be no question that Allen qualifies as an auteur.

Once again, a film made by an auteur is not necessarily a good one, even if there is agreement that the auteur is a genuine artist. In my opinion, Allen's early comedies are minor films. We may study them to help ourselves understand the themes of his more serious films, but this does not raise them above the level of slapstick comedies such as those by Mel Brooks or Monty Python during the same period. For this reason, I discuss the early films together in the first chapter.

IV. Other Critical Works on Allen

This is by no means the first serious study of Allen's work. I am indebted to the many others who have gone before me, especially Maurice Yacowar in his groundbreaking *Loser Take All: The Comic Art of Woody Allen*. I have also been influenced by the insightful comments made in a number of other works, including those by Douglas Brode, Foster Hirsch, Diane Jacobs, and Nancy Pogel. This book differs from all other critical works in that it is the first, to my knowledge, to be written by a philosopher, and, thus, the first to place its primary emphasis on philosophical themes.

While Allen's films present many other worthy areas of interest, such as his directorial and technical approaches, I will not be discussing those here. I am sure there are others much better qualified to discuss those facets of his films.

There are instances where the insights of others have affected my thinking. Where I agree with those earlier insights, I have been careful to indicate their source. Where I disagree with an earlier interpretation, I cite that interpretation only if it seems to represent a view that is commonly held.

Finally, I wish to thank Woody Allen for his support of this book and for his answers to questions I sent him (see Appendix). This support does not imply, of course, that Allen agrees with everything I say. Indeed, there are various issues of interpretation on which I know that we disagree, and I have indicated such disagreements as they occur.

– 1 –

"A Thin Story to Hang the Comedy Sequences On": The Early Comedies

Between 1965 and 1976, Woody Allen transformed himself from a stand-up comedian into an accomplished screenwriter, actor, and director. While his early films are very entertaining, there can be no doubt that they were intended primarily to be comedies. Allen's own evaluation of his early work is revealed by his comment to Mel Gussow that he strove in these films "to have a thin story to hang the comedy sequences on" (Yacowar, 1991, p. 129). When philosophical issues are raised — and they are raised often — it is with the clear intention of provoking a laugh rather than an insight. Philosophical themes touched on in these films are inevitably dealt with more seriously in his later work. Thus this chapter briefly reviews Allen's work in a few of the most interesting of these films, with an eye towards exposing those elements which provide important clues to his later philosophical concerns.

I. *What's New, Pussycat?* (1965)

Woody Allen's work on the 1965 film *What's New, Pussycat?* is usually considered to be of importance only as his entrée into the world of filmmaking. At the time, his career had focused primarily on nightclub work and secondarily on comic writing. In 1964, Allen was appearing as a stand-up comic at a New York club called the Blue Angel when the producer Charles K. Feldman caught his act and hired him to write the screenplay and appear in the film (Hirsch, 1981, p. 29). Nancy Pogel states that "neither the critics nor Woody Allen considered *What's New, Pussycat?* an artistically important movie, but it was such a commercial success that Allen's managers, Joffe and Rollins, were able to launch Allen as a director, actor, and writer of his own films" (1987, p. 34).

In this first effort, despite Feldman's interference, Allen reveals a great deal concerning his reactions to the cultural changes taking place in the mid-sixties. This was a time when American culture was becoming much more open about sexuality, a time when such magazines as *Playboy*, with their celebration of male sexual fantasy were becoming popular. Traditional mores were challenged by the so-called sexual revolution and the emergence of the youth "counterculture," with its acceptance of hedonism as an overriding value.

While *What's New, Pussycat?* is unquestionably inferior to all of Allen's later serious films, it introduces many of the themes which pervade those films. In *Pussycat*, the roles of men and women in the search for romantic and sexual fulfillment are hopelessly confused. The film's characters present us with two mutually exclusive models for behavior: the search for sexual satisfaction (represented by Fritz, Renée, Phillipe, Rita, and Victor) and the search for romantic fulfillment through marriage (represented by Carole, Liz, Renée's husband, and Fritz's wife). No one gets what they want. The men believe that all they want from women is sex; yet when one of them, Michael, is magically able to attract women sexually, he finds (like Jack in *Husbands and Wives*) that he really wants the one woman able to resist that sexual attraction. Indeed, *Pussycat* is a vaudevillian version of the view of sex and love presented in many of Allen's films, culminating in the pessimistic vision of *Husbands and Wives*.

Michael's use of the deprecating term "pussycat" to refer to all women — a habit of the actor Warren Beatty, who was originally intended to play the part (Yacowar, 1991, p. 26) — dehumanizes women by trivializing each one's uniqueness as well as her nonerotic substance and value. Michael is interested in Liz's poetry only as part of his transparent attempt to get her into bed. He praises her "Ode to a Pacifist Junkie" as being "very sexy," when in fact, as Liz tells him, it is "a plea for better housing." Yacowar interprets the whole film as a plea for "better housing, either physical or psychological" (1991, p. 26). In his words, "Liz Bien's point is that the soul needs 'better housing' than the body, which is subject to vagrant needs and unsteady devotions. Nothing is really new, Pussycat. We have always been tormented by the opposing appeals of protective shelter and uninhibited freedom" (1991, pp. 34–35).

My primary disagreement with Yacowar's analysis of this film (and of Allen's contributions to the unwatchable 1967 follow-up film, *Casino*

Royale) stems from my contention that Allen's themes here represent not simply a timeless dichotomy but a new and, to Allen, frightening conflict, which burst upon the social scene of the sixties with the full blooming of the sexual revolution and the women's movement. Many of Allen's later films are equally obsessed with the problems of sexual identity and romantic fulfillment, which have their origins in these cultural changes.

II. *Take the Money and Run* (1969)

Allen's live-action directing debut tells the story of Virgil Starkwell, an incompetent criminal played by Allen himself with most of the characteristics of his "little man" persona. In this film Allen experiments for the first time with techniques that parody the documentary format. The story is narrated by Jackson Beck in a manner which lends a mock tone of seriousness and realism to the piece. Indeed, much of the film's humor derives from the paradoxes created by the use of formal conventions to convey absurd messages. Again and again, the tone of the soundtrack seems to be in direct contradiction with the visuals which accompany it.

Allen juxtaposes formal structures of behavior with inappropriate content in order to create many of the film's funniest scenes. For example, Virgil's first attempt at bank robbery is foiled when the bank tellers are unable to decipher his handwriting. Once they understand that he is robbing the bank, he is required to have his note initialed by a bank supervisor. This comedic juxtaposition is repeated throughout the film, including its final setup, when Virgil discovers that the victim of his armed holdup is a childhood friend. They reminisce over old times as Virgil periodically interrupts to demand his friend's watch and wallet. Just as he is about to depart, the friend remembers that he is a cop and arrests Virgil.

The film also parodies the documentary format in its frequent interviews with witnesses or experts who try to shed light on the events in Virgil's criminal career. These interviews are humorous in that their supposed insights inevitably fail to shed any light on Virgil's behavior. Periodically, Virgil's parents appear, wearing Groucho Marx glasses to hide their shame. As their appearances continue, their input deteriorates from a debate over Virgil's true nature into discussions of irrelevant issues (e.g., the father offers to show us his stamp collection), and finally into a marital quarrel which the father vows to continue once the interview is over.

Allen ridicules the supposed authority of psychiatry, this time in an interview in which a psychiatrist who once treated Virgil seems to attribute his problems to his decision to study cello in his youth. Like

Fritz in *Pussycat*, this psychiatrist is shown willfully violating his professional responsibilities. He allows himself to be interviewed while one of his patients is clearly visible on his couch, and he even makes derogatory comments concerning that patient's sexual problems.

By the film's end, the fictional documentary maker has become so disgusted with the quality of the information he is receiving from his subjects that he, too, acts unprofessionally, putting the label "cretin" in parentheses beneath the name of one particularly long-winded witness. He also frequently interrupts this witness to demand that he "get to the point."

By using these techniques, Allen suggests that reality is too complex and multi-layered to be portrayed accurately in any one documentary or scientific study. He will make this same point more seriously, and effectively, in later films such as *Zelig* and *Husbands and Wives*. The device of showing his audiences early scenes from the boyhood of his characters will reappear again and again in his films, perhaps most famously in *Annie Hall*.

Despite the fact that Allen's character is given a non–Jewish name, Virgil Starkwell, the film presents us with a number of clues suggesting that the character is really Jewish. Yacowar points out that Virgil's last name is probably meant to remind us of Charles Starkweather, a famous murderer of the 1950s (1991, p. 120). Yet, the only side effect of the experimental drug Virgil takes in prison is to turn him into an Orthodox rabbi, complete with appropriate beard and clothing, who sits in his cell explaining the meaning of the Passover seder before the shocked eyes of prison officials. Virgil's choice to see a psychiatrist named Julius Epstein, his obvious discomfort in a scene where he pretends to worship in a prison chapel in order to plan an escape, and the mysterious reference to his grandfather as being "of German extraction" likewise suggest that the film is hiding Virgil's true Jewish identity, and, perhaps, the real reason for the persecution he suffered growing up.

III. *Bananas* (1971)

Working again with Mickey Rose, his co-writer on the previous film, Allen presents us with another slapstick comedy in which he plays an incompetent product tester named Fielding Mellish who becomes the Castro-like leader of a revolutionary movement in a fictional Latin American country called San Marcos. Early scenes in the film reinforce Allen's distrust of technology as Fielding is overwhelmed by the product he is supposed to be testing, just as Virgil was unable to control the shirt-folding machine he encountered in prison.

Fielding, like Virgil, is a person with no self-confidence or personal convictions. He sees himself as an outsider, someone with nothing genuine to offer, and so he must always pretend to be something he is not (Yacowar, 1991, p. 129). Complaining about his job to fellow workers, he is asked what he might have become if he had not dropped out of college. He replies that he was in the Black Studies Department so by now he might have been black.

When he meets Nancy (Louise Lasser), a parody of a feminist political activist of the early seventies, he pretends to know all about yoga, Kierkegaard, and philosophy, but it is clear that he knows nothing of any of these subjects. Nancy is initially fooled, however, because even though she is a philosophy major at City College, she knows nothing about these subjects either. Throughout the film, characters who preach the importance of abstract concepts such as freedom, love, or patriotism are inevitably shown to be fools or hypocrites. Esposito (Jacobo Morales), the rebel leader who claims to be fighting for the independence of his people, embodies this hypocrisy when he reacts to the success of his movement by immediately denying all the principles for which he was fighting. Now that they are no longer in his interest, he jettisons his earlier views in exchange for the egotistical demands of a despot. In a sense, he, like Fielding, is an outsider who wishes to be accepted. Yet, once he becomes leader, his only goal is to turn others into outsiders.

None of the film's characters seem to have any clear sense of identity. Strangely, the inhabitants of the supposedly Spanish-speaking nation of San Marcos all speak English (albeit with a Spanish accent). When Fielding, as the new president of San Marcos, arrives in the United States for a visit, he is greeted by an official and an interpreter. When the interpreter simply repeats the conversation in English, we are led to think for a moment that perhaps Fielding's encounters in San Marcos were supposed to be taking place in Spanish, but Allen destroys this temporary illusion by having the interpreter chased away by white-coated men with a butterfly net.

Allen's exaggerated portrait of American society does convey the sense of hopelessness and confusion many felt as a result of the political and cultural changes which tore apart the country during the sixties. This confusion is further emphasized by a number of other clashes of style and content, such as a conservative-looking jury that passes around a joint, and a commercial on television in which a Catholic priest hawks "New Testament" cigarettes as he dispenses communion. At one point during the trial, a man bursts in, loudly confessing his guilt for some crime, only to realize that he's in the wrong courtroom ("Isn't this Epstein v. Epstein?").

Allen's most ingenious symbol of the identity crisis racking America during this period is a black woman with an afro (Dorthi Fox) who takes the stand only to reveal that she is really J. Edgar Hoover. Asked to explain her appearance, she responds, "I have many enemies, and I rarely go out unless I'm in disguise."

Bananas implies that in a world where every philosophical, political, and religious system has been found to be inadequate, all sense of identity will be lost, and the most important decisions will be made in a whimsical fashion on the basis of personal preference without recourse to either reason or memory. For example, despite the fact that Fielding is found guilty on all counts, the judge suspends his sentence on condition that Fielding not move into *his* neighborhood.

Now freed, Fielding asks Nancy to marry him, and, irrationally, she agrees to do so, despite her repeated acknowledgments throughout the film that she doesn't love him. Interestingly, throughout this scene, Nancy's face is obscured from our view. We never get the sense that any genuine discourse is taking place between the two supposed lovers. When Nancy asks Fielding what he means when he says that he loves her, Fielding responds, as he did when he was initially trying to impress her, with a stream of meaningless but profound-sounding gibberish similar to the nonsense Allen will present at even greater length in *Love and Death*. Nancy acknowledges the worthlessness of his response by changing the subject to ask a question he can actually answer: "Do you have any gum?"

The lack of true feeling in their relationship is reinforced in the film's last scene, in which the consummation of their wedding vows is shown on television as part of ABC's *Wide World of Sports*. The film began with Howard Cosell covering an assassination as though it were a sporting event. By having their lovemaking appear on TV, Allen implies that even the most intimate of activities is now fodder for the media as part of the ongoing public spectacle that has come to pass for history. Cosell covers this event as he would a boxing match, and after the bout (which Fielding wins by successfully "making it" despite a cut above his eye), the participants reveal the antagonism between the genders which, Allen will contend in his more serious films, has eliminated the possibility for authentic, long-term romantic relationships.

IV. *Play It Again, Sam* (1972)

In this 1972 filming of his stage play, Allen worked under the direction of Herbert Ross, although Allen adapted his play for the screen and appeared as the main character, Allan Felix. As his character's surname indicates (*felix* is a Latin word for "happy"), this is one of Allen's more upbeat projects. In fact, the character even has Woody Allen's original first name, spelled as it was when he was born Allan Stewart Konigsberg.

Allan Felix is a film critic going through a recent divorce from Nancy (Susan Anspach), paralleling his own life in the late 1960s when Allen was an aspiring filmmaker going through a divorce from his second wife, Louise Lasser (who played Nancy in *Bananas*). The play's connection to Allen's personal life is not our concern here, but the film's philosophical themes are of greater interest than any of Allen's work during his pre–*Annie Hall* period.

As Yacowar points out, the play was theater about film, while the movie is film about film. He asserts that "the film of the play assumes an additional element of self-reflection because a film about film is an experience different from that of a play about film, even if the text were the same" (1991, p. 57).

The film begins, without credits, in the midst of the final scene from *Casablanca*. Allen knows his audience will be familiar enough with the film to immediately recognize it and be able to enter into it yet again. We watch and listen as Rick (Humphrey Bogart) explains to Ilsa (Ingrid Bergman) why she must join him in heroic self-sacrifice for the good of all:

> I'm no good at being noble, but it doesn't take much to see that the problems of three little people don't amount to a hill of beans in this crazy world. Someday you'll understand that. Now, now, here's looking at you, kid!

As we watch, the borders of the screen contract, letting us know that we are not in the film, but watching it on a screen. Then the camera draws back to show the shadow of a person watching *Casablanca* with us. Finally, as the scene moves into the crucial dialogue, we cut to Allan Felix, watching the film with his mouth open, mesmerized by the action. The film's title, *Play It Again, Sam*, appears on the screen almost as though it were a cartoon balloon indicating speech coming from Allan's mouth. We watch Allan doing what many a man has done, identifying with Bogart even to the point of mimicking his trademark mouth movements.

When the lights go up, we are jerked back, with Allan, into the world of the movie theater. We see Allan sitting by himself in the middle of the theater as the other people in the audience yawn, stretch, rustle about, and begin to get up. Allan blows air out of his mouth in a gesture which indicates his reluctance to leave the world of fantasy.

The themes of appearance versus reality, self-deception versus authenticity, and watching versus doing are thus established for the rest of the film. Allan tells himself, and us, as he leaves the theater, "Who am I kidding? I'm not like that. I never was, I never will be. That's strictly the movies." We next see Allan lying in his bed beneath a huge poster from Bogart's *Across the Pacific* as he complains to himself about how depressed he is. A memory of Nancy tells him, "You like movies because you're one of life's great watchers. I'm not like that. I'm a doer. I want to live. I want to participate."

Allan holds himself up to impossible standards. He judges the success of his life by comparing himself to the lives of fantasy characters from the movies he loves. Like Binx Bolling, the protagonist in Walker Percy's memorable first novel, *The Moviegoer* (a novel which begins with a quote from Kierkegaard about despair), Allan wallows in a pool of existential anxiety and self-pity, making demands of life which can only be fulfilled in fantasy. In a reverie worthy of Allan Felix, Binx describes himself this way:

> Other people, so I have read, treasure memorable moments in their lives: the time one climbed the Parthenon at sunrise, the summer one met a lonely girl in Central Park and achieved with her a sweet and natural relationship, as they say in books. I too once met a girl in Central Park, but it is not much to remember. What I remember is the time John Wayne killed three men with a carbine as he was falling to the dusty street in *Stagecoach*, and the time the kitten found Orson Welles in the doorway in *The Third Man* [Percy, 1961, p. 14].

Allan gauges the meaning of his life by comparing himself to the unreachable Bogart persona epitomized in Bogart's signature role as Rick in *Casablanca*.

The use of *Casablanca* at the beginning of the film is a change from the play, which began with Allan watching the climactic scenes from *The Maltese Falcon* on television in his apartment. This change, made by Allen but possibly suggested by Ross, has two effects on the film. First, placing Allan in a movie theater emphasizes the fact that we are watching a film about film's effects on its audience. Second, though we may miss hearing Bogart himself remark that the falcon, like film, is "the stuff dreams are made of," the use of *Casablanca* draws our attention more directly not just to the influences of film, or the Bogart mystique of male heroism, but, more specifically, to the impact of *Casablanca* itself. *Casablanca*, after all, is often cited by critics and the public alike as their favorite film of all time.

Yet the *Casablanca* of the first few minutes of *Sam* is not the "real"

Casablanca. Film buffs in the audience will have noticed that the scene we watch with Allan is shortened and edited. Major bits of action and dialogue are left out. For example, we see no Major Strasser, nor do we hear the famous line, "Round up the usual suspects." What we are being shown, then, is the *myth* of the film *Casablanca*, not its reality.

This is further emphasized by the fact that our film's title, "Play It Again, Sam," is the most famous line ever *not* spoken in film. Despite the fact that the line is instantly recognizable, admirers of the film know that the closest Bogart ever comes to saying it is when he tells the character named Sam (Dooley Wilson), "You played it for her, you can play it for me. Play!"

One primary theme of Allen's film, therefore, has to do with whether such mythical paradigms are a help or a hindrance to us in the living of our lives. Ultimately, the film argues that success will always elude those who wear a mask, who assume a persona in order to impress others and satisfy imaginary needs. This is a theme which may also be found in the writings of such existential thinkers as Nietzsche, Heidegger, or Sartre.

Much of the film's humor comes from watching Allan attempt to act as he imagines the mythical Bogart persona would act in the situations he encounters. We know from the beginning, of course, that the Allen persona (the "little man") is incapable of truly acting like Bogart, so his perpetual romantic failures do not surprise us. Yet, by the film's end, Allan has managed to put himself into the shoes of Bogart sufficiently to replay for "real" the final scene from *Casablanca*. Thus, Allan's request to "play it again, Sam" in this film's opening credits is fulfilled by its conclusion.

Two questions arise, however. First, how has Allan managed to overcome his ineptness sufficiently to recreate the *Casablanca* scenario, and second, is there anything about the *Casablanca* scenario that makes it particularly susceptible to being recreated in life?

Upon reflection, one sees that *Casablanca* itself is filled with a kind of existential ambiguity. After all, Rick Blaine is not really a heroic figure until the film's end. He starts the film as the hard-boiled expatriate café owner who believes in nothing and only looks out for himself. In the film's first scenes, he ignores Peter Lorre's pleas for help, and then watches passively as Lorre's character is dragged out of the café by police. His justification of his inaction is stated simply: "I stick my neck out for nobody!"

Rick pretends not to care what happens to the people he meets or even to care if the Nazis invade his own country. In one famous exchange, his only response to a Nazi's suggestion that the Germans might soon occupy New York City is to warn the Nazi humorously of the dangers of entering certain sections of the city, a line Woody Allen himself might have used.

He maintains an attitude of cultivated indifference and witty amusement towards the suffering he sees all around him. From the Heideggerean perspective, he is a classic example of an inauthentic person, one who appears to hide the "care" (*sorge*) that is within each of us. Yet we find out very soon that Rick is the proverbial tough guy with a soft heart, who cannot resist helping innocent people in trouble — whether a young married couple desperately in need of money, or Victor Laslo himself, the husband of his beloved Ilsa, for whom he eventually risks everything he has, including his life. Rick is one of the first American film antiheroes, the paradigm of the film character who will dominate the film noir movement and its descendants, including Godard's famous homage in the 1959 film *Breathless*, with Jean-Paul Belmondo in the "Bogie" role.

The same is true for the French police chief, Louie (Claude Rains), who pretends to knuckle under to the Nazis while caring only for gambling and women. In fact, however, all of us know that when the chips are down, he will stand up and fight for what's right, and, of course, for his friendship with Rick. Others in the film engage in pretense as well. The Nazis and Louie initially pretend that Casablanca is a neutral city, yet everyone knows it is under Nazi rule. Major Strasser pretends to be civil to the Laslos even though he is barely able to keep his animosity from breaking through.

Most importantly, we learn that even during that purer, more innocent time in Paris, before the Nazis marched in, when Rick was a young man with few emotional defenses, Ilsa was already pretending. When she first met Rick, she pretended to be unmarried and emotionally available, yet we eventually learn that she was in mourning for Victor. Later, when she knows she must leave Rick to go to Victor's side, she lets Rick think she will meet him on the train. It is this last pretense which sets up all the drama in *Casablanca*, and whose ambiguity carries over into *Play It Again, Sam*. In a sense we never know what Ilsa's genuine feelings are, or what Victor and Rick really believe about those feelings. Clearly, Ilsa is playing false with either Victor or Rick (or possibly both). Initially, she tells neither about the other. She pretends to love each exclusively and fully. Rick only learns of Victor's existence in Casablanca and, amazingly, Victor only learns of Rick's existence there as well. Ilsa tells Rick in Casablanca that she never really knew what love was until she met him in Paris, that all she felt for Victor was affection and gratitude. Yet she allows Victor to believe, even in Casablanca, that she loves him exclusively, and that Rick was never important to her.

One cynical acquaintance once suggested to me, after seeing the film for the first time, that Ilsa was only playing an entertaining game. The film's true message, she maintained, is that love and heroic struggles are no more than pleasant little lies which we tell ourselves to fill our empty lives with some form of meaning, no matter how artificial. As if to confirm this interpretation, a cloudy haze of romantic fog envelops Rick and Louie as they walk off the airport tarmac into "the beginning of a beautiful friendship." This obscuring haze, which has been palpably present throughout the whole film, fully reveals itself as the characters walk into the mists of fantasy. Interestingly, Allan walks off into a similar fog at the end of *Sam*.

Thus, from *Sam*'s very beginning (*Casablanca*'s finale), the clouds of pretense are exceptionally heavy as the film exploits a cinematic environment which was already self-consciously mythological. The film's very title suggests that it will be a retelling of the story which has just ended in the film's opening credits. The differences between the two stories are more stylistic than substantive, with the comedic style of the contemporary Allen persona playfully emulating the equally exaggerated style of the now nostalgic Bogart persona.

Yet we are made subtly aware of the fact that if the Bogart persona, as represented by the spiritual Bogart (Jerry Lacy) who advises Allan, were actually present in the film's contemporary setting, he would be almost as comic as Allan himself. The film understands, even if Allan Felix initially does not, that the problem with adopting the Bogart persona is not just Allan's unsuitability for the role, but the inappropriateness of the persona itself in a social and political environment that differs dramatically from the beginning of World War II.

The success of the Bogart persona has always been a matter of style, not substance. At a number of points, most notably in the last scene, Allan himself remarks on Bogart's own shortness and ugliness. In *Casablanca*, the "Richard" with whom Ilsa falls in love in Paris is much more like the Allan who is so attractive to Linda than Rick's "tough guy" persona in Casablanca. The film acknowledges that the Bogart persona is a defensive covering that Rick wears like a scab to protect the more vulnerable "Richard" from the pain of emotional involvement. Rick's success at the end derives from the fact that by playing the hero and the martyr, he regains his self-respect, as well as the admiration of those around him. Thus, at the film's conclusion, he walks into the mist a more complete "Richard" who might be able to commit himself authentically the next time around. The ending of *Casablanca* leaves us with a pleasant sense of anticipation of the more genuine actions in which the new, more mature Richard will now be able to engage. *Casablanca*, therefore, is the tale of an immature man who chooses to grow up. *Sam* tells the same story in contemporary terms.

The trick for Allan Felix is to avoid Richard's mistake of responding to rejection (Ilsa's rejection of Richard in Paris, Nancy's rejection of Allan in San Francisco) by becoming inauthentic, someone other than himself, in order to "attract babes" and thereby avoid true emotional involvement. It is to Allan's credit that he is so feeble in his attempts to artificially appeal to women for whom he feels nothing. It is his authentic vulnerability which attracts Linda (and us) to him.

As all of this eventually dawns on Allan in the course of the film, his attitude towards the Bogart persona changes. At first, Allan respects Bogart and tries to emulate him in all things, even drinking bourbon (which he can't stand) and calling women "dames" (a term recognized as derogatory and very much out of step in the hip surroundings of San Francisco in the early seventies). Later, as Allan rebuilds his self-confidence by winning Linda's affection and respect, he is more critical of Bogart's advice, more willing to show the impracticality of the Bogart style.

Thus, at the film's end, when Allan worries about how to break off from Linda as he rushes to the airport in a cab, Bogart's solution is a melodramatic scene in which he disarms Linda and turns her over to waiting police. Allan also has fantasies about a similarly attired and armed Linda facing the real Allan in the airport. Allan has sufficiently grown in his own eyes, and Bogart has sufficiently shrunk, that Allan can play himself in his own fantasies.

After the recreation of the final scene of *Casablanca*, in which Allan himself is able to say Bogart's lines and really mean them, the Bogart persona is reduced to playing Louie's role of the faithful friend. Bogart acknowledges that Allan doesn't need him anymore as he has developed his own style, and the film ends with Bogart telling Allan, "Here's looking at you, kid!" It is only at this point that we realize that Bogart has been calling Allan "kid," the same affectionate nickname he had for Ilsa, throughout the entire film.

By his last scene with Linda, Allan has become so authentic, so honest, that he admits that the lines he's reciting come from *Casablanca*, and that he has waited his whole life to say them. By this time, it doesn't matter that Linda was planning to go with Dick anyway, just as it doesn't matter whether Ilsa really wanted to go with Rick or Victor, because the real point of both stories has to do with being true to oneself.

The play ends with Allan meeting his beautiful new upstairs neighbor who appears to be his perfect mate. She loves film and admires his writing. The suggestion that she is the fulfillment of his every fantasy of romantic love is enhanced by the fact that she is played by the same actress who earlier played his fantasy ideal of Sharon, the first date Linda arranged for him. By removing this artificially happy ending from the film, and allowing Allan to walk alone into the airport fog, Allen implies that even though Allan is now sufficiently mature to build a real relationship, that process is the stuff of a new and different story.

In analyzing this film so extensively, despite the fact that it was not directed by Allen, I am varying slightly my use of the auteur theory. In this case, Allen's contributions to the film (authorship of both the play and the screenplay, the use of his hand-picked cast, his own roles as main actor and, unquestionably, as chief advisor to the director), make him here the most important contributor to the aesthetic value of the film. Yet Herbert Ross's more experienced directorial guidance, and his obvious willingness to offer constructive collaborative criticism to Allen, make this film, in my view, Allen's finest and most important effort prior to *Annie Hall*, clearly outshining his entertaining but less serious work in his other early comedies.

V. *Sleeper* (1973)

Writing for the first time with Marshall Brickman, Allen in *Sleeper* takes us two hundred years into the future, plunging us into a totalitarian society based entirely on a celebration of hedonism and the avoidance of genuine commitment. In his previous films, Allen suggested that the hedonism and moral cowardice of his "little man" persona is rapidly becoming the accepted norm in contemporary society. *Sleeper* reinforces that contention by placing a typical Allen persona, the Jewish owner of a Greenwich Village health food store named Miles Monroe, into a society which distracts itself from its political oppression at the hands of a Great Leader by endlessly pursuing impersonal sensual gratification through drugs, sex, food, and popular culture.

The cryogenically preserved Miles is resuscitated by scientists allied with a political Underground seeking to overthrow the government and restore power to the people. The scientists hope to persuade Miles, who has no official identity, to travel to the Western Reserve, where he can help the movement to uncover the Aries Project supposedly aimed at destroying the rebels. However, when the scientists are captured by the government's inept security forces, Miles is able to escape by disguising himself as a robot, assigned to the shallow and politically uncommitted Luna (Diane Keaton).

When his deception is uncovered, Miles kidnaps Luna and forces her to lead him to the Western Reserve. Eventually, he is captured by the government and brainwashed into submission, while she is transformed into a revolutionary. The film ends with a restored Miles leading Luna in a successful operation to steal the nose of the dead Great Leader, which is being used in an attempt to clone a new tyrant.

The film's title suggests that all of the characters, and perhaps the audience members as well, are being lulled to sleep by the mindless pursuit of pleasure while avoiding the necessary commitments which give life its meaning (Yacowar, 1991, p. 152). Although the future society is presented as unconnected to our own (because it arose from the ashes of a war which destroyed many historical records), as the film progresses it becomes clear that Allen views this society as very much like the one we currently inhabit. Indeed, the attitudes and activities of normal inhabitants of the future, like Luna, prevision the parodies of the Los Angeles "lifestyle" as it will be so memorably presented in *Annie Hall* and other Allen films. Indeed, the party given by Luna at the film's beginning is remarkably similar in look and style to the one which will take place at Tony Lacy's house in *Annie Hall*, even down to the use of white clothing to represent the characters' acceptance of hedonism.

Allen's own character, however, is by no means exempt from criticism. For the first time in a film which he himself directs, Allen criticizes his "little man" character for his unwillingness to take life seriously. After all, it is Miles who is the "sleeper" of the title; he is the one who has consistently refused to commit himself to any principle which might require sacrifices contrary to his self-interest. This point is made abundantly clear when the scientists attempt to persuade Miles to risk his life for the restoration of moral values and political liberty. When Dr. Melik (Mary Gregory) asks Miles if he has "ever taken a serious political stand on anything," he responds, "Yeah, sure, for twenty-four hours once I refused to eat grapes." When pressed to join them he says, "You've got the wrong guy. I'm not the heroic type. Really, I was beaten up by Quakers."

Yet, in his attempts to persuade Luna to believe in his innocence and to understand the shallowness of her lifestyle based on its use of "the orb, the telescreen, and the orgasmitron," Miles discovers his own need to become more authentic. Thus, surprisingly, we hear Miles, the Allen persona, telling Luna that sex should not be merely mechanical but should be based on genuine emotion. In Luna's society one can satisfy physical needs by creating enormous fruits, instant orgasms, and immediate intoxication, but one does so at the expense of individual identity and true creativity. In the future society, everyone is reduced to a stereotype, and even the robots are programmed to act archetypically. In a gay household, the robot mimics the mannerisms of its owners, while the mechanical tailors to which Miles is sent for new clothes speak with Jewish accents. When

Miles is brainwashed by the government, part of the process involves his acting out the fantasy of winning a beauty pageant, for what could be better training for instilling the ability to conform to the expectations of others? Once he has been reprogrammed, he is given an apartment complete with a robotic dog that talks. His life has been entirely reduced to the artificial.

Yet one of the more hopeful aspects of the film is the suggestion that no government will ever be sufficiently efficient to succeed in draining the quirkiness from human life. Unlike the terrifyingly impersonal structures portrayed in such dystopias as Orwell's *1984* or Huxley's *Brave New World*, Allen's future government is run by incompetent clods whose success in using their own technology is no greater than Miles's own. At the film's end, the individual initiative of Luna and Miles overthrows the system entirely. Optimistically, the film tells us that as long as apparent losers like Miles and Luna can bring down totalitarian regimes, there is hope that the rest of us can rediscover our humanity.

VI. *Love and Death* (1975)

Moving from the future into the past, Allen here creates a hilarious parody of serious philosophical and literary works set in the world of Tolstoy's *War and Peace*. Allen plays Boris, a Russian, and this time definitely a Christian, who struggles with issues of mortality, love, duty, and violence against the backdrop of the Napoleonic Wars. Fueled by his love for his distant cousin Sonia (Diane Keaton), Boris becomes a hero, fights duels, has mystical visions, and eventually is executed for his part in a failed plot to assassinate the emperor.

While the tone throughout is comic, sometimes descending into slapstick, the average viewer may also be awed by the many references to serious philosophic issues and concerns. Throughout the film, the characters periodically enter into theoretical disputes littered with obscure jargon which often sounds genuine and serious. In fact, however, while Allen certainly demonstrates his familiarity with the fundamental issues explored by such thinkers as Kant, Hegel, Kierkegaard, Nietzsche, and others, the dialogues themselves are clearly intended to be no more than clever gibberish, vaguely reminiscent of important insights, but on their own completely unconvincing.

Thus Allen suggests here, as he will again in so many of his later films (e.g., *Manhattan*), that no amount of abstract intellectualizing will ever resolve the fundamental questions of human life, including (1) Is it possible to create a deeply satisfying romantic relationship with just one person? (2) Is there one set of absolutely true moral principles, or is ethics simply a matter of opinion? (3) Is there a God? and (4) What will happen to me when I die?

Using parodies of situations from classic literary and cinematic sources, Allen touches on all these issues without taking a stand on any of them. Indeed, despite his condemnation of the cowardice of his persona in *Sleeper*, Allen again plays a "little man" initially unwilling to take a stand on any issue or risk himself for any cause. Yet, by the film's end, Boris does take a risk. He chooses, without any of the empty debate which has characterized his earlier actions, to voluntarily return to the chamber in which he left an unconscious Napoleon. There, he finds in himself the resolve to pull the trigger and premeditatedly kill another human being in order to prevent the continuation of an oppressive war in which so many innocent people have already suffered.

No explanation is given for Boris's apparent change of heart. There are no high-sounding arguments or soul-searching insights. This decision is perhaps the first example in Allen's work of a character seriously choosing to make a moral commitment with real consequences. As the price of his selfless action, Boris is condemned to death.

In his cell awaiting execution, he is visited by his loony father, with whom he engages in banter highlighted by a dialogue in which each manages to include the name of a character, novel, or story created by Dostoyevsky. Later, as he sits alone in his cell, the shadow of an angel falls on the wall. He hears a voice telling him that his life will be spared by the emperor at the last second. This mystical revelation, the last of many he has experienced throughout the film, allows him to face the firing squad without fear the next morning.

However, it turns out that the angel lied, and we next see Boris accompanied by the white-clad figure of Death, who has appeared to him periodically throughout the film in a parody of Ingmar Bergman's black-clad figure in *The Seventh Seal* (1956). He appears outside the window of Sonia's room just in time to interrupt another Bergman parody, this time of the women in *Persona* (1966). Sonia asks him to describe what it is like to be dead, but all he can tell her is that it's worse than the chicken at a lousy restaurant.

In his concluding monologue, spoken directly to the audience, Boris shares his final reflections from beyond the grave on the philosophic issues raised in the film. Unfortunately, death seems to have done little to deepen his understanding. His insights at the end of his life are just as ludicrous and no more compelling than his earlier remarks. At the end, we see Boris comically dancing with Death as they move away from us. It is the last time Allen will ever leave his audience with so little of substance to reflect upon. Indicative of the fact that Allen had, during the making of this film, already decided to explore these same themes more seriously in his future work is the way in which he departs, speaking directly to the audience and actually telling us that we will never see this exclusively comic persona again: "Well, that's about it for me folks. Goodbye."

The next time we see him in a project of his own, he will again be speaking directly to us—not, however, in the role of the "little man," but as a character much closer to himself, Alvy Singer.

VII. *The Front* (1976)

In his last film work before *Annie Hall*, Allen agreed to play the role of Howard Prince in *The Front*, a condemnation of McCarthyism produced and directed by Martin Ritt with a script by Walter Bernstein. Howard, a sleazy version of Allen's "little man," makes his living as a cashier and bookie until he is approached by a group of blacklisted TV writers who ask him to act as their front. Allen does a good job in his first appearance as an actor in a primarily serious film. Although he maintains the usual stream of comedic observations which we associate with his persona, Ritt is successful in using him as a symbol of an everyman who eventually comes to realize that he must make a commitment to some set of moral standards or his life will be empty of meaning.

By this juncture in his career, Allen's persona was associated in audience's minds with the "outsider" who wants to become an "insider," a desire which Prince explicitly concedes (Yacowar, 1991, p. 40). Initially, Prince is happy to accept the praise and rewards that come from his supposed success as a TV scriptwriter. Like David Shayne in Allen's later *Bullets Over Broadway*, Prince could continue to reap the benefits which derive from his unearned status as a successful writer; instead, he eventually chooses authenticity over dishonesty, even though it means making sacrifices.

While Allen's participation in this project was limited to acting, it is clear that this experience strengthened his resolve to move in more serious directions. One indication of the film's impact on his work can be found in *Manhattan*, where Allen reverses the roles played by himself and actor Michael Murphy. In *The Front*, Murphy's character, Miller, tells Prince, "You always think there's a middle you can dance around in, Howard. I'm telling you, this time there's no middle." *Manhattan* casts Murphy as Yale, a man who betrays everyone important in his life. In that film's most dramatic scene, Allen's character, Isaac, will tell Yale, "You cheat a little bit on Emily and you play around the truth a little with me, and the next thing you know you're in front of a Senate committee and you're naming names, you're informing on your friends."

– 2 –

A THERAPEUTIC AUTOBIOGRAPHY: *Annie Hall* (1977)

Annie Hall was Allen's breakthrough film. It introduced, for the first time in a serious manner, many of the most important philosophical themes that would concern Allen throughout the next two decades. These themes include the following:

1) preoccupation with existential issues of freedom, responsibility, anguish, guilt, alienation and the role of the outsider; bad faith; and authenticity;
2) obsession with the oppressiveness of an awareness of our own mortality;
3) concern about issues relating to romantic love, sexual desire and changing cultural gender roles; and
4) interest in, and suspicion of, the techniques of Freudian psychoanalysis as a method for better understanding human thinking and behavior.

While many of the elements of the look and spirit of *Annie Hall* are present in Allen's earlier work, especially in *Play It Again, Sam*, it is in *Annie Hall* that it all comes together most satisfyingly. The organization of *Annie Hall* may be viewed as a series of therapy sessions with Alvy Singer (Woody Allen) as the patient and the audience as analysts. Like many psychotherapy patients, Alvy is always trying to put the best possible face on his actions in order to legitimize his choices. Our job in the audience is to act as good analysts and perceive, through the clues he has

35

left us, his true feelings. While Freud's theories would obviously apply to this analysis, Allen's own fascination with existential themes, and the specific reference to Ernest Becker's *The Denial of Death*, encourage us to augment Freud with these additional approaches.

It has now become legend that Allen's original title for the film was *Anhedonia*, defined by Webster's as the "lack of pleasure or of the capacity to experience it." Had this title remained, it clearly would have applied to Allen's character, Alvy Singer, not to the character played by Diane Keaton for whom the film was eventually named. What brought about Allen's decision to shift our attention from his own character and make Annie the film's central figure?

I. "Boy, If Life Were Only Like This!"

The film starts with white titles on a black background. While this form of opening credits has become one of the signatures of an Allen film, this was his first use of it, with its characteristic small type and with no music or sound. Earlier Allen films used the white titles on a black background — *Love and Death* and *Sleeper* — but in both cases, the titles were much larger, and lively music accompanied them. This opening to *Annie Hall* immediately focuses our attention by suggesting that we are about to witness something different, something more serious, than Allen has ever showed us before.

We next see Allen standing in front of a solid orange background, dressed in sports shirt and jacket. He immediately begins speaking directly to the camera:

> There's an old joke. Two elderly women are at a Catskills mountain resort and one of them says, "Boy! The food at this place is really terrible!" The other one says, "Yeah, I know. And such small portions!"
> Well, that's essentially how I feel about life: full of loneliness, and misery, and suffering, and unhappiness, and it's all over much too quickly!
> The other important joke for me is the one that's usually attributed to Groucho Marx but I think it appears originally in Freud's *Wit and Its Relation to the Unconscious*. And it goes like this, I'm paraphrasing. I would never want to belong to any club that would have someone like me for a member! That's the key joke of my adult life in terms of my relationships with women.

Allen goes on to tell us that he just turned forty and he is going through a "life crisis," although he is not worried about aging. After a brief routine on how he will probably get better with age (unless, of course he gets worse), Allen sighs and finally tells us that this self-examination is prompted by his breakup with Annie. Claiming that he is not a "depressive character" and that he was a "reasonably happy kid," he cuts to a scene from his childhood where this claim is immediately contradicted. A boy, obviously Allen's character as a child (he has red hair and the trademark glasses), is slouched on a sofa as his mother tells the doctor, "He's been depressed. All of a sudden, he can't do anything." We learn that the cause of his depression is the fact that the universe is expanding. He explains in a monotone to Dr. Flicker, "Well, the universe is everything, and if it's expanding then someday it will break apart and that will be the end of everything." His mother agitatedly replies, "What is that your business?" To the doctor, "He's stopped doing his homework!"

> CHILD: What's the point?
>
> MOTHER: What has the universe got to do with it? You're here in Brooklyn! Brooklyn is not expanding!
>
> FLICKER: (gesturing with lit cigarette in his hand) It won't be expanding for billions of years yet, Alvy. And we've got to enjoy ourselves while we're here, huh? huh? (laughs)

In this prologue, all of the film's main concerns (mortality, low self-esteem, romance, and existential anxiety) are laid out. At first, we may think the character speaking directly to us is Woody Allen himself—as the film's writer-director introducing the film, as other directors have done in the past (e.g., Hitchcock in the opening of his pseudo-documentary *The Wrong Man* in 1956). It is only when Allen mentions his breakup with Annie that we suspect he is in another character.

This is finally confirmed when the doctor calls the child Alvy, yet our identification of this character with the real Allen remains throughout the film and is stronger than in any of his previous films. The first name, Alvy, sounds like Allen, and the "y" on the end of the name fits with the "y" at the end of "Woody." Furthermore, Alvy Singer started as a gag writer for others until he built up the courage to perform his own material as a stand-up comic; now he has become a playwright and a popular television performer. All of this can be said as well of Woody Allen. (In fact, early in the film, we see a clip of Alvy as a guest on the Dick Cavett show which we could easily mistake for a genuine clip of Woody Allen.) When Alvy is recognized on the street while waiting for Annie in front of a movie theater, we cannot help thinking that his obvious discomfort reflects Allen's real feelings about fame, just as we may believe he is venting his real irritation with critics and fans in the later *Stardust Memories*.

This sense that art is imitating life is further confirmed if one knows that Allen and Keaton really were once involved romantically, and that Keaton's real name at birth was Diane Hall (Annie's first name may well be a tribute to a character in Jean-Paul Sartre's first existential novel, *Nausea*). Yet, according to Yacowar:

> Allen denies that the film is autobiographical, beyond the fact that "there have been a couple of true facts in nearly every movie I've done." His affair with Keaton was not like Alvy's with Annie; nor were their meeting and parting as depicted in the film [1991, p. 172].

This initial identification of the characters with actual people counteracts our expectation of just another funny movie. It contributes, along with many other elements, to the effort of persuading us that this film, though quite funny, is more "real" and deserves more serious attention than its predecessors.

Alvy clearly has problems with his self-esteem. Throughout the film, he swings back and forth between arrogant self-confidence and submissive self-hatred. Like many people who suffer from low self-esteem, Alvy often overcompensates by judging others as harshly as he judges himself. In such moods, Alvy is a proud man who does not suffer fools gladly.

We see an example of this in Alvy's impatience with the boorish Italian men who bother him in front of a movie theater, not because they know who Alvy is, but simply because he is famous, he's "somebody." Our first look at Annie occurs in this scene. We share Alvy's irritation with her for making him wait under this barrage of attention from cretins, but we are also aware that he is treating Annie in an obnoxious, even sexist manner, attributing her bad mood to menstruation and refusing to go into the movie two minutes late. Alvy concedes that he's "anal," and Annie responds, "That's a polite word for what you are."

The film they were supposed to see was Ingmar Bergman's *Face to Face*, which Leonard Maltin describes as a "drama about [a] woman psychiatrist who suffers [a] severe nervous breakdown. As harrowing as they come..." (1990, p. 337). Alvy insists they go once again to see Marcel Ophuls's *The Sorrow and the Pity*, which Annie describes as "a four-hour documentary about Nazis." We can now see that Alvy's childhood pessimism and depression have continued into adulthood. He's obsessed with exploring his despair over the apparent meaninglessness of life and, as we shall soon see, his terror of death. Both films mentioned describe the plight of very successful people (a psychiatrist in *Face to Face*, well-established citizens in Nazi-occupied France in *The Sorrow and the Pity*) who collapse under the weight of life's burdens. Alvy has already hinted at his fear of doing the same when he jokes earlier that he might end up as a drooling old man who wanders around spouting about socialism. Underneath Alvy's arrogance and self-assurance is a man overwhelmed by his fears, one who resents others' claims to intellectual insight, yet desires adulation for his own views.

This is driven home in the film's most famous scene, in which Alvy and Annie wait in line for *The Sorrow and the Pity* as a man behind them (Russell Horton) arrogantly instructs his date on the inadequacies of Fellini, Beckett, and television. With the man's pedantries as a backdrop, Annie and Alvy argue about her having slept late and missed her therapy session.

When Alvy interprets her actions as hostile gestures towards him, Annie correctly points out that he is only capable of viewing her problems and behavior in the context of himself. He has no respect for her as an independent person. (The film will soon show us that Alvy sees himself as the center of Annie's life, almost her creator.) Annie sarcastically tells Alvy that she knows he believes she is hostile to him because of "our sexual problems." When Alvy denies this, she changes her phrasing to "my sexual problems," demonstrating her resentment towards Alvy's claim that he is "normal" and, that, therefore, their problems must be her fault. As the man behind them continues to pontificate, it becomes clear that Alvy resents him because he embodies many of Alvy's own worst traits.

This man, who claims to teach at Columbia, spews an endless stream of insights onto his date (who never says a word). Like Alvy, he believes himself an intellectual and emotional mentor for his female companion. The scene's famous payoff comes as, in another fantasy sequence, Alvy directly addresses the audience looking for our confirmation of the man's obnoxiousness. When the man defends his knowledge of Marshall McLuhan (telling us that he teaches a course in "TV, Media, and Culture"), Alvy crushes him by bringing the real Marshall McLuhan from behind a lobby poster. Alvy smirks in satisfaction as McLuhan tells the professor, "You know nothing of my work, you mean my whole fallacy is wrong. How you ever got to teach a course in anything is totally amazing!" "Boy, if life were only like this!" Alvy joyfully exclaims to the audience.

What Alvy means is, "If only I ruled the world!" Those familiar with McLuhan cannot fail to notice that the professor's statements do in fact show some awareness of his theory. Further, McLuhan's condemnation of the man ("you mean my whole fallacy is wrong") is so oddly constructed, with its double negation, that it is virtually meaningless. The real McLuhan, we suspect, would never actually talk to anyone in such a derogatory, obfuscated way. This fantasy McLuhan is completely at Alvy's command; he acts and speaks as Alvy wishes. Thus we see that Alvy wants to be the focus not only of Annie's world, but of the entire world. Again and again, he uses the comic device of having strangers in the street comment on the events in his life, answering his questions and offering suggestions. Like the protagonist in the later "Oedipus Wrecks" sequence in *New York Stories*, Alvy imagines a world where everyone is interested in his private dilemmas, while, simultaneously, he neither knows nor cares about the lives of others. Alvy's anhedonia results from this self-obsessive *bad faith* (a Sartrean notion).

II. Sartrean Influences

Using the existential philosophy of Jean-Paul Sartre to interpret Alvy's behavior (and to define "bad faith"), we can come to a better understanding of Alvy's condition. Sartre describes the human condition, that of the *for-itself*, as one of emptiness and nihilation in the face of a world, an *in-itself*, which is both complete and meaningless. The for-itself has no essence and no being, which is why it is able to comprehend the in-itself. For Sartre, only "what is not" is able to understand "what is." It is through this nihilating capacity that the for-itself is able to distinguish itself from the in-itself. The for-itself always retains the possibility of negating the in-itself. While the in-itself is always complete in its existence, the for-itself is always incomplete due to its isolation and non-being.

Sartre concludes from this examination of negation that the for-itself is perpetually lacking and envious of the completeness of the in-itself. The for-itself exists without essence and with total possibility to accept or negate what appears to him as the in-itself. At the same time, however, because of the for-itself's lack of essence, each human being is also totally responsible for his or her acts. One does what one does because one has chosen to do so.

When a person comes to really understand and experience this total freedom and responsibility, as Alvy clearly has, he is filled with anguish. Anguish is the apprehension born of the realization that you must make choices—not to choose is a choice in itself—and that there is nothing to guarantee the validity of the values you choose. Values must be chosen without reference to any ultimate guideline, since we are unable to prove that such guidelines exist. Each person creates value by choosing to cherish those things which are seen as desirable. Each seeks to make himself complete or fulfilled in the sense that the in-itself is fulfilled. Thus each person completely creates an individual being by the way in which he constitutes his values.

Out of this anguish there often arises what Sartre calls *bad faith*. Bad faith occurs when a person lies to himself and thereby refuses to accept his freedom and the responsibility which goes with it. One common form of bad faith discussed by Sartre derives from our desire to become simultaneously conscious (that is, free) and complete. We want to control everything, especially the reactions of others to ourselves, while maintaining the fiction that they choose to be with us, and admire us, of their own free will. In acting as though this desire were realizable, and in punishing others, especially Annie, when they fail to participate in this fantasy, Alvy chooses to engage in self-deception. He clearly knows that his goal of being godlike is unattainable, yet he pretends to himself that his egocentric actions are somehow justifiable.

Elements of Alvy's paranoid bad faith litter the film. When we first see Alvy with his best friend, Rob, he is humorously accusing everyone he meets of anti–Semitism. He claims that a man muttered "Jew" under his breath after the completion of a mixed doubles tennis match. He also insists that a "guy" from NBC named Tom Christie (Dick's last name in *Play It Again, Sam* and a clear sign of his gentileness), when asked if he had eaten lunch, responded, "'No, Jew'? Not 'did you' but 'Jew'? Jew eat? Do you get it? Jew eat?" Rob sees Alvy's paranoia as one of the effects of living in Manhattan. The solution, in his view, is to move to California. This suggestion appalls Alvy, whose hatred of California, especially Los Angeles, becomes a major theme of the film. From Alvy's perspective, the possibility that living in New York accentuates one's sense of persecution and awareness of life's final futility is an important reason for remaining there. To move to Los Angeles would be to abandon both the best and worst elements of civilized human life. It would be a betrayal of the human obligation to deal "face to face" with one's deepest anxieties. For, despite the evidence that Alvy is ultimately in bad faith, there is also no doubt that Alvy, like Allan in *Play It Again, Sam*, has a deep sense of personal integrity and honor. He punishes himself, and those around him, out of this sense of duty. It is wrong, in his view, to enjoy life once one has recognized its fundamental horror.

The three major characters in this film are played by the same actors who appeared in *Play It Again, Sam*. In fact, *Annie Hall* is a reworking of the themes of *Sam* in the context of the self-confident Allan Felix of that film's ending. Once again, Tony Roberts plays his best friend, and through this friend Allen's character meets the Diane Keaton character, again initially presented as insecure and even more neurotic than Allen. Once more, their characters develop a Pygmalion-Galatea relationship in which Allen educates Keaton and helps her to become a more fulfilled person, until finally she chooses to leave Allen in favor of a return, of a sort, to Roberts by following his lead in moving to Los Angeles.

In this film, however, the relationship between the characters played by Keaton and Roberts is quite different. In *Sam*, they were married, which ostensibly presented the major obstacle to the Keaton-Allen romance. In *Annie Hall*, Annie and Rob are just friends; yet an obstacle does destroy the Keaton-Allen romance, and that obstacle is again thematically identified with Roberts's character. This character is named "Rob," a name which again suggests close identification between a character and the actor playing him.

Rob tells Alvy that he wants to move west — "California, Max, we get the hell out of this crazy city and move to sunny L.A. All of show business is out there, Max." In this film, as in other Allen movies (e.g., *Manhattan*), the city of New York is itself a character. For Allen, it is the only place where life may be faced honestly.

In this conversation, we hear Rob call Alvy "Max" for the first time. Alvy tells Rob not to call him that, but Rob responds, "Why not? It's a good name for you." Alvy retaliates by calling Rob "Max" as well, but we know it's really Rob's name for Alvy. Why is Max a good name for Alvy? Well, knowing Allen's universe of allusions, the name is suspiciously reminiscent of the famous Swedish actor Max von Sydow, who played the morose, anguished protagonist in so many of the films of Ingmar Bergman. Later, in *Hannah and Her Sisters*, Allen will actually use von Sydow himself to play a role very much like Alvy.

Returning to Alvy's exclamation in the theater lobby — "Boy, if life were only like this!" — the film responds by cutting to a clip from *The Sorrow and the Pity* in which the narrator describes the way life is more likely to be: "June 14, 1940. The German army occupies Paris. All over the country, people are desperate for every available scrap of wood." Not only are we not able to magically win every argument, but at any time, through no fault of our own, we may find our nation occupied by an evil enemy and ourselves struggling to survive. The real human condition is a bitter disappointment to an Alvy who dreams of godlike powers; nevertheless, like the women at the Catskills resort, no matter how bad things get, Alvy wants life to go on forever.

Alvy believes that Annie's appearance is primarily determined, not by any of her own characteristics, but instead by the qualities of the man who accompanies her. We enter Annie's memories of her earlier boyfriends, including a hippie artist of whom Alvy is obviously jealous. As in his fantasy of Nancy's biker boyfriend in *Sam*, Annie's flame is a tall, blond, hip-looking actor named Jerry (John Glover). Alvy and Annie visit a memory of a party where they watch Jerry come on to a very insecure Annie. With his usual condescension, Alvy exclaims, "Look at you, you're such a clown!" Annie responds, "I look pretty!" to which Alvy says, "Yeah, but look at that guy with you!"

Just as Alvy believes that Annie now looks great because she is under his tutelage, he devalues her earlier worth in accordance with his opinion of her male companion. Later in the film we will see him do this again as he analyzes evidence in her apartment to construct a negative picture of her new boyfriend. (Finding a copy of the *National Review* and a program from a rock concert, he concludes that she is going out with "a right-wing rock and roll star." Annie gives in to his rewriting of her history by agreeing that Jerry was "creepy," as Alvy happily tells her that she was lucky he came along. This leads to Annie's first use of her trademark expression, "La-de-da!" which, of course, Alvy ridicules.

Later, we see Alvy and Rob preparing for a game of indoor tennis as Alvy resumes his ranting about the anti–Semitism that surrounds him. Now he claims that the rest of the country hates New York City because they perceive it as a hotbed of "left-wing, Communist, Jewish, homosexual pornographers," admitting that even he "thinks of us that way sometimes and I live here!" Rob perceptively remarks, "This is just a very convenient out. Whenever any group disagrees with you, it's because of anti–Semitism." Rob returns to his campaign for the West Coast, pointing out that if they lived in California, they could play outside all the time.

It turns out that the game of tennis marks Alvy's first meeting with Annie. After the game, Alvy and Annie run into each other in the lobby of the tennis club. Their interaction is dramatically different from the usual Allen persona pick-up scenes from earlier films. If this were any of Allen's previous films, especially *Sam*, Alvy would be nervously trying to impress an uninterested Annie, but that situation is here reversed. As we have repeatedly seen, Alvy is a much more self-assured person than is his usual "little man." He is the confident Allan of *Sam*'s ending, a more mature man (we are told he's forty) who has experienced the dissolution of two marriages (as had the real Allen by 1977). In this film's only earlier pickup scene (with Alvy's first wife Alison), Alvy was more arrogant than Allan would have been, but in his nervousness (either partially or mostly caused by stage fright) he was both rude and patronizing.

This time, however, Annie plays the role of nervous suitor, while Alvy is calm, cool, and collected. Her body language, her fumbling for words, her self-derision, and her confusion over who should give a ride to whom, all underline her desperate desire to make a good impression on Alvy. That she is taking the mating role usually reserved for males in our society is emphasized by her unusually masculine attire. Annie Hall's look in this film started a fashion craze, which may partially obscure the fact that when the film was released, it was by no means common for a woman to wear a man's tie and vest. Her gender-crossing clothing, which contrasts dramatically with Alvy's traditionally male white sports shirt and beige slacks, emphasizes their differences.

When Rob and Alvy first appear on the tennis court, it is obvious that the two women (the other presumably Rob's girlfriend) have been discussing Annie's nervousness about meeting Alvy. We know that Alvy is a famous comic who has appeared on television, so in a sense Annie already knows and admires him from afar; but Alvy doesn't know Annie, again the reverse of the clichéd boy-girl meeting.

Alvy is older and more experienced than Annie. In an earlier high school flashback, Annie was shown meeting a date in front of a movie theater with her hair in a beehive looking like what Alvy describes as "the wife of an astronaut." On the theater's marquee, we can see that *The Misfits* is playing, a film released in 1961. We already know that by 1956 Alvy was a professional stand-up comedian meeting his first wife. So far as we know, Annie's romantic experience prior to meeting Alvy was limited to a few adolescent boyfriends and Jerry, the overbearing actor. Alvy is already a professional success, while Annie has little confidence in her abilities in the areas in which she "dabbles" — acting, photography, and singing. Thus the scene is set for Alvy to move completely into his favorite role, that of the romantic mentor taking in hand his younger, less sophisticated female protégée.

We are introduced to Annie's terrible driving as Alvy admits that he can't drive because he uses driving to express hostility, a claim resoundingly confirmed later in the film. We are also introduced to Annie's eminently Waspish background, which Alvy describes as being out of a Norman Rockwell painting. She's from Chippewa Falls, Wisconsin, and she calls her grandmother "Grammy Hall." Annie emphasizes the cultural gap between them, and confirms Alvy's obsessions about anti–Semitism, when she confesses to Alvy that he is what Grammy would describe as "a real Jew."

Alvy talks openly about his fifteen years of analysis. Later, when he acknowledges that he is still sweaty after the tennis game because he never showers in a public place in front of other men "of the same gender," Annie emphasizes the neurotic nature of his homophobia by commenting, "Fifteen years, eh?"

We watch as the two of them traverse the comic terrain of the first stages of a relationship. Allen cleverly shows us their feeble attempts to impress one another as subtitles tell us their real feelings and fears. Both of them worry that they will appear shallow as the scene perfectly captures the interaction which Sartre describes as "the look." While this scene is a stroke of genius in its universal appeal (we have all been there), it also serves to emphasize the artificiality of their relationship's beginnings.

From the start, their romance is more contrived than spontaneous. Annie arranges to meet Alvy. Her efforts to continue their interaction after the tennis match and outside her apartment are blatantly strained. When they finally make a date to go out (on the very night of her audition as a lounge singer), Alvy suggests that they kiss on their way to dinner so they can get it over with and enjoy the rest of their evening without anxiety.

Annie's audition is everyone's nightmare of a first performance, with crashing plates, ringing phones, and an inattentive audience. It will be contrasted later in the film with her more polished performance as she grows into her professional self and out of her need for Alvy as a mentor. But at this early point in their relationship, we watch Alvy encourage and mold her into the person he thinks she should be.

III. Death and Denial

In a bookstore, Alvy wants Annie to read two books on death titled *Death and Western Thought* and *The Denial of Death*. The second book, which won a Pulitzer Prize, is Ernest Becker's analysis of the inherent terror of dying. Becker, through an analysis of such thinkers as Kierkegaard and the psychologist Otto Rank, contends that a Heideggerean dread of death is the most natural human condition, and that we engage in actions which we perceive as "heroic" or "spiritual" in order to inauthentically escape that fear as opposed to honestly confronting it.

Here is Alvy's real answer to those (like Rob) who propose flight from the depressed craziness of Manhattan in search of a mellower, less stressful life in more idyllic surroundings. To Alvy, New York symbolizes authentic acceptance of the human condition. Trying to escape that awareness results in a form of self-deception akin to Kierkegaard's life of the esthetic, the hedonist who believes the search for pleasure alone is ultimately life's goal.

Like Kierkegaard, Alvy believes that such a lifestyle only momentarily diverts one from the abyss. It is better, and more moral, to live life with a grim recognition of one's inalterable condition, exercising one's free-dom in aesthetic pursuits. Alvy fully reveals his ethical commitment to anhedonia when he tells Annie:

> You know, I'm obsessed with death, a big subject with me, yeah. I have a very pessimistic view of life. You should know about this if we are going to go out. You know, I feel that life is divided up into the horrible and the miserable. Those are the two categories. The horrible would be like, um, I don't know, terminal cases, you know, and blind people, cripples. I don't know how they get through life. It's amazing to me, you know. And the miserable is everyone else. So, so, when you go through life, you should be thankful that you are miserable because you are very lucky to be miserable.

Becker combines existential and psychoanalytic themes to suggest that the natural way to deal with this pessimistic yet honest realization is through "transference," the drive to create meaning for one's life by pro-jecting one's own chosen values onto the rest of the world:

> As Rank so wisely saw, projection is *a necessary unburdening* of the indi-vidual; man can not live closed upon himself and for himself. He must project the meaning of his life outward, the reason for it, even the blame for it. We did not create ourselves, but we are stuck with ourselves. Tech-nically, we say that transference is a distortion of reality. But now we see that this distortion has two dimensions: distortion due to the fear of life and death and distortion due to the heroic attempt to assure self expan-sion and the intimate connection of one's inner self to surrounding nature. In other words, transference reflects the whole of the human con-dition and raises the largest philosophical question about that condition [1973, p. 158].

The most obvious way to engage in this creative transference is by shaping another person into a replica of oneself with all of one's judgments and values. We see Alvy doing this with Annie as they sit in the park and Alvy neatly sketches the characters of passersby, sticking them into this or that clever category, just as we saw him reduce Alison to a cultural stereotype. Alvy succeeds in taking control of all of Annie's thoughts and actions at this point; when she says she likes him, he ups the ante by ask-ing if she *loves* him. When Annie asks if he loves her, he says his feelings for her go beyond love; a new word is needed to describe his feelings.

His exhilaration derives from his success at fulfilling his deepest god-like fantasy of creating another person in his own image. Becker states that this is a way of attempting to achieve immortality by perpetuating one's own admittedly idiosyncratic neuroses through another person. Traditionally, one accomplishes this through marriage and family. After all, the most obvious way to strive for immortality is by producing and rearing physical copies of oneself.

The problem with this solution, according to Becker, is that it stems from our species sameness; it submerges one's individuality. Becker puts it this way:

> Although he perpetuates himself in his offspring, who may resemble him and carry some of his "blood" and the mystical quality of some of his ancestors, he may not feel that he is truly perpetuating his own inner self, his distinctive personality, his spirit as it were. He wants to achieve something more than mere animal succession. The distinctive human problem from time immemorial has been the need to spiritualize human life, to lift it onto a special immortal human plane, beyond the cycles of life and death that characterize all other organisms [1973, p. 231].

One way of doing this, Becker points out, is through what he calls "perversions" and "fetishisms." By departing from the accepted norm of reproductive behavior, one asserts one's individuality, one's stamp of uniqueness. This accounts, in Becker's and Rank's view, for the Greeks' high regard for homosexual relationships, especially boy-love, as an idealization of romantic love because they have no specific reproductive purpose. The sole goal of a man-boy relationship lies in the man's attempt to fashion the boy into a spiritual reproduction of himself:

> In terms of our discussion we can see that this attempt represents the complete *causa-sui* project: to create all by oneself a spiritual, intellectual, and physically similar replica of oneself: the perfectly individualized self-perpetuation or immortality symbol [Becker, 1973, p. 232].

This may account for Alvy's sensitivity about appearing naked in front of other men and his avid acceptance of the *Playboy* mentality with its glorification of "scoring" with women and its thinly disguised gay bashing. This is not to suggest that Alvy has any more repressed homosexual urges than do most heterosexual men. Rather it implies that, although Alvy is not physically attracted to men, he is at some level aware of the Greeks' approach to such idealized love and wishes to mimic its metaphysical advantages in his relationship to women. Alvy is aroused by the existence of the women's movement in general, with its insistence that women are the equal of men, just as he is specifically attracted to Annie, who by her dress, manner, and aspirations seeks to be his equal. The rest of the film chronicles the results of Alvy's attempt to mold Annie into a replica of himself while maintaining his individuality, and without allowing her to become her own person and realize that she no longer needs him.

This analysis explains Alvy's reluctance to allow Annie to move into his apartment. He insists that she maintain her own place as "a free-floating life raft so that we know we are not married." Confirming this view is the fact that there has been no mention of the possibility of children with his two previous wives, nor is the matter ever discussed with Annie. We will have to wait for *Hannah and Her Sisters* to see this issue dealt with seriously in an Allen film.

At their beach house, we see Annie and Alvy reclining on the bed as Annie consults Alvy about the proper college courses to take to expand herself. By this point, he's giving her reading lists, and is even presumptuous enough to insist that she stop her habit of smoking grass to relax her before they make love. According to Becker (1973, pp. 235–6), Annie's need to smoke grass would be an example of the kind of perversion or fetish discussed by psychologists such as Freud, Boss, and Greenacre. From this perspective, taking a pill, or smoking a joint, acts as a kind of magic potion, relieving Annie's anxieties about the loss of the uniqueness of her individual identity in the common species activity of intercourse.

This analysis is similar to Sartre's interpretation of the use of emotion as a tool for entering a magical realm where one's dreams may be fulfilled, even if they are self-contradictory. By insisting that Annie give up her magic charm, Alvy is attempting to strip her of the last remnants of her individuality, like Scotty in Alfred Hitchcock's *Vertigo* (1958), who insisted that Judy put her hair up like Madeleine's. Judy thoroughly gave in to Scotty's demands, and thereby lost her soul; Annie, however, responds in a healthier way by splitting herself in two during their lovemaking. In a brilliant scene, we see Annie's spirit jump out of her body and move over to a chair, where she asks the lovers if they've seen her sketch pad so that she may develop her artistic side while her body is possessed by Alvy.

Alvy is dissatisfied with this arrangement because, as usual, he wants everything. In Sartrean terms, he wants to control Annie both sexually and spiritually, while at the same time he wants to feel that Annie's submission to him is entirely voluntary. When Annie demands to know why he's so threatened by her use of her charm, he compares it to performing before an audience that's stoned. He wants to know that the laughs he gets are solely the results of his talents and not of intoxication. By comparing her to an audience member, he confirms her fears that he has no respect for her as an individual, as well as her awareness that he sees her as an onlooker there to appreciate him, as opposed to an active participant in their relationship.

We next see the successful Alvy performing his material to an enthusiastic college audience at the University of Wisconsin, near enough to Annie's home to allow for a meeting between him and the Halls. Alvy's dinner with the Halls reemphasizes the cultural gulf that separates him from Annie. Earlier, when they went out to get sandwiches at a New York deli, Alvy had been amazed when Annie ordered a pastrami sandwich on white bread with mayonnaise, lettuce, and tomatoes. Now, he sits at the dinner table in a sunny dining room with a family he describes this way:

> I can't believe this family! Annie's mother is really beautiful, and they're talking swap meets and boat basins and the old lady at the end of the table is a classic Jew-hater. They really look American, you know, very healthy, like they never get sick or anything. Nothing like my family, you know, the two are like oil and water.

At this comment, a scene of Alvy's extended family arguing, yelling, and gossiping at a meal takes up three-quarters of the screen. Mom Hall (Colleen Dewhurst), still visible in the screen's left-hand corner, asks the Singers how they plan to spend the holidays (it's Easter weekend). Alvy's mother (Joan Newman) and father (Mordecai Learner) take the question in a Jewish context, assuming that she is referring to the most important Jewish holidays, Rosh Hashanah and Yom Kippur. They tell her that they will fast to atone for their sins, and when Mom Hall says she doesn't understand, Alvy's father says, "To tell you the truth, neither do we!"

From Alvy's perspective, Annie's family lives in a bright, sunny world which supplies them with good health, economic well-being, and a sense of belonging. Alvy, who fantasizes that the Halls see him in the garb of a Hasidic Jew, is the perpetual outsider from the hated New York City, a world of darkness and pessimism, a world where people fast to atone for sins they don't understand. Alvy sees his world as the real one, and he feels a moral duty to bring Annie into it.

The next scene belies the assumptions of its predecessor (for example, that the Halls never get sick) when we learn that Annie's brother, Duane, suffers from obsessions which exceed even Alvy's own dark pessimism. Sitting on his bed in his dimly lit room, Duane tells Alvy that he wants to confess something because he believes that Alvy, as a "fellow artist," will understand. He describes his desire to kill himself by driving into the headlights of an oncoming car, and shares his images of the horrible nature of such a crash. Alvy is shaken by this revelation, telling Duane that he has to leave because he's "due back on the planet Earth," even though we know that Duane is correct in assuming that Alvy shares his obsession with death.

Here Allen again reveals his agreement with Becker and the existentialists in their claim that the horror of living is a human universal, not a viewpoint limited to any particular cultural or religious group. He also cracks open the door to an analysis of such themes in the context of an all–American Waspish family, an analysis which he will pursue in much greater and more serious detail in his next film, *Interiors*.

We next see Mom and Dad Hall saying goodbye to Annie as she prepares to leave for the airport. This is presumably taking place while Alvy is still in Duane's room. If we listen closely, we can hear Mom Hall telling Annie that she thinks he's adorable as Annie responds, "Do you really think so?" As Annie goes to get Alvy, we see Mom and Dad Hall happily kissing.

This scene further undermines Alvy's assumptions at the dinner table about who the Halls are and what they are feeling. In fact, it appears that the Halls liked Alvy, and they share a more complex emotional life than he imagined. After the obligatory gag scene of Duane driving Alvy and Annie to the airport in the rain as Alvy glances nervously over to Duane, we move forward in time to the deterioration of Alvy's and Annie's relationship.

IV. Love's Lessons

Alvy has taken to spying on Annie, following her from the very class that he encouraged her to take, because he is afraid that she is having an affair with her professor. Annie is appalled by this invasion of her privacy and vehemently denies any romance. She is hurt by Alvy's assumption that the professor would take interest in her only if they were having a sexual relationship. To him, she complains, it is unthinkable that the professor would want to talk with her after class just because he thinks she's "neat."

Alvy derides the course's content by making up a phony name for it ("Contemporary Crisis in Western Man") when in fact the real course title — Existential Motifs in Russian Literature — is right down Alvy's alley, as we know from Allen's previous film, *Love and Death*, a send-up of such motifs. Here again, we see Alvy's need to be the source of Annie's intellectual views. He rejects any intellectualism other than his own, describing it as "crap" and "mental masturbation." To Annie's insightful rejoinder that the latter is a subject on which Alvy is expert, he responds honestly, "Hey, don't knock masturbation. It's sex with someone I love."

Annie reminds Alvy that he is the one who didn't want to make a commitment, who wanted to keep the relationship "flexible." She reminds him of their discussion at the beach house the month before following Annie's first therapy session, therapy that Alvy encouraged her to enter and is paying for. Alvy is shocked to learn that Annie made more progress in one session than he's made in fifteen years (she even cried) and that the therapist is interpreting her dreams in ways that are critical of Alvy.

Annie describes a dream in which she is being suffocated by Frank Sinatra with a pillow. Alvy wants to interpret this to mean that Annie is suffocating herself, but according to the analyst, Alvy is suffocating Annie. The analyst pointed out that Alvy's last name is Singer and that in Annie's dream she breaks Sinatra's glasses. Alvy is also unpleasantly surprised to hear that in the dream Annie "does something" to Sinatra so that he's singing in a very high voice. The scene ends with Alvy encouraging Annie to take the very adult education courses that he is shown criticizing in the previous scene.

We return to that scene for a continuation of Alvy's diatribe against adult education. As Annie gets into a cab, we hear her suggest, for the first time, that they break up. Alone on the street, Alvy lapses back into fantasy, stopping passersby to get their insights on love. An elderly woman pessimistically tells him that "love fades." An average-looking older man reveals that Annie's marijuana fetish is not as strange as Alvy thinks; he informs us that he and his wife use "a large vibrating egg" to enhance their sex.

In a famous moment, Alvy stops a young, attractive couple to ask the secret of their apparent happiness. The woman (Shelley Hack) responds, "Oh, I'm really shallow and empty, and I have no ideas and nothing interesting to say." The man (James Burge) adds, "And I'm exactly the same." This confirms Alvy's earlier view that life is composed of the horrible and the miserable. Alvy would probably put this couple in the first category.

What happens next further confirms the contention that *Annie Hall* is a more sophisticated remake of *Sam*. Once again, as in *Sam*, the Tony Roberts character tells Alvy to forget Annie and let him fix Alvy up with a "dynamite woman," just as Dick told Allan to forget about Nancy as he offered to fix him up with empty-headed women like Julie. In fact, Annie's complaints about Alvy perfectly mimic Nancy's condemnation of Allan when she told him, "I don't find you any fun. I feel you suffocate me."

While his date with Pam (Shelley Duvall), the reporter for *Rolling Stone*, ostensibly goes better than the date with Julie in *Sam* (he even "scores"), emotionally it is an empty experience. Pam is accurate when she describes sex with an Alvy who detests her "as a Kafkaesque experience."

As he lies next to Pam in the middle of the night, Alvy receives a phone call from Annie and promptly rushes to her apartment. In a reenactment of the romantic lobster scene, Alvy rescues her from a spider "the size of a Buick." Annie confesses that she misses him. Alvy lies when she asks if he was with anybody (in his book, being with Pam was like being alone), yet he has no qualms about jealously sniffing out the clues lying around her apartment that suggest she has dated another man.

To celebrate the reconciliation, Alvy and Rob drive Annie out to Brooklyn to show her their old neighborhood. The scene is reminiscent of the same group's drive to the beach in *Sam*, except that Annie is now in the driver's seat. The nostalgic mood of this scene continues into the next as we revisit Annie singing in a nightclub (she even sings "Seems Like Old Times"). But, we soon discover, times have changed. Annie now is an accomplished performer, so accomplished in fact that a famous singer, Tony Lacy (Paul Simon), comes over with his entourage to congratulate her and ask her if she wants to join them for a drink with "Jack and Anjelica" (presumably Nicholson and Huston). Alvy, typically, forces Annie to refuse ("Remember, we have that thing?"), wanting to keep Annie for himself, but we can see that Annie is flattered and excited by the attention. Tony even suggests that he would like to talk to her about a recording contract and working together.

Annie berates Alvy for turning down the offer, and he responds with a diatribe on Tony's comment that the evening would be "mellow." Returning to the Manhattan-versus-L.A. dichotomy, Alvy says, "I don't think I could take a mellow evening. I don't respond well to 'mellow.' I have a tendency, if I mellow, I get too ripe and then I rot." When Annie asks Alvy how he wants to spend the evening, the answer comes when the screen fills again with *The Sorrow and the Pity*. Alvy can't give up his rituals of pessimism and despair.

During the Christmas season we travel with Annie and Alvy to Los Angeles, where Alvy is supposed to give out an award on television. Alvy's reaction to California is exactly what we would expect. Rob has now moved there, and he brags that he has never been more relaxed. He even lives right next to Hugh Hefner: "And the women, Max, are just like the women in *Playboy* magazine except they can move their arms and legs." Alvy is disgusted by the hodgepodge of architectural styles, and he responds to Annie's observation that everything is so "clean" (sterile, in Alvy's terms) by saying, "They don't throw their garbage away. They make it into television shows."

Alvy is literally nauseated as he watches Rob use a laugh track to manufacture phony appreciation for the lousy jokes on his "hit sitcom."

Alvy goes to a Hollywood party, where Allen's relentless mocking of the "mellow" lifestyle hilariously continues. (In a cameo, Jeff Goldblum worriedly tells someone on the phone that he forgot his mantra.) The party is at the house of Tony Lacy, who uses his time with Annie to try to convince her to move into his house for six weeks so they can make an album. He says he used to live in New York, but now there's too much "garbage"—in other words, it's too real and depressing. Alvy accurately responds, "I'm into garbage."

On the plane back, they both realize that they want to break up (Annie because even though she "adores" Alvy, their relationship "doesn't seem to work anymore"; Alvy because he found it fun to flirt with other women). Alvy negatively compares a relationship to a shark: "It has to keep moving or it dies. What we've got on our hands is a dead shark."

We see Alvy coming out of a movie theater alone, depressed about the breakup and missing Annie (we watched Allan do the same in reaction to his breakup with Nancy in *Sam*). Fantasy passersby tell him that Annie is living with Tony Lacy and advise him to date other women. Alvy flies back out to California to try to get Annie to return with him, but the trip is a disaster.

The meal Alvy and Annie share in Los Angeles parallels their earlier meal at the deli on their first date (Yacowar, 1991, p. 176). At that first meal, Alvy was the comfortable insider and Annie was the outsider, ordering improperly. Now Alvy is the alienated one. He tells Annie on the phone that he can feel the return of his "chronic Los Angeles nausea." He rents a car, which we see him driving haltingly to the restaurant where they are to meet. Of course, it's an outdoor health food restaurant (everything Alvy hates). Annie shows up looking very "L.A." in a flowing white dress and stylish sunglasses.

Alvy tries to be nice (he tells her she looks "pretty"—again judging her by her appearance), but they soon fall back into their bickering as Alvy fails to convince her to come back with him. He even wants her to marry him, but she has gone over to the other side. She professes satisfaction with her hedonistic lifestyle of endless parties and tennis, and explicitly identifies Alvy with a New York which she describes as an island cut off from everything and "a dying city." Alvy tries to define his philosophy by saying he can't be happy if even one person is suffering, but we know this is a simplistically distorted version of his true views. Annie acknowledges Alvy's role in molding her into the person she's become, but she refuses to deny her feelings for his sake. Finally fed up, Annie leaves the table, with Alvy trailing her desperately as he continues to bicker.

After she's gone, Alvy proves his much earlier claim that he uses driving to take out his hostility as he bashes his rental car into other vehicles in the parking lot. He compounds his difficulties by defying the traffic cop who comes on the scene demanding his license. The cop epitomizes everything Allen hates: a fascistically dressed symbol of male Californian order who sees him as just another bad driver. In response to his demand that Alvy "just give me your license, not your life story," Alvy tears the license into tiny pieces, saying, "I have a terrific problem with authority. It's not your fault. Don't take it personal" (a retread of the gag from *Sam* in which Nancy tells Allan everything that's wrong with him, but says, "Don't take it personal"). Rob bails Alvy out of jail wearing a bizarre sun protection outfit that looks like a reject from *Sleeper*. Legalistically and stylistically, Allen suggests that California is rapidly becoming the empty society depicted in that earlier film.

We next see actors rehearsing the scene just played out between Alvy and Annie, except that in this version, the Annie character says she is going back to Alvy because she loves him. Alvy justifies this to the audience by saying, "What do you want? It was my first play. You know how you're always trying to get things to come out perfect in art because it's real difficult in life?" It's interesting that this is the only one of Alvy's fantasies played out by people identifiable as actors in the film's "real world," instead of in a fantasy sequence. This and Alvy's bittersweet but undeniably happier manner suggest that, as at the end of *Sam*, he has learned from his experiences and is now mature enough to accept the inevitability of his breakup with Annie. We suggested earlier that the entire film is in the form of a kind of therapy session. At its end, the therapy has apparently worked, as Alvy has overcome the anxiety of his opening monologue.

He tells us of running into Annie years later, dragging the guy she was living with in Soho into a showing of *The Sorrow and the Pity*, something he describes as a "real triumph." While Annie is now clearly her own person (she's the one doing the dragging), she has returned to Alvy's values of existential authenticity as represented by living in Manhattan and feeling obliged to make regular pilgrimages to Ophuls's film. Alvy describes a lunch where they kicked around old times. We see them laughing together hysterically, and then we are presented with a montage of scenes from their relationship, as we hear the swelling tones of Annie's voice reprising her version of "Seems Like Old Times" on the soundtrack. Alvy has overcome his anger at Annie and accepted the fact that romance often confuses and disappoints us. But, as with life itself in the opening joke about the Catskills resort, we cling to the magic of love in dread of the alternative. He now realizes:

what a terrific person she was and how much fun it was just knowing her and I thought of that old joke, you know? This guy goes to a psychiatrist and says, "Doc, my brother's crazy, he thinks he's a chicken. And the doctor says, "Well, why don't you turn him in?" And the guy says, "I would, but I need the eggs!" Well, I guess that's now pretty much how I feel about relationships. You know, they're totally irrational, and crazy, and absurd, but I guess we keep going through it because most of us need the eggs!

In a written exchange with me in 1994 (see Appendix), Allen says this about romance:

In relation to impossibility of authentic romantic commitment — this is a question of pure luck, the interfacing of two enormous complexities and the delusion that it can be "worked at" is just that. Efforts by the parties may aid in a small way but have the same relation to the success of a relationship that a writing class has to a real reader.

– 3 –

THEMES OF REDEMPTION:
Manhattan (1979)

While *Annie Hall* was in the form of an extended therapy session, *Manhattan* resembles a novel. The film begins with black-and-white scenes of Manhattan set to the glorious strains of Gershwin's *Rhapsody in Blue*. For the first time in an Allen movie, there are no titles at all. The flashing lights of a marquee spelling "Manhattan" are the closest thing to a title. A smaller sign saying "Parking" invites us to stay for a while.

In a voice-over, Allen reads five different versions of the beginning of a novel. One is rejected as too corny, another too preachy, still another too angry. Each beginning emphasizes the narrator's love for New York, and in more than one version he eagerly confesses that he is a romantic and that the city is a metaphor for his dreams and fears.

These introductions effectively summarize the themes to be explored in this film. In *Annie Hall*, the city of New York came to stand for an authentic acceptance of the sometimes harsh truths about life, as opposed to the hedonistic illusions of Los Angeles. In *Manhattan*, Allen explores a corrupting influence which he fears is undercutting everything he loves about the city and himself. One version of the novel begins:

> Let me try and make it more profound. Chapter one: He adored New York City. To him it was a metaphor for the decay of contemporary culture. The same lack of individual integrity that caused so many people to take the easy way out was rapidly turning the town of his dreams.... No, it's going to be too preachy. I mean, you know, let's face it, I want to sell some books here.

As in the opening sequence of *Annie Hall*, the audience doesn't know whether Allen is speaking as himself or as a character in the film. In any

56

case, the clear implication of the voice-over is that Allen will explore serious themes while, at the same time, attempting to be entertaining in order to "sell some books." The trick for both Allen himself and his character in the film is to do both without allowing the commercial motive to taint the more serious one.

And so Allen returns as an actor, playing the primary role in a film for the first time since *Annie Hall*. His name is Isaac Davis, another name (like Alvy Singer) with the same cadence as his own. (The name Isaac also suggests a parallel to the story of Abraham and Isaac, a theme to which we will return.) In *Annie Hall*, Alvy's best friend, Rob, hypocritically exploited success with a hit television sitcom; now it is Allen's own character who works on such a show. Isaac tortures himself with guilt for selling out his talents to television's mediocrity. In the course of the film he quits his job, a melodramatic gesture which instantly terrifies him. In fact, reflexively, he quits his job to write the very book which we are now experiencing as a film, for in today's culture, film is the world's literature.

The other major characters are his best friends, a married couple named Yale (Michael Murphy) and Emily (Anne Byrne); Tracy (Mariel Hemingway), a seventeen-year-old girl whom Isaac is dating; and Mary Wilke (Diane Keaton), a woman romantically involved with both Yale and Isaac. We also meet Isaac's young son, Willie (Damion Sheller); his ex-wife, Jill (Meryl Streep), and her lesbian lover, Connie (Karen Ludwig); and, briefly, Mary's ex-husband, Jeremiah (Wallace Shawn).

I. Yale

In the first scene, we see Isaac, Tracy, Yale, and Emily at the then-chic, crowded club Elaine's. Yale is arguing to Tracy that "the essence of art is to provide a kind of working through of a situation for people so that you can get in touch with feelings you didn't know you had." Isaac responds that "talent is luck. The important thing in life is courage." Like Joey in *Interiors*, Isaac views the possession of artistic ability as happenstance; what's important for everyone, talented or not, is the courage to act with integrity. Emily tells Tracy that Isaac and Yale have been having this argument for twenty years. Isaac raises the example of the stranger drowning, and asks which of them would have the "nerve" to risk life and limb to attempt to save that person. He quickly defuses the seriousness of his question by confessing that, of course, for him, this is not an issue since he can't swim.

For Isaac, being the head writer for a popular television show looks good and brings in lots of money, but it leaves him feeling empty and shallow. He demonstrates his fundamental integrity when he abandons the show in favor of a book that might not succeed. The parallel to Allen's own work is obvious. With the making of *Interiors* (1978), Allen gave up the job of making lucrative, entertaining, but (in his own opinion) shallow comedies, in favor of making serious films which are not as appealing to the general public, but which satisfy his belief that, in art, what counts is the courage to do what you think is right.

When Tracy excuses herself, Yale praises her beauty ("she's gorgeous"), indicating that Yale, like Alvy in *Annie Hall*, primarily judges women by their appearance. When Isaac reveals his guilty anxiety about Tracy's extreme youth compared to his forty-two years (exactly the same age as Allen himself) and jokes that he is older than her father, Yale and Emily conclude that he is drunk, and Yale tells him he should never drink. This implies that Isaac's concern is not important, that a man would have to be drunk to worry about the morality of dating a teenager and engaging in statutory rape.

Isaac also tells them about his concern that his second ex-wife, Jill, is writing a tell-all book about their marriage and breakup. While Isaac claims that he has nothing to hide, he is upset that Jill will publicly reveal "all the little details about my idiosyncrasies and quirks," and "a few disgusting moments" that he would rather keep private. Returning to an earlier theme, Isaac desperately wishes to maintain his individuality in the face of the onslaught of a culture that attempts to turn private experiences into the common experience of the species. Only by retaining one's uniqueness through aesthetic creation, such as his proposed book, can Isaac distinguish himself from the rest of society. Yale agrees that "gossip is the new pornography."

After joking more about Tracy's youth (she has to get up early the next morning for an exam), they leave the club. As he is walking with Isaac, with the women walking together safely out of earshot, Yale shares some of the "new pornography" with Isaac by telling him that he's having an affair with Mary, a high-strung, beautiful journalist.

In this discussion, Yale reveals the extent of his moral hypocrisy. He says that the affair is very serious, yet he acknowledges that he still loves Emily and has no intention of telling her about it. He admits that what he is doing is wrong, and that this is not his first affair. He also claims that he hates what he is doing, and hates himself for doing it, but it never seems to occur to him that these are good reasons to simply stop doing it. Yale feels justified in indulging all of his desires without any concerns for the pain he causes others.

Throughout the film, Yale manipulates everyone he supposedly cares for in order to satisfy his own yearnings, no matter what the consequences. Yale rationalizes his choices by mocking legitimate moral concerns while pretending to himself that humans, being inescapably flawed, are not really responsible for their acts. Thus he thinks nothing of encouraging Isaac to get involved with Mary, only to betray him by continuing to date Mary behind his back. In this sense, like Nick in *Broadway Danny Rose*, Yale may consciously be using Isaac as a "beard," a cover for his own romantic interest in Mary so that he can keep track of Mary through Isaac and ensure that she doesn't get seriously involved with anyone else.

In their apartment, Yale and Emily disagree about whether to have kids and whether to leave Manhattan for a more rural life in Connecticut. Emily obviously senses that something is wrong with their marriage, but Yale encourages her to continue to live in self-deception (pretending to herself that his affairs don't matter). We see the depth of his own bad faith in his willingness to construct a variety of phony reasons for not having kids or moving. We learn that Yale has a number of projects planned (a book on O'Neill and the establishment of a new literary journal) which he uses as excuses for his behavior despite the fact that he never works on them. Later, we will see Yale squander the money he has been saving for the journal to buy a used Porsche, an astonishing self-indulgence for a low-paid professor living in a city with excellent public transportation and horrendous traffic and parking problems. In fact, throughout the entire film, the only work we ever see Yale doing is when Isaac interrupts his teaching of a class at the film's end. Yet another sign of Yale's lack of seriousness about his work is the fact that he immediately abandons his class without a word of explanation to them.

In that scene, Isaac is stunned by the immensity of Yale's betrayal. In a climactic dialogue in an empty classroom, he challenges Yale's lack of moral perspective and his unwillingness to take responsibility for his acts. Yale uses every kind of excuse to defend himself, obviously lying about the frequency and types of encounters he's had with Mary since she's been involved with Isaac. He tells Isaac not to make this "into one of his big moral issues," as though morality were a boring and unimportant hobby Isaac imposes on his friends the way someone else might force people to look at his stamp collection.

When Yale acknowledges he is no saint and says that we are all just human beings, he implies that integrity and moral virtue are attributes beyond the scope of mere people. He discounts Isaac's demands that he be harder on himself and is unmoved when Isaac analyzes his character (and the degenerate character of the times) this way:

> But you're too easy on yourself! Don't you see that! That's your problem, that's your whole problem. You rationalize everything. You're not honest with yourself. You talk about you want to write a book, but, in the end, you'd rather buy the Porsche, you know? You cheat a little bit on Emily and you play around the truth a little with me, and, the next thing you know you're in front of a Senate committee and you're naming names, you're informing on your friends.

This last comment reminds us of Allen's and Murphy's participation in the film *The Front* (1976), a gritty portrayal of the moral complexities of the McCarthy era. To Yale's accusation that Isaac is too self-righteous, that he thinks he's perfect, that in fact he thinks he's God, Isaac jokes that he has to model himself on someone — showing how far Allen's characters have grown since *Sam*, where his highest goal was to model himself on Bogart.

Standing in front of a skeleton of an ancient man, Isaac argues for our fundamental duty to preserve moral standards for the generations that follow:

> What are future generations going to say about us! My God, you know someday we are going to be like him. You know, I mean, he was probably one of the beautiful people. He was probably dancing and playing tennis and everything! And now! This is what happens to us! You know, it's very important to have some kind of personal integrity. I'll be hanging in a classroom one day and I want to make sure that when I thin out that I'm well thought of.

In a sense, Allen himself is already hanging in a classroom, in the form of the many film courses and books in which his work is studied seriously. In his portrayal of the ethical differences between Yale and Isaac, Allen emphasizes his commitment to a deontological approach which values the intrinsic worth of one's acts over the pursuit of hedonistic ends. Like the philosopher Immanuel Kant, Isaac recognizes that ethical behavior demands both a respect for the dignity of others and a willingness to sacrifice personal pleasure for the sake of duty.

II. Mary

Mary is introduced in an art gallery, in a scene that begins with Isaac pontificating about the meaning of the pictures as he asks Tracy if she has been using the camera he bought for her (so she can become a photographer like Annie Hall). When she tells him that she's had fun using it — implying that she doesn't take his instruction too seriously — he retaliates by telling her that her voice sounds like the mouse in the *Tom and Jerry* cartoons, an attempt to put her in her place by reminding her of her youth. Although Isaac's relationship with her is another of the Pygmalion-Galatea variety (like the one between Alvy and Annie), Tracy is better able to defend herself than the more vulnerable Annie; she responds by pointing out that his voice is nothing to brag about.

To their mutual surprise, Tracy and Isaac run into Yale and his girl-friend, Mary, as they try to sneak by without being spotted. While Yale introduces both Mary and Isaac by their full names, he introduces Tracy only by her first name, implying that, because of her age, she is less worthy of consideration than the grown-ups.

Isaac finds Mary opinionated and pretentious. Her view of the artwork is diametrically opposed to his own, and she uses meaningless, pseudointellectual jargon to justify her own views while she crudely dismisses his:

> To me, [the steel cube] was very textual. You know what I mean? It was perfectly integrated and it had a marvelous kind of negative capability. The rest of the stuff downstairs was bullshit!

As the four of them walk down the street after leaving the museum, Mary asks Tracy what she does. When Tracy honestly answers that she goes to high school, Mary makes an unintelligible but obviously snide comment to Yale. They then discuss their "Academy of the Overrated," which comprises many of the figures Allen himself admires, including Gustav Mahler, Isak Dinesen, Carl Jung, F. Scott Fitzgerald, Lenny Bruce, and Norman Mailer. When Isaac protests that he likes all those people, Mary doubly offends him, first by mentioning Vincent Van Gogh (pronouncing it Goch in the most pretentious manner), and then by naming Ingmar Bergman, whom Isaac immediately defends as "the only genius in cinema today."

Mary's and Yale's willingness to trash the names of great artists in order to make themselves feel superior will be recalled subtly later in the film: first, when Isaac accuses Yale of being the kind of person who would have been willing to "name names" in the McCarthy period in order to protect and promote himself; and second, when Isaac comes up with his own list of people and things that make life worth living. Mary reacts negatively to Isaac's defense of Bergman by comparing him unfavorably to Isaac's own work:

> God! You're so the opposite. I mean, you write that absolutely fabulous television show! It's really really funny and his view is so Scandinavian. It's bleak! My God! I mean all that Kierkegaard, right? It's real adolescent,

you know, fashionable pessimism. I mean the silence, God's silence! OK,
OK, OK! I mean I loved it when I was at Radcliffe but, I mean, all right,
you outgrow it! I think you absolutely outgrow it!

This interchange is one of the two key discussions of the film (the
other being Isaac's condemnation of Yale at the film's end). Mary's attitude represents to Isaac (and Allen) the kind of pseudointellectualizing
that is destroying the moral fabric of the city he loves. By identifying
Bergman's genuine existential *angst* with the faddish rebellion of her
undergraduate days at Radcliffe, during which she evidently mimicked
anguish for fashion's sake without any actual suffering, Mary illustrates a
mentality which, again, mistakes appearance for reality. In her view, all
serious philosophizing is just a mask to disguise Freudian hangups. If only
Kierkegaard or Bergman had spent a few years in analysis, she seems to
be suggesting, they too could be writing successful sitcoms. Again, we
have a major character (like Rob in *Annie Hall*) glorifying hedonism as
the only plausible approach to life, while she pays lip service to platitudes
("I'm just from Philadelphia, you know, and we believe in God").

In a grocery store with Tracy, Isaac rages against Mary. Tracy tries
to calm him down by insightfully pointing out that Mary's exaggerated
manner is a defense which she uses to hide her vulnerability, what Tracy
calls her "nervousness." Isaac attacks Mary as too cerebral, and speculates
that she and Yale sit around at night sipping wine and mispronouncing
intellectual terms. It's not that Isaac is anti-intellectual; it's that he believes,
in the manner of Kierkegaard, Nietzsche, or Camus, that every insight of
real importance has its origins in our intuitions, not in our minds alone.
Dread's emotional reality must, after all, be ontologically prior to its status as an idea if it is to have any real significance. Intellect without instinct
leads to a kind of moral relativism in which everything becomes permissible and no one can be held accountable for his actions.

Repeatedly in the film, Isaac describes his views as old-fashioned. He
says he opposes extramarital affairs and favors mating for life ("like pigeons
or Catholics"). Yet we know he has been divorced twice, and he is constantly
urging Tracy not to take their affair seriously. When Tracy speculates that
perhaps we are meant to have a series of meaningful romantic relationships with different people throughout our lives, Isaac strongly disagrees,
despite the fact that he used the same arguments in an earlier scene in order
to justify his unwillingness to make any kind of commitment to her. Like
so many of Allen's characters, especially Alvy, Isaac has strong moral views
to which he believes himself committed, yet he is sufficiently dishonest
with himself to ignore his own hypocrisy while attacking it in others.

We see Isaac in the control room during the filming of his hit television program, some form of satirical variety show. As a parody of a talk show called "Human Beings— Wow!" it features an interviewer who doesn't know if it's day or night (he starts the show by saying "Good Morning," yet a second later mentions the names of the guests he has with him "this evening"). The guests are a married couple in which the wife is catatonic ("Well, we don't consider her catatonic, we just kind of consider her quiet"). In a society where the private has become public and everyone uses everyone else, especially the ones they supposedly love, to get what they want, a man is willing to exploit his wife's illness to make fools of them both on TV.

As this contribution to the decline in values goes on literally beneath him, Isaac rails against a culture that rewards him for creating such trash. When his colleagues try to convince him that everyone finds it very funny, Isaac tells them that an audience conditioned by a lifetime of television-watching is so corrupted that "their standards have been systematically lowered over the years. These guys sit in front of their sets and the gamma rays eat the white cells of their brains out." His colleagues, on the other hand, are such full participants in the hedonistic culture that they have fried their minds with drugs, so, of course, whatever he writes seems funny to them. After all, it is in their collective interest to find it funny. In *Annie Hall*, Rob used a machine to simulate laughs for his unfunny material. Now, a laugh-track is unnecessary because audiences are so well trained that they fully participate in the sham experience of television, artificial entertainment for people seeking any excuse to avoid dealing honestly with their lives.

We mentioned earlier that Isaac's name recalls the story of Abraham and Isaac, the story of a man who decides, against both his desires and his reason, to blindly follow God's command to sacrifice the life of his son. This story was used extensively by the existentialist Søren Kierkegaard (already attacked by Mary) to illustrate his belief that the only life worth living, and capable of delivering us from despair, is one that results from a "leap of faith" into an intuitive belief in God, into what one knows in one's heart is right, despite the fact that society will ridicule those few who make such a choice, and that no empirical evidence exists to prove such a choice is justified.

Isaac has chosen to take just such a leap into the belief that he will create a work of art of significant moral worth. In addition to following Kierkegaard's lead by sacrificing material success as well as a traditional family life (Kierkegaard was publicly ridiculed for his views, and he also gave up his engagement to the woman he loved), Isaac also follows

Kierkegaard by inviting the wrath of accepted religious authorities. Isaac tells Yale that he won't be able to send as much money to his parents, which will result in his father's inability to purchase a good seat in his synagogue. He will be forced to sit "in back, away from God, far from the action."

Kierkegaard contended that traditional religious institutions were actually more of a hindrance than a help in coming face-to-face with God. Isaac indicates his agreement by his scorn for religious institutions that reward material rather than spiritual worth. Kierkegaard contrasts the leap of faith with two other unsuccessful ways of living, the aesthetic and the ethical. Those in the aesthetic lifestyle, like Yale and Mary, seek fulfillment solely through the gratification of their senses. This way of life will ultimately return one to despair as the empty pursuit of pleasure alone always leaves one hungry for more.

Kierkegaard sees the ethical life as equally unsatisfactory. Building on a foundation of hypocrisy, the ethicist pontificates about life's eternal truths while simultaneously realizing that such unfounded claims are dependent upon one's subjective perceptions. Mary represents this choice. Like Linda (in *Sam*) and Annie Hall, she has been molded in her views by an intellectually controlling man, in this case her former husband, a professor fittingly named Jeremiah. Like the prophet of the Scriptures, Jeremiah demanded of his listeners (his students) that they give up all their old ways to follow and obey him. Thus even though he failed her in his course — or perhaps precisely for that reason — Mary chose to be dominated by him completely. We become aware that all of her pseudointellectual mumbo-jumbo is an imitation of the ideas to which she was exposed when married to Jeremiah. When we devote our souls to a false ideology, no matter what its source, we give up our uniqueness and destine ourselves to an unsatisfying life of pretension.

Mary is an Annie Hall still living in the shadow of her Alvy. She strains to maintain the illusion of her intellectual sophistication as she searches for a new mentor to follow, finally settling on Yale, another professor. In the interim, she lives her life in a pointless charade in which she waffles from one chic activity to another (her dog is even named Waffles). Isaac encounters her at one such event, a benefit for the ERA. When Isaac asks, "What are you doing here?" she responds, "Well, of course I'm here!"

One party conversation concerns a group of Nazis who plan to march in New Jersey. Isaac, favoring action over intellectualization, suggests confronting the Nazis with bricks and baseball bats. To another guest's observation that the *Times* had a "devastating, satirical piece on that on its op-ed page," Isaac responds that that's all well and good, but bricks and baseball bats get more to the point. A woman counters that "a biting satirical piece is always preferable to physical force," to which Isaac says, "No, physical force is always better with Nazis. It's hard to satirize a guy with shiny boots." She comes back one last time, saying, "You're emotional, I know, but...." We never hear the end of her argument, but we can guess the rest. The party guests are all like Mary: they mistakenly believe that ideas by themselves have more force and are somehow morally superior to emotional commitment. Isaac forcefully disagrees. Some issues are so important that one must risk all of one's self, not simply hide behind a facade of intellectual superiority. This is Allen's answer to those who criticize him for leaving behind the comedy genre. "Biting satire" constitutes an unwarranted self-indulgence in the face of society's collapsing values.

After the party, Isaac and Mary spend the night together, talking and walking around the city that he loves. They are both swept up in the magic and romance of Manhattan at night. Isaac mistakenly attributes some of this magic to Mary and believes himself smitten with her, even though her conversation reveals her instability and her acceptance of the ethic of popular culture and narcissism. Where previously she listed such notables as Mahler and Fitzgerald as candidates for her "Academy of the Overrated," now she contends that everyone she met through Jeremiah is a "genius." Despite their breakup, and her claim that she no longer wanted to live a life submerged in the identity of "a very brilliant, dominating man," she still hangs out with his friends and accepts their views as gospel.

In the film's most memorable image, we see them sitting on a bench facing a bridge just at dawn as we hear the beautiful melody of "Someone to Watch Over Me." Isaac gushes in his praise for the beauty of New York, making it clear that the one "watching over" him and the real source of the evening's romantic magic has been the city, not Mary. Jealously, Mary interrupts his paean to Manhattan by announcing that she has to get home.

Still in the grip of his romantic intoxication, Isaac is disappointed when he calls Yale hoping to find out that his affair is over. In fact, learning that Isaac is interested in Mary simply increases Yale's ardor. Indeed, Yale is so affected by Isaac's call that he can't resist arranging to meet Mary at lunchtime at Bloomingdale's, where he insists on checking into a hotel for a quickie—a request that even Mary finds sleazy, given the purity of her Platonic night with Isaac.

Later in the film, brooding alone in her apartment on a Sunday, Mary calls Yale at home—something they obviously had agreed she would not do—to ask him to get away for a walk. Yale is irritated by her invasion of his private domain in which he pretends to be a happily married man. However, once Mary becomes involved with Isaac, he will think nothing of calling her at Isaac's to ask her to go out. Yale perpetually expects others to follow imperatives from which he himself is exempted. From a Kantian perspective, Yale's willingness to make a moral exception of himself underlines his lack of character.

In her frustration, Mary next calls Isaac. In contrast to Yale, Isaac is pleased and flattered by her call, never suspecting that he is Mary's second choice. Unfortunately for Isaac, his self-confidence and moral naivete blind him to his true status with Mary until, in the end, he is stunned by her betrayal.

Mary tells Isaac that it's a beautiful day for a walk, yet we immediately see them running from an electrical storm. As we have already noted, Mary's judgment is not to be trusted. Furthermore, she is a bad influence on Isaac because she is even more pessimistic. After he jokes that the sound of thunder is the Chrysler Building exploding, she tells him that "every year one or two people are killed by an electrical storm in Central Park." In *Sam*, the fact that Linda shared Allan's neurotic anxieties was positive because she looked to him as a mentor to guide her out into greater self-confidence. In *Manhattan*, however, Mary's despair is so deeply rooted in such fundamental bad faith that her companionship affects Isaac entirely negatively.

They escape the storm by running into a planetarium. Once in the building, Mary makes a point of telling him how ridiculous he looks, while a moment later she fishes for compliments on her own appearance.

With a model of the moon taking up most of the screen, Isaac and Mary, appearing as small figures walking in the distance, seem to have left this world, their conversation detached from earthly reality. Mary lies to Isaac, telling him that Yale cancelled their plans for the afternoon when we know that they had no such plans. She also tells him that they were supposed to go to a Vivaldi concert the night before, a very suspicious claim. What husband would be able to take his mistress to a concert on a Saturday night while his wife sat at home?

When Isaac starts to respond, Mary interrupts him by finishing his sentence, saying that's what happens when you have an affair with a married man. She then immediately chides him: "What a terrible way to put it!" when it was she, not he, who put it that way. Mary seems to be having an internal dialogue in which Isaac's job is to play the role of sympathetic audience. There is a certain irony to this as Isaac himself has treated Tracy in this same condescending fashion.

As Isaac and Mary walk across a darkened, gloomy, and artificial lunar terrain, Mary tells him of her first husband's affairs and her decision to say nothing about them based on her belief that Jeremiah cheated on her because of some deficiencies in herself. Mary seems not to care that she is putting Yale's wife, Emily, through exactly the same sort of suffering that she herself endured. A further indication of the fact that they are now traversing an alien, inhuman (and immoral) terrain comes as a solitary tourist, slowly walking in the foreground, turns to photograph the audience. For those out of touch with moral intuition, it is we, the supposedly average people sitting in the audience, who are so out of place that we become the oddities, the tourist attraction worthy of a picture.

Mary labels Jeremiah as a "louse" (Isaac adds, "an intellectual louse"), yet she praises him for opening her up sexually and says that "women found him devastating." The relationship among Isaac, Mary, and Jeremiah has a certain resemblance, albeit in a more serious context, to the relationship among Victor, Carole, and Michael in *Pussycat*. Like Michael, Jeremiah is described as both irresistible to women and incapable of resisting the temptation to capitalize on this appeal. Mary, like Carole, toys with the affections of the Allen character in an attempt to validate herself by doing to him what she feels has been done to her.

The situation in *Manhattan* is further complicated by the fact that Mary has partially transferred her adoration for Jeremiah to another manipulating pseudointellectual, namely Yale, who is allowing her to relive her negative experiences with Jeremiah from the perspective of the mistress rather than the wife. Given the twisted psychological neuroses that dominate her life, there is no chance for Isaac to engage in an authentic relationship with her.

When Mary says, "There's Saturn, the sixth planet from the sun. How many of Saturn's moons can you name?" and then commences to name them without pausing for breath, she sounds like a little girl having an imaginary conversation with herself. Isaac acknowledges the oddness of this apparent monologue by saying, "I can't name any of them, they never come up in conversation." He tries to break through Mary's introversion by trying to convince her that facts don't mean a thing because "nothing worth knowing can be understood with the mind. Everything valuable has to enter you through a different opening."

As the screen gets darker and darker, and their voices are lowered seductively to whispers, Mary tries to disagree by asking where we would be without rational thought. Isaac transforms the conversation from an abstract philosophical debate into an analysis of Mary's character. He tells her that she relies too much on her brain. When she reacts defensively, as usual, by exaggerating his comments to imply that she has no feelings, Isaac is manipulated into praising her, eventually telling her that she's terrific, although he admits she's too sensitive and insecure. Mary reciprocates, first by asking Isaac if he wants to get something to eat; then, when he refuses, she reverses the traditional sex roles by aggressively asking if she can call him to get together next week. Despite her tantalizing appeal for him, he tells her it wouldn't be a good idea because of his loyalty to Yale, a loyalty which Yale himself will later violate without a second thought.

In these scenes, Isaac agrees with Nietzsche, Heidegger, Camus, and Kierkegaard in his rejection of the intellect in favor of nonrational intuition. All four of these philosophers "rebel" (Camus's term) against the traditional societal and religious reliance on reason in favor of a highly personalized "transvaluation" (Nietzsche's term), in which one overcomes "dread" by harking to the "call" of one's "authentic self" (Heidegger's terms). Ultimately, such a choice requires a "leap of faith" into some form of transcendent spirituality. Isaac has already made one such leap in his decision to quit his job in order to fulfill himself artistically and morally. At the film's conclusion, he will make an even greater leap when he chooses to believe in the spiritual purity symbolized by Tracy.

There are also elements of Eastern mysticism, particularly Taoism, in Isaac's approach. Simply stated, the early Chinese Taoists, inspired by the writings of Lao-tzu (literally, "old boy"), believed that within each person, from birth, there is an "uncarved block" (*pu*) of innocence and moral purity which should guide one in all one's acts. Appeal to this instinctual inner core gives one the power (*te*) to overcome life's apparent difficulties and put oneself on the correct "tao" or path. These early Taoists had no affection for the use of reason, the discoveries of science, the intrigues of politics, or the demands of institutionalized religion. Like Allen himself (for example in *A Midsummer Night's Sex Comedy*, "Oedipus Wrecks," and *Shadows and Fog*), the Taoists are fascinated by the powers of magic and alchemy, which they use not to gain material wealth or position, but to strengthen their spiritual ties to the natural forces of the universe.

Mary's bad faith is reemphasized when she does not acknowledge that her desires are contradictory. On the one hand, she describes herself as being beautiful and bright, and therefore deserving of better; yet her strange assertion of a conventional social ethic ("I'm from Philadelphia and we don't have affairs") results in her insistence that she not be the cause of the breakup of Yale's marriage. Where Tracy is willing to support Isaac and encourage him to disregard his anxieties, Mary's primary concern is always for herself, and she thinks nothing of making derogatory remarks that only feed into Isaac's neurotic tendencies. Isaac accurately points out that her therapy has been so unsuccessful that her self-confidence is "a notch below Kafka's," and we see that when Isaac and Mary are together it is Isaac's role to constantly reassure her.

Isaac and Mary develop a relationship as they go to a double bill of foreign films (over which we see them arguing as they leave the theater). As they enter Mary's dark apartment, we hear Isaac praising W.C. Fields (a reference to his recent wonderful evening with Tracy) and films like *The Grand Illusion* (another film, like the one we are watching, that depicts the collapse of traditional standards). Douglas Brode has pointed out that Allen uses food as a symbol for a fulfilling sexual relationship; the same symbolism appears to apply to spiritual fulfillment. Thus it is no surprise when Isaac complains that Mary has nothing worth eating in her refrigerator; all he can find is a rotted corned beef sandwich. Nevertheless, he insists on kissing her. Mary's reaction to Isaac's sexual advances is completely uninterested and remote; she even asks him what he is doing, as though the thought of a romantic relationship has never entered her mind. Yet, a second later, when Isaac confesses he's wanted to kiss her "for the longest time," Mary says she thought he was going to kiss her that day in the planetarium. Isaac's explanation that he would never have done that to Yale is of no interest to her. Isaac's further confession — that he would have liked to throw her down on the fake lunar surface and commit "interplanetary perversion"— suggests again the unnaturalness of any relationship between them.

Mary demonstrates ambivalence about getting involved with Isaac, admitting that she has no idea whether she is interested in him, and that she has too many problems. Finally, she warns him that she is nothing but trouble. Despite this disclaimer, she does not protest when Isaac jokes that trouble is his middle name and starts kissing her again.

Once again, as in earlier films, a flawed relationship is portrayed by showing a scene in a car. Isaac halfheartedly complains to Mary about the exorbitance of taking a $14 cab to eat at a restaurant (something he told Yale he would no longer be able to afford). He confesses that he is so drunk, and Mary looks so beautiful, that he can't pay full attention to the meter. The implication of this scene is that his relationship with Mary will be so costly that it will destroy his ability to forgo material luxury for the sake of his novel.

In a montage of scenes, we see Isaac and Mary dancing in her apartment, window shopping, and rowing on the water (when Isaac trails his hand in the water, he pulls it up covered, significantly, with muck).

When Emily complains to Isaac that she and Yale never see him anymore, Isaac confers with Yale, asking whether it would bother him if Isaac brought Mary along on a double date. Yale claims this would not bother him, and Isaac tells him that Mary said the same thing. Nevertheless, their discomfort is palpable as they pretend to meet for the first time in front of Emily and squirm awkwardly in their seats at a concert.

In Isaac's apartment, we learn that Mary spends her time reviewing books and creating novelizations of other people's films. When Isaac complains about her doing such junk, she responds that "it's easy and it pays well," suggesting that this should be enough. Isaac disagrees, accusing her of complicity in "another contemporary American phenomenon that is truly moronic" and urges her to return to her work in fiction.

When the telephone rings, Mary answers, and Yale tells her, "I hoped that you would pick up." As noted earlier, Yale has so little integrity that not only does he not share Isaac's reluctance to pursue his best friend's love interest, but he thinks nothing about calling Mary at Isaac's apartment. When she rejects his advances—at least for now—and tells Isaac that the call was from a dance studio wanting to know if they want free dance lessons, we know what kind of dancing she has in mind. Unknowingly, Isaac is correct when he states that the lessons may be free now, but later on, they will cost a great deal.

When Mary finally tells him that she and Yale are getting back together and that Yale has decided to leave Emily, Isaac is stunned by the immensity of this betrayal and Mary's inability to consider the possible consequences of her actions. Isaac says he feels like a character in a Noel Coward comedy ("Someone should go out and mix the martinis"). When Isaac points out all of the possible pitfalls in a relationship with Yale, telling Mary that he gives the whole thing four weeks, she demonstrates her instability and lack of commitment by saying she can't plan that far in advance.

III. Jill

We first see Isaac's ex-wife Jill when he accosts her on the street, demanding to know if she is really writing a book about their relationship. His method of speaking to her is reminiscent of the scene in *Annie Hall* where Alvy follows Annie from a class because he suspects that she is involved with her professor. Jill reinforces this association when she accuses him of spying on her. We get the first hint of the real reasons for their breakup when Isaac inquires about their son, Willie, asking if he is wearing dresses. As they part, Isaac denies that he is threatened by the book because he was not the "immoral, psychotic, promiscuous one."

We meet Connie, Jill's lover, when Isaac arrives at their place to pick up Willie for his visitation. Isaac's contradictory emotions are evident as he discounts the possibility that Willie's ability to draw could come from his exposure to Connie ("There's no way you could be the actual biological father"), even though we know he is worried about Willie growing up in a lesbian household. Just as Mary represents one variation on Annie Hall, Jill represents another. In the split-screen analysis scene in *Annie Hall*, Annie wonders if she would be better off with another woman. We suggested that this would be Alvy's worst nightmare. That nightmare has come true for Isaac. Furthermore, when Annie rejects Alvy in Los Angeles at the film's conclusion, Alvy takes out his hostility by crashing his rental car into other cars in a parking lot, reliving his childhood mechanism for releasing aggression at his father's bumper-car concession. Isaac, who appears to resemble Alvy more and more as the film goes on, took out his hostility towards Jill and Connie in the same fashion, although with a more murderous intent.

Douglas Brode insightfully points out that in this film, Allen takes his usual inability to deal with any form of machinery and

> turns it into a motif that suffuses every aspect of the film: imagery, dialogue, and plot. A car, of course, is what Yale is going to waste his money on; a car is what Isaac apparently used to try and kill the lesbian lover of his ex-wife.... Throughout the film, we see each significant set of characters try, without much luck, to cement a relationship while driving. In each successive scene, Allen's camera is behind the car, doggedly following them, as we hear their conversations in a voice-over technique. The failure of each of these affairs to amount to anything thus appears to grow from the fact that they were developed in that vehicle which has always been associated with Los Angeles, a city Allen despises, and actually seems out of place in his beloved New York: It is no small matter, then, that at one point in the film Isaac/Allen claims all cars should be banned from Manhattan. The only relationship in the film that is not developed in a car is the Isaac/Tracy one (they are always seen walking places) and significantly, when Isaac at the end wants to get to Tracy's house as quickly as he can, he cannot flag down a cab. He cannot get there by car, and is forced to make the journey by foot [1985, pp. 197–98].

Thus automobiles are symbolic of the degradation of our national cultural values, a degeneration which began in Los Angeles (the source of most fads) and has now spread even to Manhattan. Allen argues that we should resist the selfishness of the so-called Me Decade (the seventies) and return to old-fashioned notions of honesty and honor, which each of us experiences directly and instinctively. Yet Isaac is seduced by the apparent sophistication of the new morality. How else can one account for his attraction to Mary and his willingness to implicate himself in Yale's deception of Emily?

Back in a car (Yale's Porsche this time) we see Emily, Yale, Mary, and

Isaac spending a day together. Mary buys Isaac a present, some sort of picture, which is so inappropriate for him that he immediately throws it away — unlike the harmonica he received from Tracy, which he treasures.

Passing a bookstore window, they see copies of Jill's book (pretentiously titled *Marriage, Divorce, and Selfhood*). Isaac groans as his supposed friends enjoy themselves by reading aloud painful passages which make clear the many similarities between Isaac and Alvy. When Mary happily tells Emily and Yale about his attempt to run down Connie, Isaac asks her whose side she's on. We can't conceive of Tracy taking such unabashed pleasure in publicly sharing Isaac's most vulnerable and painful memories.

As Emily and Yale pass out of the screen's frame, eagerly perusing the book's pages, we see a tortured Isaac grimace as Emily reads this Alvy-like description of Isaac:

> He was given to fits of rage, Jewish liberal paranoia, male chauvinism, self-righteous misanthropy, and nihilistic moods of despair. He had complaints about life, but never any solutions. He longed to be an artist but balked at the necessary sacrifices. In his most private moments, he spoke of his fear of death which he elevated to tragic heights, when, in fact, it was mere narcissism.

IV. Tracy

While Jill represents Isaac's worst nightmares, Tracy symbolizes an innocence so overwhelming that Isaac spends most of the film fleeing her. In their first scene alone together, in his apartment, they discuss their relationship to the accompaniment of "Our Love Is Here to Stay." When Tracy tells Isaac that she thinks she loves him, he pushes her away by telling her that she should think of their relationship as only a pleasant interlude and that she shouldn't get "too hung up" on him. Throughout the film, we watch Isaac using Tracy's age as an excuse to keep their relationship casual, as a sexual relationship with a minor could only be justified by lust rather than genuine emotion. In Allen's view, this reversal of morality is yet another result of the degradation of values occurring in contemporary life — even in Manhattan, the city that once epitomized the tough smart-aleck exterior that hides authentic moral sensibility.

Worried about what others would think if he acknowledged that he was falling in love with a seventeen-year-old, Isaac forces himself to pretend that he is exploiting Tracy for sexual reasons alone. To make matters worse, he pretends to Tracy that his unwillingness to make himself emotionally vulnerable is based on his concern for her interests rather than his own. Later in the film, Tracy accurately accuses him of using her age as a justification for his own selfishness.

Isaac's relationship with Tracy is another of Allen's Pygmalion-Galatea romances. He tells Tracy that he is going to take her to see a Veronica Lake picture (at the same theater where Alvy met Annie for *Face to Face*). As Isaac instructs Tracy, she feigns ignorance about the identity of Rita Hayworth. Unlike Annie, who at the beginning of her film was extremely unsure of herself, Tracy, despite her age, exudes self-confidence and a playful acceptance of Isaac's need to play the role of mentor and professor.

Their most important scene together begins when Isaac impulsively calls Tracy and offers to spend the evening doing anything she wants. In contrast to the gloom of many of Isaac's scenes with Mary, Isaac's scenes with Tracy are brightly lit and often associated with food (Brode, 1985, p. 198). Over a pizza with everything including anchovies (Isaac says they forgot the coconut), Tracy tells him about the offer she's received to study acting in London for six months. Isaac encourages her to go for it all, just as with the pizza, and ridicules her concerns about the effects on their relationship ("Well, we'll always have Paris," he cracks in a reference to his intoxication with Bogart in *Sam*). He doesn't disagree when Tracy accuses him again of refusing to take their relationship seriously because of her youth. When he tries to demonstrate the impracticality of it by calculating his age when she is thirty-six, he gets lost in the arithmetic. Tracy, with a quicker mind than Isaac's, tells him he'll be sixty-three, and in spite of himself, Isaac realizes that the age combination would be both socially acceptable and sexually exciting.

Tracy's choice of activity, in the film's second unabashedly romantic scene, is to take a horse-drawn carriage through Central Park. As before, with Mary by the river, the real star of this scene is Allen's beloved Manhattan. In fact, we learn of her choice by seeing a panorama of the New York cityscape through the branches of the park's trees as we hear the romantic sounds of horse's hooves and the glorious strains of Gershwin's "He Loves and She Loves."

Unlike the scene with Mary, who violates the magic by leaving just as Isaac is reveling in his love for the city, Tracy is such a natural part of the environment that Isaac wonders at her absence when he remembers that he last circled the park in a carriage on his prom night — unfortunately alone. Thus, despite his protests about the activity's corniness, by unselfishly giving in to another's desires he has reaped rich spiritual benefit; he is able to transform an unhappy adolescent memory into a moment to be cherished.

In this sense, Tracy has allowed Isaac to experience what the existential novelist Walker Percy has called "a successful repetition." In Percy's first novel, appropriately titled *The Moviegoer*, the narrator, Binx Bolling, describes "a successful repetition" in this way:

> What is a repetition? A repetition is the re-enactment of past experience towards the end of isolating the time segment which has lapsed in order that it, the lapsed time, can be savored of itself and without the usual adulteration of events that clog time like peanuts in brittle [Percy, 1980, p. 68].

In the film's most beautiful imagery, Isaac, buoyed by the exhilaration of his repetition, associates Tracy with images of religious redemption:

> You know what you are? You're God's answer to Job. You would have ended all argument between them, I mean, He would have pointed to you and said, you know, I do a lot of terrible things but I can also make one of these!

Tracy is so moved by this that she joyfully buries her head on Isaac's shoulder.

Another uplifting scene shows them happily eating Chinese food in bed, watching television and commenting on the phoniness of newscasters who wear bad toupees and get endless facelifts. Again revealing her inherent honesty, Tracy asks why people can't "just age naturally instead of putting all that junk on." Like a happily married couple, they delight in simple pleasures. When a W.C. Fields film comes on the late show, Isaac innocently expresses his joy in the moment by squeezing Tracy's arm and kissing her shoulder.

The moral consequences of Isaac's decision to reject Tracy for Mary are vividly illustrated in the scene in the ice cream parlor, in which Isaac's response to her gift of a harmonica (she wants to open up the happy, musical side of him) is to tell her that he's in love with someone else. Once again, Tracy demonstrates her moral superiority over all the other characters by responding both naturally and wisely. Dismissing Isaac's claim that no one really knows what love is, Tracy gives this film's best definition of it:

> We have laughs together. I care about you. Your concerns are my concerns. We have great sex.

Unlike Mary, who reacts to Yale's rejection with controlled bitterness and sarcasm, Tracy cries openly. When Isaac pleads with her to stop crying (because, we suspect, he is embarrassed that she is being emotional in a public place), she demands that he leave her alone so she can continue to respond spontaneously. Isaac then lies on his bed alone in his apartment, blows a single note on the harmonica, and sighs. Clearly, he knows the horrible thing he has done.

Towards the film's end, Isaac has lunch with Emily, who reveals her complicity in the many levels of self-deception. Like Mary earlier, she acknowledges that she knew her husband was having affairs but ignored them in the belief that compromise was required and in the blind hope that things would work out somehow on their own. After Isaac lectures her on the sins of compromise and brags that he has the values of an earlier age, he is reminded of his own guilt (and the hypocrisy of his last remarks) when Emily tells him that she was angry with him at first for introducing Yale to Mary. In this scene, Isaac also confesses that he realizes now what a good thing he passed up when he left Tracy. He tells us that, despite everything, Tracy left a message on his service to tell him that *Grand Illusion* was on television — a phone call, he regretfully admits, that he never bothered to return.

Back in his apartment, we see his tape recorder going and hear Isaac talk about an idea for a short story (very much like the film we are watching) in which a group of people in Manhattan are shown creating needless neurotic problems for themselves in the attempt to inauthentically escape from life's more fundamental, and more terrifying, genuine philosophical concerns. Expanding on this idea, he composes his list of things that make life worth living (the counterlist to Yale's and Mary's earlier Academy of the Overrated). On this list, he moves from the work of a few of those who, like his skeleton, have left us a legacy of honest achievement (from Groucho Marx to Willie Mays, Flaubert, and Cézanne) to his favorite place for crabs, to Tracy's face. As the strains of "He Loves and She Loves" draw us back to the scene in the park where he explicitly associated Tracy with God's redemptive power, he longingly fondles the harmonica.

Unable to reach her by phone or catch a cab, he runs to her place (to the tune "Strike Up the Band"). He arrives to find Tracy in the process of leaving to catch her flight to London. We watch with Isaac as Tracy combs out her hair until she catches sight of him through the door (now to the accompaniment of "But Not for Me"). Like the romantic cinema beauties mentioned earlier (Veronica Lake and Rita Hayworth) her hair falls over one eye as she explains that, just like in the movies, he really did arrive just in the nick of time to catch her before she left for England.

Isaac immaturely tries to convince her to change her plans and stay.

He acknowledges that he made a mistake as she tells him how much he hurt her. When he repeatedly asks her if she still loves him, she asks the more important question: Is he now willing to say that he loves her? When he professes his love and continues to try to persuade her to stay, warning her that in six months she might find someone else, or become such a different person that she will lose that innocence that he loves in her, she chides him by pointing out that "not everyone is corrupted."

For the first time in the film, Isaac really listens to Tracy. He realizes that he has the power to let go of his anxieties in order to make a leap of faith into a commitment of love from which he will gain no immediate gratification. As Tracy utters the film's last line, "You have to have a little faith in people," Isaac slowly smiles. Returning to the film's beginning, "Rhapsody in Blue" again accompanies romantic images of Manhattan, a city still deserving of our love and faith, despite the inadequacies of some of its residents.

V. Themes of Redemption

As one way of portraying Isaac's transformation in the course of this film, I will now refer to ideas presented by Rabbi Joseph B. Soloveitchik in his lengthy 1965 essay, "The Lonely Man of Faith." While Allen has not to my knowledge made a scholarly study of the works of Soloveitchik, there are some important similarities between the two. This compatibility adds to the richness of our understanding of Allen's work.

Soloveitchik, an Orthodox rabbi who wished to reconcile the demands of faith with those of life in contemporary secular society, writes of two fundamentally opposed images of humanity which can be found in the Orthodox Halakhic Scriptures. He refers to these as Adam the first and Adam the second.

Adam the first, whom he also calls "majestic man," is motivated by his natural desire to fulfill his freedom through the creation of dignity in a human community. This he achieves through teleological behavior which strives to control his environment using the tools of his mind and his creativity. Adam the first (somewhat like Kierkegaard's aesthetic and ethical persons, represented here by Yale and Mary) believes that one can come to learn everything, to penetrate the secrets of the universe, if only one persistently accumulates enough data, enough of Mary's "facts." Yet Adam the first is also aware of his freedom and the responsibility which flows from that freedom to create meaning for the world both in work and in one's relations with others. Adam the first is a social-contract theorist who constructs a stable social environment through the creation of laws and institutions to enforce those laws.

Soloveitchik states:

> Adam the first is not only a creative theoretician. He is also a creative aesthetic. He fashions ideas with his mind, and beauty with his heart. He enjoys both his intellectual and his aesthetic creativity and takes pride in it. He also displays creativity in the world of the norm: he legislates for himself norms and laws because a dignified existence is an orderly one.
>
> Anarchy and dignity are mutually exclusive. He is this-worldly-minded, finitude-oriented, beauty-centered. Adam the first is always an aesthete, whether engaged in an intellectual or in an ethical performance. His conscience is energized not by the idea of the good, but by that of the beautiful. His mind is questing not for the true, but for the pleasant and functional, which are rooted in the aesthetical, not the noetic-ethical sphere [1992, pp. 18–19].

Thus, while Soloveitchik's description of Adam the first might apply to the classical notion of teleological humanity, it also applies to the Cartesian, Kantian, and even existential notions of the human condition. At the beginning of *Manhattan*, Isaac may be identified with this notion of humanity. Like many of Allen's protagonists, especially those played by Allen himself, Isaac's method of maintaining his dignity and expressing his freedom and aesthetic creativity is initially through his humor.

As stated earlier, Allen's distinctive wit is the thread running through all the characters he has played. Allen's humor imposes an existential running commentary on all the events in his films, a commentary which proclaims his autonomy. Yet there is never a claim that humor can fulfill his character's goals. Isaac's disgust with his television work and the degenerate contemporary lifestyles represented by Mary and Yale lead him to quit a successful career grounded in the exploitation of his humor in order to seek the things that make life worth living. Thus, by the end of the film, he is ready to begin to travel down a different path.

For Soloveitchik, Adam the second

> sees his separateness from nature and his existential uniqueness not in dignity or majesty but in something else. There is, in his opinion, another mode of existence through which a man can find his own self, namely, the redemptive, which is not necessarily identical with the dignified [1992, p. 25].

Unlike Adam the first, the "ontologically perfectible" individual of the Enlightenment — or, as Soloveitchik tells us in a footnote, of Marxist philosophical anthropology (1992, p. 30) — Adam the second experiences himself as incomplete and fundamentally alone. For Soloveitchik, "loneliness is nothing but the act of questioning one's own ontological legitimacy, worth, and reasonableness" (1992, p. 31).

According to Soloveitchik:

> Adam the second suddenly finds out that he is alone, that he has alienated himself from the world of the brute and instinctual mechanical state of an outward existence, while he has failed to ally himself with the intelligent, purposive inward beings who inhabit the new world into which he has entered. Every great redemptive step forward entails the ever-growing tragic awareness of his aloneness and only-ness and consequently of his loneliness and insecurity... [1992, p. 37].
>
> At this crucial point, if Adam is to bring his quest for redemption to full realization, he must initiate action leading to the discovery of a companion who, even though as unique and singular as he, will master the art of communicating and, with him, form a community. However, this action, since it is part of the redemptive gesture, must also be sacrificial. The medium of attaining full redemption is, again, defeat. This new companionship is not attained through conquest, but through surrender and retreat.... Thus, in crisis and distress there was planted the seed of a new type of community — the faith community which reached full fruition in the covenant between God and Abraham [1992, p. 39].

In *Manhattan*, this new covenant results from a leap of faith in the redemptive power of love with a teenaged innocent. That Isaac must also deal with his loneliness is illustrated by the fact that, at the film's end, he must go through a six-month period of solitary penance while Tracy is in England and he works on his book. In this sense, Isaac's leap is not solely towards fulfillment through a romantic relationship; it could also be interpreted as a more private quest which will require his withdrawal from practical society.

For Allen and Soloveitchik (unlike Kierkegaard) this choice does not rule out a return to the world of the practical or the renewal of romantic involvement upon Tracy's return. For Soloveitchik, the relationship between Adam the first and Adam the second is a dialectical one which requires an ongoing interplay between the two. Soloveitchik states that

> since the dialectical role has been assigned to man by God, it is God who wants the man of faith to oscillate between the faith community and the community of majesty, between being confronted by God in the cosmos and the intimate, immediate apprehension of God through the covenant, and who therefore willed that complete human redemption be unattainable [1992, p. 86].

– 4 –

BETRAYAL AND DESPAIR:
The Purple Rose of Cairo (1985)

Allen frequently reminds us of the magical escape the movies can provide for those dissatisfied with their lives. Many of Allen's personas (e.g., Alvy, Isaac, Mickey, and Cliff) anchor elements of their lives in the meaning and pleasure that moviegoing affords. *Play It Again, Sam* focuses on Allan Felix's attempts to augment his disappointing romantic life with his fantasies of transforming himself into the successful Bogart persona. In that film's opening scene, Allen demonstrates both the wonder of the filmgoing experience and the awful letdown that occurs when the movie ends and one must go back out into the world.

Allan Felix is able to retain some of that magic by internalizing the Bogart persona and relying upon it for advice in dealing with his many frustrations. Thus, like Tom Baxter in *The Purple Rose of Cairo* (the film within the film; hereafter referred to as "the inner *Cairo*"), Bogart is able to step off the screen and into the life of a fan. This use of fantasy becomes therapeutic in *Sam*, with Allan slowly weaning himself from his daydream until he is able to leave it behind in the fog of the San Francisco airport. In *Cairo*, Cecilia's experience with the magic of film is less satisfying.

I. Kugelmass and Cecilia

Perhaps Woody Allen's most famous story is "The Kugelmass Episode," which first appeared in *The New Yorker* (May 2, 1977, pp. 34–39) and later in his book *Side Effects* (1980). The story describes an English professor named Kugelmass who is able to transport himself into the literature of his choice with the help of a magician named Persky the Great. Kugelmass, who has always romanticized his feelings for Flaubert's Emma Bovary, is thus able to fulfill his dreams by entering the novel and engaging in a passionate affair with the woman of his dreams. But, as Madame Bovary learns more about Kugelmass's "real" world, she longs to enter it and seek its pleasures. Persky is able to make her dream come true by bringing her into the real world for a weekend, but when Persky has trouble sending her back, the romance fades. Once Persky has finally removed Emma, Kugelmass resolves to be satisfied with reality as it is. Eventually, however, he reneges on his vow and has Persky send him into other books. At the story's conclusion, when Persky dies of a heart attack, Kugelmass is stranded in *Remedial Spanish*, where he is doomed to be chased forever by the irregular verb *tener* (to have). *The Purple Rose of Cairo* reverses and expands this entertaining idea into the realm of film, with much more serious philosophic and moral overtones.

After *Stardust Memories* (1980), many critics accused Allen of showing disdain for his fans and demonstrating a lack of empathy for ordinary people in love with the escapist magic of the cinema. Anyone who thinks that Woody Allen scorns the cinema fan should see *Cairo*, a film with a starstruck moviegoer as its sympathetic main character.

This is also Allen's first film with a female protagonist. While it might be said that the most important characters in *Interiors* are women, that was more of an ensemble piece. In *Cairo* there is no question that Cecilia (Mia Farrow) is the central figure in the plot. In fact, it is even possible to interpret the story of Tom Baxter's descent from the screen as no more than a fantasy in the mind of Cecilia while she watches the film-within-the-film (the "inner *Cairo*") for the fifth time. It is interesting to compare Cecilia to the typical Allen personas that have appeared in his films.

Cecilia can accurately be described as the female equivalent of the "little man," a person victimized by an unfeeling world more interested in the material manifestations of success than in the imaginative sensitivities of someone easily defined as a "loser." Like Allan Felix or Danny Rose, Cecilia is a person whose dreams far outdistance the harsh realities of her life, and who, through an unusual situation, is given the opportunity to make some of her dreams come true.

With Danny she shares a nurturing spirit. Just as he devoted his life to looking after the interests of others, often getting very little in return, so Cecilia, in the film's opening scenes, is depicted as someone whose primary role is to look after the needs of others. However, Cecilia's role seems less chosen, less a function of her own urges and aspirations, than Danny's.

After all, Danny, in the final analysis, hugely enjoys his job as a personal manager, even to the dismal performers he usually represents. Further, he views his sacrifice as a worthwhile and necessary one, not only for moral reasons, but because he truly believes that one day he could be transformed from a "bum" into a "showbiz hero." Of course, the very telling of his story is evidence that this dream has come true.

Cecilia, on the other hand, is a Depression-era waitress in New Jersey, the sole wage-earner for herself and her husband, Monk (Danny Aiello), an unemployed lout who pitches pennies all day and carouses at night. Her sole pleasure comes from the world of fantasy she enters when she goes to the movies. During her days at the restaurant, she talks endlessly with her sister, another waitress, about the details of each of the films and the gossip she has read in the picture magazines. Her constant daydreaming makes her so slow and clumsy at her job that her boss is always after her to quit socializing and get back to work.

Cecilia's jobs as waitress and wife are not, by any stretch of the imagination, capable of fulfilling her dreams. If anything, they are impediments to the one activity that offers her any hope of escape or stimulation, namely moviegoing. The film makes clear that whatever romance was connected with Monk's initial courting was short-lived and woefully beneath her cinematic standards of romance. Their marriage is really one of convenience — his convenience. Cecilia is a resource Monk can exploit for financial support and for her services as maid and cook. Alternating between his two strategies of groveling and intimidation, he is able to keep her "in shape" so that he can pursue his real interests in life: drinking, gambling, whoring, and eating.

One night, Cecilia comes home from her solitary evening at the movies to discover her husband engaged in drunken revelry with another woman. Her initial reaction is to pack her bags and leave, but with nowhere to go, in the end she returns home. Her glimpse of a prostitute (Dianne Wiest) entering a bar and an overheard remark about making some money frighten her about the possible consequences of leaving her husband for good. The next day, back at her job, when her sister tries to get her to leave Monk by fixing her up with an eligible exterminator, Cecilia is so flustered that she drops a plate and is fired on the spot.

Cecilia was given the waitress job not on her own merits, but through the influence of her sister (played by Farrow's actual sister, Stephanie). Her boss also works to keep her "in shape" so that he can accomplish his aim, the running of a profitable business. That his interest in her is determined by how much she can contribute to that aim is demonstrated by his willingness to fire her — and her more efficient sister as well, as soon as he decides that she is more trouble than she is worth. Not that Cecilia's firing isn't justified. She returns her boss's indifference in equal measure. Indeed, her primary goal at work is to become so absorbed in her gossiping and daydreaming that she is effectively able to forget where she is.

In describing Cecilia, Douglas Brode remarks

> In true Woody Allen fashion, her plight is schematized through her relationship to food. It's not for nothing Allen makes her a waitress rather than assigning her some other equally drab job (sales clerk, secretary). Early on, we see her mumbling mindlessly about her movie-fed fantasies even as she none too effectively serves food to a very real, and, very hungry, clientele. At the greasy spoon diner, Cecilia daydreams about those people glimpsed eating at the Copacabana. Understandably, then, her relationship with her husband is defined by images not of affection or even marital responsibility but of food: "Any more meat loaf left?" is all Monk (Danny Aiello) wants to know. The highest compliment he can extend refers to a successful meal: "That stuff you made yesterday was delicious." When Cecilia considers leaving him, he's less worried about losing her sexually (he's already sleeping with someone else) or even her financial support (she works, he doesn't) than about his stomach: "I want my supper" is all he can say to a wife desperately walking out the door [1985, pp. 247–248].

Later, in her relationships with both Tom and Gil, she always seems to be the one providing the food. We watch her drinking champagne with Tom, and we hear Gil offer to take her to lunch, but we never see her actually eating.

II. The Ephemeral Tom Baxter

After losing her job, needing to escape more than ever, Cecilia returns to the one film playing in town, the inner *Cairo*. She spends the afternoon sitting through it again and again, until a startling thing happens: one of the film's characters, the idealistic explorer and adventurer Tom Baxter (Jeff Daniels), pauses and addresses her directly from the screen. To everyone's amazement, including that of the other characters in the film, Tom is able to come off the screen and run into the night with Cecilia. This rip in the fabric of reality creates a multitude of complications.

Unlike Allan Felix's conversations with the Bogart persona in *Sam*, Tom Baxter's departure from the screen is not portrayed as a private event affecting the life of only one person; nor is Tom solely a fantasy figure who appears and disappears when needed by the main protagonist. On the contrary, Tom becomes a character in his own right in the supposedly "real world." However, being viewed as "fictional" by others who regard themselves as "real" (although, of course, they are equally fictional) leads to his victimization and eventual destruction, a destruction for which Cecilia shares responsibility.

For Cecilia, although unquestionably the primary protaganist, is not the only Allenesque "little man" in the film. Tom is perhaps the ultimate little-man character. With a childlike innocence and naiveté which surpasses even that of Chaplin's little tramp, Tom is a spunky explorer with a streak of impulsiveness who lives by a firm code of traditional moral values, the same values for which Allen's other personas often yearn when faced with a modern world corrupted by hedonism.

We first see Tom as a character in the inner *Cairo*, a carefully constructed homage to the wildly escapist Hollywood films of the thirties in which sophisticated men and women, for whom money never seems to be a problem, move through a world of witty conversation, champagne dinners, nightclubbing, and exotic locales. The plots of such films (epitomized by the Astaire-Rogers musicals) often turned on minor romantic difficulties, which always resolved themselves happily by the final reel.

The inner film begins with the credits presented on engraved white calling cards as lively and exotic music plays (in contrast to the credits of the outer *Cairo*, which conform to Allen's custom of white titles on a black background). We see a playwright, Henry (Edward Herrman), dressed in black tie and tails, smoking a cigarette while seated at a white piano in a stylized movie apartment. His opening speech typifies the superficial concerns that drove the plots of so many such films. Complaining that he is bored with "cocktail parties and opening nights," Henry rejects Jason's suggestion that they book their "usual suite" at the Ritz in Paris in favor of an exotic trip to Egypt. While this beginning superficially has the light, airy touch of the Astaire-Rogers musical, the playwright's attitude also manages to convey an element of mock-existential *ennui* similar to that of an Alvy or an Isaac.

Cutting to the interior of a Pyramid obviously filmed on a Hollywood soundstage, we see our heroes dressed causally, and impeccably, as they inspect the ruins. Just as the faithful sidekick Jason (John Wood) expresses comic concern about the possibility of feeling the Mummy's hand around his throat, out pops Tom from a small opening in the chamber wall. He completely defines his character in his opening lines:

> Tom: Oh! I'm awfully sorry! Tom Baxter, explorer, adventurer. I'm doing a little archeological work.

RITA: A real-life explorer!

TOM: I've come in search of the Purple Rose of Cairo. It's an old legend that has fascinated me for years. A pharaoh had a rose painted purple for his queen, and now the story says purple roses grow wild at her tomb.

RITA: How romantic!

TOM: And you?

HENRY: We're going back to New York tomorrow. It's been a refreshing two weeks.

JASON: Say, we could bring him back to meet the countess! She loves anything in a pith helmet!

HENRY: Right!

TOM: I will say it's tempting.

HENRY: Then it's all settled. You can explain to us what we have been looking at for the past two weeks, and we can go take you nightclubbing!

TOM: It's so impulsive, but I'll come! Why not? What's life without a little risk-taking! Who knows, a fortuneteller predicted I'd fall in love in New York.

The incongruity and artificiality of this interchange demonstrates the peculiar tone of films in which every line must advance the plot. Thus Tom Baxter is quickly categorized as an aging Tom Swift, an all–American boy accustomed to the good life and ready for anything. His fascination with the legend of the Purple Rose of Cairo symbolizes both his and Cecilia's most desired dream: to transform a work of art, such as the pharaoh's painted rose (or, for our purposes, tinted celluloid), into something miraculously real, like living purple roses or a liberated fictional character.

When Tom magically develops the ability not only to come alive and look back at the audience watching him, but also to choose his own actions outside the context of the inner film's script, he fulfills his character's inherent romanticism by again acting impulsively. He leaves the security of the screen to learn more about the mysterious "real" woman who has come to see him so many times. Like a modern-day Pinocchio, Tom is brought to life by the loneliness and suffering of another.

Again and again, we and Cecilia have heard Tom express his surprise at the fact that only twenty-four hours before he was alone in an Egyptian tomb (metaphorically dead), and now (still dressed in his pith helmet and safari suit), he is surrounded by new friends and "on the verge of a madcap Manhattan weekend." This time, however, after pausing in the middle of his lines, Tom directly addresses Cecilia, then chooses to leave the tomb represented by the fixed structure of the film in order to pursue the liberty and romance suddenly available to him.

Yelling, "I'm free, I'm free!" he begs her to hide him and tells her that because he's managed to get out of the film before the Copacabana scene, he no longer has to marry Kitty Haynes (Karen Akers). In fact, now that he's met Cecilia, he can rid himself of the charade of romancing and marrying a woman who he says isn't even his type. ("She's too boney!")

III. Trapped in a World They Didn't Create

Missing a crucial character, the rest of the inner film's cast is at a loss. Because none of them were written with Tom's idealism or his impulsive streak, they are trapped within the film, unable to escape. They bicker among themselves like critics over the film's real meaning and their relative importance as characters. Each argues that his own role carries the weight of the movie's meaning and that the others' roles are subordinate.

The theater manager (Irving Metzman) tries to ease the characters' confusion and concerns, but when an usherette suggests to him that he consider turning off the projector, Henry (a playwright like Allen and clearly the film's deepest thinker) begs him not to do so:

> HENRY: No, no! Don't turn the projector off! No, no, it gets black and we disappear.... But you don't understand what it's like to disappear, to be nothing, to be annihilated!

Here Henry demonstrates that he is plagued by the same sorts of existential ghosts that haunt "real" contemporary artists such as Alvy and Isaac. Like them, he is filled with Heideggerean dread at the prospect of death (non-being). However, unlike "real" people, he has had the added misfortune of actually experiencing nothingness and returning to tell the tale. His terror at the prospect of the projector being turned off, a fate which we know befalls him after the last show every night, only confirms our human fears that even a momentary stoppage of being is a horror beyond our collective imagination.

As we find out more about the fate of those trapped onscreen, we learn their existence is like that of the mythical Sisyphus (or the characters in Sartre's *No Exit*), doomed to repeat the same tasks again and again with no hope of completion or escape. Given this condition, it is not surprising that the denizens of such a land envy the mortals in the audience. They envy us for our lack of foreknowledge concerning our fates, and especially for our ontological freedom to choose our own acts. We, unlike them, can have some impact on the roles we play in a picture shown only once.

Eventually, the theater manager complains to the film's producer, Raoul Hirsh (Alexander Cohen), whose name is a play on that of Raoul Walsh, a well-known filmmaker of the era. Fearful of the economic and legal consequences of characters walking off the screen and getting into who knows what kind of trouble, the studio sends a group of representatives, including Gil Shepherd (Jeff Daniels), the actor who plays Tom, to get everything back under control.

Meanwhile, Cecilia hides Tom at the local amusement park, which is closed for the season, and goes home, where she conceals from Monk everything that has occurred. Later that evening, the naive Tom, believing himself to have fallen in love with Cecilia, takes her out for an expensive evening of dinner and dancing at a local club. However, when the time comes to pay the bill, Tom discovers that his pockets are filled only with stage money, and they have to make a run for it.

From this point, the film, like the Kugelmass story, shows the results of tinkering with the line separating reality from fantasy. Tom is baffled by all the things he doesn't know about: the Depression, the Great War, and the mysteries of childbirth, death, and God. He is astonished to discover that cars don't just move on their own (they need keys to start), and that there are women who are willing to engage in sex for money with men they don't love. Despite these revelations, Tom keeps his idealistic spirit and clings to his moral principles.

IV. Gil Shepherd and the Theme of the *Doppelgänger*

Cecilia is hysterical with pleasure when she meets Gil Shepherd, the actor who played Tom Baxter in the inner film. We first see Gil boasting to a reporter about his abilities and his great plans for his future, especially his desire to play Lindbergh in an upcoming film. When his agent (Michael Tucker) tells Gil about the problem with Tom Baxter, they worry that this could mean the end of Gil's career just when it was starting to take off. Overcoming his fear of flying, Gil rushes to New Jersey, where he searches frantically for Tom so that he can get him back onto the screen.

When Cecilia mistakes Gil for Tom in a shop, he begs her to take him to his double, promising that he is not angry with him. But when Gil confronts Tom, he is very angry indeed, berating him for the damage done to his career, threatening to get lawyers, the police, and even the FBI after him. Eventually, however, Gil appears to be attracted by Cecilia's "magic glow," and he claims to have also fallen in love with her.

In a reversal of the usual Pygmalion relationship between the Allen persona and a woman, this time the woman is in the role of mentor. We see Cecilia taking Tom on a tour of the town as she explains various puzzling aspects of the real world: a line at a soup kitchen, a pregnant woman with a child, and a church. In the church, Tom examines a crucifix as Cecilia tries to explain the meaning of religion:

> TOM: It's beautiful. I'm not sure exactly what it is.
>
> CECILIA: This is a church. You do believe in God, don't you?
>
> TOM: Meaning?
>
> CECILIA: That there's a reason for everything, for our world, for the universe!
>
> TOM: Oh, I think I know what you mean: the two men who wrote *The Purple Rose of Cairo*, Irving Sachs and R. H. Levine, they're writers who collaborate on films.
>
> CECILIA: No, no, I'm talking about something much bigger that that! No, think for a minute. A reason for everything. Otherwise, it would be like a movie with no point, and no happy ending!

Yacowar points out that

> Allen's absence from this film coheres with the theme of an absent maker in the fictional cosmos. The inner film credits producer Raoul Hirsh but no director; there is no director in a world where God is dead.... To Cecilia, a world without God would be "a world without point and no happy ending"—i.e., the world in which Allen leaves her, with only the idol worship of the silver screen to console her. Without God behind the creatures, the only good shepherd is the culpable Gil Shepherd [1991, p. 249].

Monk discovers them and tries to get Cecilia to come home. When he starts pushing her around, Tom declares his love for her and challenges Monk to a fight. Initially, Tom is able to defeat Monk, but when Monk appears to be beaten and Tom offers to help him up like a gentleman, Monk takes advantage of Tom's naiveté and knees him in the groin. With his new advantage, Monk is now able to easily defeat Tom, and continues to beat him until Cecilia intervenes and talks him into leaving. Tom is limited by his insistence on fighting fair, playing by the rules; Monk, with no interest in morality, is just concerned with winning. Tom, however, is not hurt. As a fictional character, no physical beating can hurt him.

Only Cecilia, when she rejects him at the film's end, has the power to hurt Tom in any way that matters.

Meanwhile, his double, Gil, has shown himself to be more like Monk — a person not to be trusted. Arrogant and selfish, he displays only a superficial resemblance to Tom, a character he initially claims to have "created." When it is pointed out to him that the film's scriptwriters actually created Tom, he backtracks, asserting that he is the one who "breathed life" into the character, who "fleshed him out." Yet, as Yacowar points out, Gil "denies responsibility when Tom claims independence" (1991, p. 249). With many such hints (e.g., Gil wants to play Lindbergh, a man who was an apologist for the Nazis in the 1930s), Allen warns Cecilia, and us, not to mistake Gil for Tom. But, gullible as she is — after all, she has been fooled repeatedly by Monk's tired little deceits — she falls for Gil's line.

In a music store, Gil buys her a ukulele, and they bang out songs accompanied by of an old lady on the piano. It is like a scene from one of Cecilia's movie musicals — so much so that she, and we, should realize that it is too perfect not to have been staged by Gil for a reason. Gil and Cecilia then reenact a scene from one of his films where a man says goodbye to his girl. Cecilia has seen the film so many times that she has memorized the lines, yet she keeps herself blissfully unaware of the possibility that Gil's behavior towards her may be a sham. In fact, as things turn out, their reenactment of the farewell scene is actually a more honest portrayal of Gil's real intentions than the words of love with which he deceives her. Cecilia is not even suspicious when Gil tells her that his apparent passion on the screen for an actress meant nothing ("It was just a movie kiss") at the very moment when he pretends to kiss her for real. In this film, it is the fictional character, Tom, who behaves authentically, while his supposedly "real" counterpart, Gil, is always just acting.

This point is confirmed by Tom's scene in the whorehouse. Approached by Emma (Dianne Wiest), the prostitute who frightened Cecilia earlier, he accepts her invitation to go with her to "where I work." In the brothel, Tom innocently ignores the whores' suggestive comments and insists on interpreting all of their actions in terms of his notions of morally acceptable behavior. By his genuineness and the depth of his concern with fundamental philosophic issues, he is able to crack their artificial facade of inauthentic chatter with a prospective client:

> TOM: I was thinking about some very deep things, about God and His relationship with Irving Sachs and R. H. Levine. I was thinking about life in general, the origin of everything we see about us, the finality of death, how almost magical it seems in the real world as opposed to the world of celluloid and flickering shadows.

PROSTITUTE: Where did you find this clown?

TOM: For example, the miracle of birth. Now, I suppose some of you lovely ladies are married?

PROSTITUTE: Not any more!

TOM: No? Then the absolutely astonishing miracle of childbirth! With all of its attendant feelings of humanity and pathos! I stand in awe of existence!

PROSTITUTE: Do you want to tie me up?

Eventually most of the whores are so moved by him that they offer him a free "roll in the hay." But when Tom finally understands the true nature of their offer, he is astonished. He refuses their claim politely as he poetically describes the force of his love for Cecilia and his absolute unwillingness to betray her, even as she is betraying him at that very moment. Emma is so amazed and impressed by Tom's devotion that she asks rhetorically if there are any more like him out there. Given her dismal experiences with men of all kinds, she is better able than Cecilia to recognize Tom as a jewel (the name, by the way, of the movie theater from whose screen he descended).

This scene, juxtaposing of honestly felt intellectual probing with the surroundings of a house of illicit pleasures, symbolizes the disdain with which the modern world views sincere metaphysical exploration. Such concerns are today viewed as so self-indulgent and profitless that the most appropriate place for them is a whorehouse. Also, this scene prefigures those to come in *Shadows and Fog* (1992), a film in which the prostitutes and their clients are among the few characters concerned with metaphysical issues in a surreal village populated by bigots, corrupt officials, and crazed vigilantes.

V. Betrayal and Despair

By this point, the studio people are growing more and more worried about reports of other Tom Baxters in other theaters who are forgetting their lines or threatening to walk off the screen. The characters in the print at the *Jewel* are getting increasingly cranky. The countess (Zoe Caldwell) throws insults at everyone, including the real people in the audience; a working-class character urges his fellow characters to rebel as he is labeled a "red." Another character named Larry Wilde (Van Johnson) has the same charge thrown at him when he threatens to follow Tom and walk off the screen. One studio lackey laments, "The real ones want their lives fiction and the fictional ones want their lives real."

Indeed, the qualities of screen life (the shallowness, the glamour, and the certainty of a script which determines all of one's actions without the need for responsible decision-making) have always been very attractive to the average filmgoer, especially during the Depression when economic choices were so limited. Yet it is wrong to interpret this film, as some critics have done, as a rejection of the existence of genuine ontological freedom in the face of deterministic forces such as genetic or environmental factors.

As we have discussed in our exploration of Sartrean existential themes, no matter how constricted our choices may appear, or how surprised we may be by the unexpected consequences of our acts, what we choose to do, and why, still matters tremendously. In all of his films, including this one, Allen maintains his firm belief in the importance of moral behavior and intent, even if that behavior does not have the desired effects. It does matter whether Cecilia chooses to stay with her husband, flee to Hollywood with Gil, or risk everything by deciding, against all logic, to love a fictional character with the courage to recreate himself authentically.

The studio bosses come to the conclusion that the only thing to do is cut their losses, withdraw all prints of the film from circulation, and burn them along with the negative. Given what we have seen of Tom's sensitive nature and his genuine moral goodness, this scheme strikes us as being no better than murder. The bosses regard the film's characters with the same level of indifference that the Nazis showed to the Jews, another group of individuals who were considered less than "real."

It is a fitting irony that the movie's scriptwriters, the creators of the characters whose destruction seems imminent, should have obviously Jewish names. Even the manager of the *Jewel*, the theater where all the trouble started, is shocked and saddened by this decision. "What a shame, it was such a good picture!" he moans as he lies exhausted on a sofa with his hand on his brow and his eyes tightly shut. Before they can begin their incineration, however, they must get Tom back up on the screen.

The opportunity to do this arises when Tom takes Cecilia into the film (which has been left running endlessly in the empty theater) so that they can go out for a night on the town at places where Tom's stage money will be good. The other characters are at first shocked at the appearance of a real person in the film. However, pleased at the chance to leave the apartment in which they have been stranded since Tom left, they all go out to the Copacabana, where Tom is supposed to meet and fall in love with Kitty Haynes. The headwaiter at the club is taken aback when they ask for seven seats instead of their usual six. Drinking champagne at the table, Cecilia is disillusioned to discover it's only ginger ale; someone tells her, "That's the movie business for you."

Tom announces that he's taking Cecilia for a night on the town. When the characters complain that this isn't in the script, Tom tells them that they are all free and "it's every man for himself!" Upon hearing this, the headwaiter realizes that he doesn't have to seat people anymore and can now devote himself to doing what he really loves. Telling the band to "hit it, boys!" he begins to tap dance exuberantly across the floor to the enthusiastic clapping of the audience.

Allen uses a classic thirties cinema technique — the superimposition of nightclub signs, flowing champagne glasses, and street scenes of New York — to show us that Tom and Cecilia are having a wonderful time. Finally, back at the deserted apartment, Cecilia tells Tom how much she has always wanted to be on "this side of the screen," as she admires the beauty of the set with its white telephone and city skyline. Tom tells her he wanted a chance to talk to her alone. Just then, Gil wanders into the theater. Telling her that he is jealous, Gil begs Cecilia to leave Tom, and her husband, to come with him to Hollywood. Tom and Cecilia come back down from the screen to argue with Gil as the other characters in the film reassemble and argue among themselves over what Cecilia should do.

Urged by Larry Wilde to use her most human of abilities — the ability to choose — Cecilia is torn between her feelings for the perfect Tom, who will always love her and be faithful, and the flesh-and-blood Gil, who promises her a real-life Hollywood adventure. Only the film's blond female lead, Rita (Deborah Rush), encourages Cecilia to choose Tom and perfection. The rest of the characters, mistakenly thinking that they will be able to resume their old life if only Tom rejoins them, beg Cecilia to pick Gil. When she decides to follow their advice, Tom is stunned by her betrayal (like Isaac or Danny). He sadly returns to the screen.

Gil tells Cecilia to hurry home and pack a bag so that she can join him for the trip to Hollywood. At home, Monk at first apologizes and begs her to stay; however, when it is clear that she is really going this time, he tells her he doesn't care. Eagerly hurrying back to the theater, she is shocked when the manager tells her that all the movie people have returned to Hollywood, including Gil Shepherd. The manager also reveals that Gil was very relieved that he was able to prevent his career from going down the drain.

We are given a brief glimpse of Gil on the plane, appearing ill at ease;

however, now that we realize just how much he was simply "acting" with Cecilia, we have no clue whether his discomfort is due to his conscience or simply his fear of flying. This fear may be symbolic of his unwillingness, in contrast to Tom, to make an impulsive leap of faith. Throughout the film, he has been overwhelmed with fear that this incident might destroy his career. Given the harsh economic times in which he lives, and his earlier revelation that he once drove a cab, his obsession with material success is perhaps understandable. However, these factors no more excuse his betrayal of Cecilia than did the justifications given by Lou or Yale in Allen's previous films.

Understanding at last that Gil was only using her, Cecilia accepts the manager's invitation to go in to see the new Ginger Rogers–Fred Astaire film that has just arrived, the 1935 production *Top Hat*. Still clutching her bag and ukulele, Cecilia sits alone in the darkened theater as she watches Fred and Ginger sing and dance their way through Irving Berlin's classic number "Cheek to Cheek," the song that played over the film's opening credits. Still entranced by movie magic, Cecilia smiles slightly as her moistened eyes hungrily cling to the screen.

By her own refusal to forsake the world's "reality" for a magical chance at perfection, Cecilia has betrayed her own romanticism and condemned herself to a life even emptier than the one with which she began. Without her job, and with no illusions left about the possibilities of a decent life with Monk, she seems destined to end up with the prostitutes in the brothel.

When we last see her, Cecilia obviously hopes that what happened once may happen again, that if only she stays long enough and believes hard enough, Fred will dance down from the screen and whisk her up to "heaven." Like the children in the audience of *Peter Pan* whose faith brings Tinkerbell back to life, she cannot help praying that such a miracle will happen again. Her only other option would be to fall into the hopeless despair which must result from living in a world without God, a world she herself has described as "a movie with no point, and no happy ending!"

– 5 –

"WE ALL HAD
A TERRIFIC TIME":
*Hannah and Her Sisters
(1986)*

At the time of its release, *Hannah and Her Sisters* received unusually mixed reviews. Most critics enthusiastically praised the film, many calling it, in the words of *The Washington Post*'s Rita Kempley, "Allen's finest hour," and "the film of a lifetime" (*The Washington Post, Weekend,* February 7, 1986, p. 19). On the other hand, some critics, most notably Pauline Kael, gave the film a much lower grade. Kael, while praising the film as "agreeably skillful" and "likable," called it a "minor" effort which showed signs of being "a little stale" with "almost a trace of smugness" (*The New Yorker,* February 24, 1986, pp. 90–92).

The reason for these extreme differences of opinion lies in the different criteria that Kempley and Kael apply. If judged against the standards of most commercial films in terms of its ability to entertain, *Hannah* is unquestionably a superior picture (Kael herself concedes this point). However, if judged against the standards of the finest films made by Allen to date and the high goals which the film seems to set for itself, it is debatable how well it succeeds.

The film's plot revolves around a family of three sisters and their aging parents. Many of the film's characters, excluding Hannah (Mia Farrow), seem to be seeking greater meaning for their lives. Hannah's two sisters, Holly (Dianne Wiest) and Lee (Barbara Hershey), are desperately engaged in this search throughout the film. Because of its similar focus on the lives of three sisters, one cannot help comparing this film to Allen's earlier *Interiors*.

I. God, She's Beautiful...
We All Had a Terrific Time
The Hypochondriac

Allen's white credits on black ground are this time accompanied by an instrumental version of "You Made Me Love You." We next see the first of sixteen full-screen title cards with the same white lettering on a black background. Often, the card is then followed by a quick glimpse of an aesthetic object, anything from a painting to a wall mural, although the first such shot is a kind of cinematic photograph. "God, she's beautiful..." reads the first card, words we hear immediately repeated in a voice-over by Elliot (Michael Caine) as we see Lee posing seductively against a doorframe, staring into the camera. As we watch her move gracefully through crowds of guests at a gathering in an apartment, Elliot waxes romantic about Lee's allure, his passionate attraction to her, and his desire to take care of her — until he stops abruptly to chastise himself for lusting after his wife's sister.

In casting Caine as a successful financial adviser who lives a secret emotional life of romantic fantasy, Allen makes use of the cinematic baggage Caine carries into every new role he plays. Caine has played similar roles from his early breakthrough film triumph in *Alfie* to his embarrassing appearance as the father infatuated with his daughter's teenage friend in the 1984 film *Blame It on Rio*. He has come to embody the middle-aged adolescent, disillusioned with material success, who seeks to fulfill himself through illicit passion.

Hannah interrupts Elliot in the midst of his fantasies to bring him down to earth, urging him to eat some of the appetizers made by Holly. As they praise Holly's cooking skills, she emerges from a hallway, eating one of her own creations. When Hannah and Elliot compliment the food and suggest that she should open her own restaurant, Holly tells them that she and her friend April (Carrie Fisher) are actually planning to start a catering business and asks Hannah if she may speak to her privately.

In the kitchen, Holly asks Hannah for a loan of two thousand dollars to help her get her catering business off the ground. It is clear that Hannah has loaned Holly money many times before and has never been paid back. Also, we find out that Holly has had a drug problem when Hannah asks for her assurances that the money won't be spent on cocaine.

Holly swears that this is the last time she'll ask for money, that she is keeping strict accounts and will soon pay it all back; but it is clear that this is a dialogue that the sisters have had many times before. Yet Hannah immediately agrees to loan her the money (although she seems a little surprised by the large amount). Hannah is the strong sister, the one upon whom the other two lean for support. She asks for nothing in return from them. As the film develops, we learn that both of them, and Elliot, resent her for her seeming perfection and self-sufficiency.

We see Elliot and Lee flirting together as Lee tells him how much she enjoyed the book he lent her. Their early scenes together remind us of those between Frederick and Flynn in *Interiors*, especially one in which Frederick helps Flynn remove her boots. While Frederick feels inferior to his wife, Renata, because of her aesthetic output and the recognition she has received, Elliot feels emotionally detached from Hannah because of her success both as an actress and a mother. Like Renata's sisters Flynn and Joey in *Interiors*, Lee compares herself unfavorably to an older sister of whom she is clearly jealous.

As Holly and Hannah set the table for a large family Thanksgiving feast, Holly complains about the lack of attractive eligible men at the gathering, comparing one of them, Phil, the principal of one of her children's schools, to Ichabod Crane. We learn that Holly has been married once before, as Hannah favorably compares the principal to her former husband. Soon Holly's friend April joins them and, in a comment which suggests that she and Holly have already done a critique on Phil, uses the same Ichabod Crane analogy to describe him.

Holly says that she is sure Hannah will eventually find some attractive men to invite to these gatherings. When she lists all the different holidays at which the family gets together, we get a sense of the closeness of the family and its continuity. Despite the tensions and conflicts revealed as the film progresses, this portrayal of the extended family is Allen's warmest and most positive. We have just seen a quick cut of the sisters' parents, Evan (Lloyd Nolan) and Norma (Maureen O'Sullivan), playing and singing "Bewitched, Bothered, and Bewildered" at the piano, surrounded by hordes of relatives. Children run through the rooms as Hannah and Holly enter the dining room with the turkey.

Unlike our experience of the Halls in *Annie Hall* and the dysfunctional family in *Interiors*, we in the audience feel included in this family. We share in the sense of strength and security that comes from knowing the family is there. Later in the film, Allen's own character, Mickey Sachs, will be discouraged from committing suicide when he realizes the consequences of such an act on his family. Here the presence of family plays a moral role, reminding individuals of their duties and responsibilities, just as Danny's memories of his ancestors' words in *Broadway Danny Rose* compel him to follow moral principles. By both beginning and ending the film at family gatherings, and by using a large ensemble cast, Allen emphasizes that this is a family saga rather than the story of an individual.

Yet, if any individual is at the center of this family, it is Hannah. As the family is shown crowded together at the Thanksgiving table, Evan presents a toast to Hannah for preparing the meal and praises her for her successful year, a year in which she triumphed as Nora in Ibsen's *A Doll's House.* Hannah tells everyone how lucky she is to have been able to combine her primary love, her family, with an opportunity to dabble successfully in her former career as actress, and Norma reminisces about the time she played Nora many years ago. Hannah is the glue that holds the family together.

As Lee returns in a cab to her apartment, we hear her admit to herself that she is aware of Elliot's flirting and even feels a little high from it. She enters an apartment that appears to be in a process of permanent renovation. Large sheets of plastic separate the rooms from one another, and, initially, Lee from Frederick (Max von Sydow), who is obscured by the plastic. Frederick wants no food or drink (Allen's usual symbols of sensuality and fulfillment). He is not interested in hearing about Lee's terrific time. As he cleans his paint brushes, he tells her that he's going through a period in his life in which he can't be with anyone but her.

Lee begins the film as the disciple of this dark-souled, introspective artist. Knowing Allen's admiration for the films of Ingmar Bergman, it is easy to imagine his delight in casting Von Sydow in a role so similar to those he played as a principal member of Bergman's stock company of actors. Lee's relationship with Frederick once again epitomizes the Pymalion-Galatea syndrome. Frederick and Lee, like Alvy and Annie, or Isaac and Tracy, have a relationship grounded in an older man's intellectual and aesthetic superiority and his ability to convey this wisdom to a younger, impressionable woman. In the most pejorative sense, these relationships are a form of prostitution in that each partner exchanges whatever he or she has to offer for something in return. Usually, the man provides the woman with training and emotional support, in exchange for which he receives companionship, nurturing, and sex, until the inevitable time comes when the woman has gotten all she can from the man and is ready to move on to someone else.

When Lee tells him of Elliot's offer to find customers for his artwork from among his clients, Frederick expresses the conviction that no man does favors for a woman unless he lusts after her. Challenged to explain how he could know the motives of someone he has met so rarely, Frederick argues that Elliot, by suggesting books and films to her, is trying to step into his role as her mentor.

Like Rob in *Annie Hall* and Isaac in *Manhattan*, Mickey Sachs (Woody Allen) is yet another TV producer. Like Alvy and Isaac, Mickey is obsessed with a Heideggerean dread of death which drives him to search desperately for life's meaning. As the neurotic hypochondriac who produces a successful TV series of the *Saturday Night Live* variety, Mickey's obsessions at first seem to be a parody of his earlier roles.

When he arrives at the apartment of his ex-wife—Hannah—for a brief visit with his twins on their birthday, Hannah speaks for all of us when she says, "Hi, I'm glad that you could put in an appearance," but Allen warns us not to focus exclusively on his character by responding, "I've got two minutes. I've got two minutes. The show is killing me. I've got a million appointments today." He quickly pushes us through the scene, explicitly acting as a director, as he tells the children what to do, first getting them to hug him and then leading them through the opening of their presents and demanding their "reactions."

He also informs the audience that Elliot is the prime Allenesque character in the film by having Mickey say this to Hannah about Elliot:

> I like him. I think that he's a sweet guy, the few times that I've met him....
> Cause he's a loser. He's awkward and he's clumsy, like me, so I like that.
> I also like an underconfident person.

Mickey, holding one of his son's new footballs, then confirms this description of himself by breaking a picture as he tries to play catch.

As he goes down the street to his doctor, he intrigues us by revealing that he pays no child support (later, we find out why), and he worries about whether anything is wrong with him. In the doctor's office, he complains about dizziness and a sudden hearing loss, and then undergoes a series of tests. He refers to earlier health scares; then he displays a comical inability to remember which of his ears he is having a problem with.

To Mickey's surprise, the doctor claims to have found a genuine hearing loss and orders him to go to the hospital for more elaborate tests. When Mickey starts to panic, his doctor tells him to relax and just trust him (always an unreliable plea in an Allen film). Mickey rushes out to a pay phone and calls another doctor of his acquaintance to whom he describes the symptoms. Pressed to speculate on the worst possible scenario, this doctor concedes that such symptoms could indicate a brain tumor.

In a hilarious scene with his colleague Gail (Julie Kavner), Mickey anguishes over his possible illness as she tries to get him to concentrate on the problems with their show. He claims to hear ringing (we think it's the telephone) and later buzzing. When Gail tries to calm him down by saying the doctors want to eliminate some "things," he demands to know what kinds of "things"; yet when she mentions cancer, he tells her not to mention that word while he's in the building. We hear of a previous false health alarm when Mickey mistook a spot on his shirt for skin cancer, and we listen as he wishes it were still the morning, before he went to the doctor, when he was still "happy." But, Gail points out, he was miserable this morning. No, he responds, he was happy, but he just didn't realize it.

II. The Stanislawski Catering Company in Action
Nobody, Not Even the Rain, Has Such Small Hands
The Anxiety of the Man in the Booth

Catering at their first affair, Holly and April meet a guest named David (Sam Waterston in an uncredited role). A successful architect with a private box at the Metropolitan Opera, he invites them both to join him for a tour of New York's most memorable buildings. The scenes with David seem to have two purposes.

First, the architectural tour gives Allen a chance to lobby once again for the preservation of his favorite buildings in New York. Concern about the deterioration or downright destruction of these edifices was expressed repeatedly by Isaac in *Manhattan*. In that film and again here, these older buildings are identified with our ongoing loss of heritage and its accompanying moral perspective.

Secondly, despite their professed concern for preserving this heritage, there is no question that the underlying motivation for Holly's and April's interest in accompanying David is romantic. In scenes reminiscent of one in *Annie Hall* where Alvy and Annie pretend to discuss the finer points of photography while we read the subtext of their true conservation, the discussion of architecture here is used, especially by April, as a way to impress and attract David. April talks abstractly (and meaninglessly) about architectural theory in a manner that reminds us of Mary's treatises on art in *Manhattan*.

At the end of the tour, there follows an amusing discussion about which of them should be dropped off first, with each jockeying to grab this opportunity to be alone with David. April wins this battle, and even manages to sit up front with David as Holly, in the back seat, belittles herself for her poor performance (as though enticing a man were an Olympic event). She gives herself poor scores for her awkwardness and inability to tell a good joke. In the end, she resigns herself to going home, reading, watching a movie, and taking an extra sleeping pill.

The romantic high jinks of the last scene continue, this time with Elliot as the stalker and Lee as the prey. We watch Elliot find his place as he prepares to "accidentally" run into Lee going to her AA meeting. He spins a yarn about being early for a client and looking for a bookstore whose location he obviously already knows.

Once he succeeds in luring Lee to the store to browse with him, he, like Alvy, purchases a book for her to read. However, the differences between Alvy's concerns and Elliot's are highlighted by their choice of reading material. Alvy chose Becker's pessimistic *The Denial of Death*, while Elliot chooses a book of e. e. cummings's poetry, from which he recommends a highly romantic selection. In fact, the first shot in the bookstore is that of a painting in which a naked woman touches herself suggestively, emphasizing Elliot's sexual obsession while reminding us of Lee's own appearance in a nude painting hanging on someone's wall.

Elliot creates meaning for his life primarily through his romantic and sexual fantasies. Like Sandy Bates in *Stardust Memories*, Elliot is searching for the perfect woman, or at least the perfect erotic experience. When he offers to buy the book for Lee, he initially misspeaks, saying, "I read a poem of you and thought of his last week." Here Elliot tells the truth, since he is much more interested in Lee than in poetry. To the instrumental sounds of "Bewitched, Bothered, and Bewildered," Elliot woos Lee as she catches a cab, even telling her that he would like to attend one of her AA meetings. Responding as though he had suggested going to a concert or a movie, she says, "Yeah, yeah, you'd love it. It's really entertaining. You'd have a good time!"

As Lee lies on her bed reading the poem to herself (we hear it in a voice-over), we also see Elliot at home in his robe, no doubt imagining Lee doing just that. In the poem, clearly addressed to a lover, cummings speaks of how that person is able, through her touch, and voice, and eyes, to open him up, just as the spring opens the first petals of a rose: "...nobody, not even the rain, has such small hands."

We watch Mickey's ordeal as he goes through another series of tests to determine the source of his problems. Mickey, like all Allen personas, has a fear of technology. These tests appear to be designed solely to torture and dehumanize. The final one, in which a robotic arm swings over Mickey as he lies flat on a table seen through a window from a darkened room, suggests the scenarios often described by victims of alien abductions or the torments suffered by the victim in Poe's "The Pit and the Pendulum."

These scenes offer a penetrating critique of modern medicine's contribution to the dehumanization of society. In Heideggerean terms, it is as though doctors and patients were speaking different languages. Doctors, like repairmen of any sort, tend to speak from a present-to-hand, or calculative, perspective in which they view the body as an object to be fixed using the best technology available for the task. Patients, however, speak from a ready-to-hand, or meditative, perspective which emphasizes their more subjective, emotive concerns.

If the physical threat or damage is minimal, then the conversation resembles one between an auto repairman and a car owner: all the customer really wants to know is how quickly the damage can be repaired and how much it is going to cost. The doctor, on the other hand, feels obliged to explain the procedure by which the problem has been diagnosed and the next steps in calculating the most effective ways to fix it.

However, as the threat to the patient's continued health increases in magnitude, the communication gap widens dramatically. While the approach of the health care professional tends to remain the same (although perhaps now leavened with greater caution and less willingness to speculate), the patient's reactions are more and more driven by fear. Thus, in Mickey's situation, the doctors' dispassionate attitudes make them appear inhuman, even monstrous.

The reference to "the man in the booth" reminds us of the war crimes trial of Adolf Eichmann in Jerusalem, where he was commonly referred to in this manner because he was kept in a glass booth for security reasons. At the time of that trial, Eichmann shocked the world with his apparent lack of any of the normal human emotions of remorse or guilt at the torture and deaths of so many innocent people. Much was made of the claim that the "man in the booth" was like a member of a species different from the rest of us, a species that could concern itself with the mechanics of genocide without any corresponding sense of its horror.

In Mickey's situation, however, medical technology seems to have reversed the earlier metaphor. Mickey feels as if he were the one placed in a glass booth by an inhuman species which has allowed the impersonality of technology to become its master; a species more interested in the mechanics of discovering a brain tumor than in dealing with the inevitable feelings of terror and helplessness such a discovery elicits from its victims. These scenes with Mickey reveal the inadequacies of a system which would coolly send a patient home for the weekend knowing that he might have a brain tumor, without any counseling or support. Earlier in the film, Hannah speculated humorously over a scenario in which a lifelong hypochondriac discovered that there was really something wrong with him. As if by magic, we now see that situation played out.

Leaving the hospital, Mickey gives himself a pep talk, telling himself not to panic, that nothing can happen to him as long as he's in New York, "his town," surrounded by people and restaurants. Later that night, Mickey panics as he convinces himself that he has a brain tumor "the size of a basketball." He offers to make a deal with God: he will gratefully accept the loss of an ear, and even an eye, in exchange for continued life without the need for a brain operation. He consoles himself with the fact that he always thinks that something's wrong with him and that, usually, he turns out to be fine. Then he remembers the one time his worst medical fears were confirmed as we relive those memories with him.

We see him and Hannah in a doctor's office being informed that he is infertile. Again, the medical profession shows itself insensitive, as we hear the doctor reporting his findings in a mechanical tone, even noting that "many fine marriages" fail as the result of hearing such news. He calmly lists the possible ways that they could still have children. Although he expresses the hope that they "won't make too much of this," he is clearly incapable of helping them deal with the emotional consequences of his news. On the way home, Hannah further humiliates Mickey by asking him if he could have "ruined himself" through excessive masturbation. He defensively tells her not to knock "my hobbies." She asks him to consider the possibility of artificial insemination as she is determined to experience pregnancy and childbirth.

In expressing this desire, Hannah allies herself with the forces of impersonal technology while ignoring Mickey's sense of failure as a husband and a man. We share Mickey's sense of shame and embarrassment as he and Hannah confront his partner, Norman (Tony Roberts), and Norman's wife with the proposal that his sperm be used to impregnate Hannah. We are again reminded that impersonal professionals have pushed themselves into the most intimate aspects of our lives when Norman's wife says it is really a matter for "your analyst, and mine." Norman responds, "And maybe my lawyer." In contemporary society, procreation, the most private and primordial activity of human life, has become the domain of medical, psychiatric, and legal professionals.

Even though Mickey tells us that he and Hannah were drifting apart before all this happened, these events, and the subsequent birth of Hannah's twins (Norman's biological children), led inevitably to the breakup of both Mickey's marriage and his partnership with Norman.

Without a change of titles, we cut to a scene at the opera, where we see Holly and David sitting in his private box, toasting each other with the wine he brought. Given the pessimistic view of relationships that we have just witnessed, and the identification of Holly and Mickey in style and temperament, we are filled with misgivings about the prospects for this relationship.

III. Dusty Just Bought This Huge House in Southampton
The Abyss
The Only Absolute Knowledge Attainable by Man Is That Life Is Meaningless

Elliot brings one of his clients, a rock star named Dusty Frye (Daniel Stern), over to Frederick's apartment to look for paintings that could fill up the empty walls of his new house. Frederick is clearly in spiritual agony, from the moment Dusty gives him the "power handshake" to his demand that any purchases must first be cleared by his interior decorator. It is impossible to believe that Elliot expected any other conclusion to this enterprise, but, of course, his real motive in bringing Dusty is to put Lee in his debt.

She thanks Elliot for suggesting that she purchase an album of Mozart's music as she plays another by Bach that the man in the record store recommended. She is clearly torn within herself between her devotion to duty, as represented by the somber figures of Frederick and Hannah, and Elliot's childlike romantic wooing. We hear Elliot trying to restrain himself as he ponders the best move to make next and the delicacy of the situation; yet, when Lee approaches him with the volume of cummings in her hands, he kisses her passionately, knocking her into the turntable so that the music skips from its former peaceful strains to a more urgent and louder passage.

We hear Frederick and Dusty arguing as they come back up the stairs. Dusty and Elliot hurriedly leave as Dusty describes Frederick as a "weirdo," and worries that Elliot seems so upset. Elliot tells him to go on without him and attributes his physical state, actually the result of his encounter with Lee, to a need for fresh air. Sounding a familiar theme from many past Allen films, Elliot associates passion with food when he tells Dusty, "It must have been something I ate."

Rushing to a phone booth, Elliot tries to call Lee, but hangs up when

Frederick answers. Then he intercepts Lee on the street looking for him. He tells her of his love for her, claiming that he and Hannah are in the last stages of their marriage because "they are going in different directions" (which is what Mickey once said about his own marriage to Hannah). Lee is distraught and confused, however, and racked with guilt. She needs to be reassured, again and again, that the problems between Elliot and Hannah have nothing to do with her. When Elliot pushes her to say whether she has any feelings for him, she reluctantly admits that she does.

Elliot, exultant over her response, tells her that it is now his responsibility to work things out. Needing to escape from his passion and her own confusion, Lee again takes refuge in the mundane. She has to go, she tells him, because "I have to get my teeth cleaned." Elliot has now entered into his own private world of emotional triumph. Like a child who has finally gotten his way, he smiles broadly and laughs to himself, "I have my answer, I have my answer! I'm walking on air!"

The sounds of "Bewitched, Bothered, and Bewildered," again fill the air as we see Hannah pull up to her parent's apartment in a cab. She has been summoned by her father to umpire one of her parents' regular fights. According to Evan, he and Norma were in the process of making a commercial when Norma started flirting with a young man and drinking heavily. As they hurl accusations at one another, Hannah separates them into different rooms and persuades her mother to sober up with coffee. Each describes the other in the worst possible terms. Evan claims that Norma is just a tart and even throws doubt on Hannah's paternity. Norma calls Evan "this nonperson, this haircut who passes for a man," and suggests that he never became a successful actor because he is empty inside, he has nothing to give.

In a voice-over, we hear Hannah's thoughts about the sadness of her parents' married life. As we see photos of them in the apartment, Hannah reflects on their beginnings when they were attractive young performers who seemed to have everything ahead of them. However, as their careers never fulfilled their dreams, they fell into a tired pattern of infidelities, excessive drinking, and fights. Having never really wanted children, they weren't particularly interested in raising them.

By casting Farrow's actual mother (Maureen O'Sullivan) in the role of Norma, Allen is able to portray the relationship between mother and daughter in an especially poignant manner. The line between reality and illusion is further blurred by the fact that an uncharitable observer might describe Maureen O'Sullivan as a once-beautiful actress who never quite fulfilled her early promise. Furthermore, one could argue that Farrow has exceeded her mother's acting success to much the same degree that Hannah has exceeded Norma's. As for Lloyd Nolan, whose career could be described in much the same terms as O'Sullivan's, he has the shuffle of an elderly man and a vacant look in his eyes which is both sad and haunting.

Hannah defuses the crisis, not by seeking a genuine resolution, but simply by changing the subject. She gets her mother to talk about her sisters. Then, by playing an old tune on the piano, Evan entices them into the living room.

In the bookstore scene, Lee told Elliot that she had a terrible childhood and suggests this is what led to her drinking. Now, having been exposed to the horrors of the parents' married life, one understands why each of the sisters seems tormented and lost. Again, we are reminded of the three sisters in *Interiors*, sisters who also grew up in a troubled marriage with a strong mother and who each internalized some negative aspect of their parents' relationship.

Returning to the similarities between the families in *Interiors* and *Hannah*, it is easy to see the connections between the characters of Renata and Hannah. As the eldest of three sisters, both have internalized the pressures upon them to succeed, to fulfill the failed dreams of their parents, by becoming extremely self-controlled and driven. While both have exceeded their mothers' successes as artists— Renata as a poet and Hannah as an actress— each has achieved this success at the expense of her emotional life. Each is so focused on her role as the pillar of strength upon which the rest of the family can lean that neither is able to expose her own fears and weaknesses. As a result, they are both envied and resented by their spouses and siblings.

Lee, on the other hand, has responded to her upbringing by choosing to be weak, by allowing men and alcohol to define her character. Like Joey, she has no firm notion of her purpose in life; she drifts from interest to interest, lover to lover. She tells Elliot she is going to take some college courses, but she's not sure what she is interested in, maybe she will work with children. At present, she has no job other than that of helpmate and disciple to Frederick.

Holly, too, initially seems lost and confused. Like Hannah, and Flynn, she aspires to be an actress, but she never gets any parts, and her expectations always seem to exceed her reality. Also like Flynn, she has been a cocaine user; Hannah describes Holly's first husband as a dope fiend. Constantly borrowing money from Hannah to finance her apparently harebrained schemes for success, she nonetheless differs from her sisters in that she has somehow managed to create an independent sense of herself, an authentic voice.

Her interior monologues (for example, on the way home in the back of the car after striking out with David) remind us most of the Allen persona, an Allan Felix, Alvy Singer, or Isaac Davis. She fits Mickey's earlier description of the kind of person he likes, a "sweet" person who seems to be a "loser," who's awkward, clumsy, and underconfident; yet she never gives up or compromises her ideals. By the film's end, she will become a mature, sensitive playwright and will discover love with Mickey. One could argue that her character dominates the film because she undergoes the most positive development, and in the end, her wildest dreams seem fulfilled.

The term "abyss" calls to mind the dread of a Kierkegaard or a Heidegger, staring into the face of death's finality and life's apparent lack of meaning. We see Mickey strapped to a white slab, wearing what looks like a straitjacket, as his head is silently moved into position in the white tube of the CAT scan machine. Again, he is in a room with a large rectangular window through which we see two technicians in white coats at a console, watching a screen as Mickey's skull appears to be sliced by lines. Restrained and without his glasses, Mickey appears completely vulnerable to the heartless machinations of medical technology.

As Mickey sits gloomily waiting in the doctor's office, a doctor enters and sticks the test results on a light bar. Tall and skinny, with a protruding Adam's apple, the doctor reminds us both of traditional images of Death, and, humorously, of Holly's description of the guy who looked like Ichabod Crane at the film's beginning. The doctor calmly informs Mickey that he has an inoperable tumor. Mickey throws himself into the depths of despair:

> It's over! I'm face to face with eternity, not later, but now! I'm so frightened I can't move, speak, breathe!

Yet, as Mickey covers his face with his hand, we see a figure in a white coat enter the room. It is the same doctor, putting the results up on the same light bar, except that this time he is telling Mickey that there is nothing wrong with him and that they will probably never know what caused his hearing loss. The doctor seems flustered, almost a little disappointed, as he confides in Mickey that he was initially worried by Mickey's symptoms but now is relieved.

While we laugh in relief when we realize that the first scene was merely Mickey's fantasy, we also feel a little angry and betrayed. For an instant, we had believed that Allen was completely shifting gears on us, turning a mostly pleasant film depicting characters facing real, but not life-threatening, traumas into a tearjerking soap opera like *Terms of Endearment*.

Yet Allen has not tricked us just for the sake of a quick laugh. By making us believe, if only for a second, that Mickey's fears of imminent death are justified, he is able to elicit from us at least an inkling of genuine *angst*, which Heidegger claims is necessary before one may experience "the call."

Like Kierkegaard, Heidegger describes dread as overwhelming fear. For Heidegger, this is always a fear of death. When one comes to realize emotionally, as well as intellectually, that one's death is inevitable, one becomes filled with dread. This fear of non-being can bring about an awareness of the meaning of an authentic life. In the experience of dread, the authentic self issues a call to the inauthentic self. One is called back to one's true self. It is through such dread that authentic personhood may be obtained if one chooses to pursue it. According to Heidegger, those who experience the call but refuse to heed it fall into the *Mitsein* (the world of the other), in which one denies one's true self by acting only according to the perceived expectations of others (like Zelig).

Now that he has genuinely experienced dread and the resulting call, Mickey is obsessed with what Binx Bolling in Percy's *The Moviegoer* called the "search." After leaving the hospital, we see Mickey running down the street in ecstasy, even jumping for joy, until suddenly, overwhelmed by the call, he stops abruptly and puts his hand to his face.

He tells Gail that he is quitting the show, and when she protests that he has no reason to quit, he responds:

> MICKEY: Can't you understand how meaningless everything is? Everything I'm talking about! Our lives, the show, the whole world, it's meaningless!
>
> GAIL: Yeah, but you're not dying!
>
> MICKEY: No, I'm not dying now but, you know, when I ran out of the hospital I was thrilled because they told me I'm going to be all right. I'm running down the street and it hit me! All right, so I'm not going to go today, but eventually, I'm going to be in that position!
>
> GAIL: You're just realizing this now?
>
> MICKEY: No, I don't realize it now, I know it all the time, but I manage to stick it in the back of my mind because it's a very horrible thing to think about. Can I tell you something, can I tell you a secret? A week ago I bought a rifle. Sure, I bought a rifle. If they told me I had a tumor, I was going to kill myself. The only thing that might have stopped me, might have, is, my parents would be devastated, I would have to shoot them also, first, and then I have an aunt and uncle. You know, it would have been a bloodbath!
>
> GAIL: Well, now eventually, it is going to happen to all of us...

MICKEY: Yes, but doesn't that ruin everything for you? That makes everything, you know, it just takes the pleasure out of everything! I mean,
you're going to die, I'm going to die, the audience is going to die, the network, the sponsor...

By having Mickey mention the audience, Allen intends that we should
at first think he is talking about us, not just the audience of the fictional
television show. Although Mickey's plight has its humorous aspects, it is
not intended solely as a parody of existential concerns. Indeed, by human-
izing the somewhat abstract aspects of existential theory in the plight of
a character with whom we can all identify, Allen is at his most effective in
conveying the ontological "feel" of the existential crisis.

Like Roquentin in Sartre's *Nausea*, or Binx Bolling in *The Moviegoer*,
Mickey's concerns are genuine, and his search is real. His decision to quit
his humiliating television job resembles Isaac's, but their motivations are
quite different. Isaac quit his job because he was sick of adding to the flow
of garbage which passes for entertainment in our morally decaying society. He felt an obligation to produce serious literature with moral overtones which might help to stem the tide.

Mickey, on the other hand, does not leave his job out of a specific
disdain for television, nor does he leave with any particular project in
mind. In a sense, Mickey starts from a much more fundamental point in
the search. Like Camus's "absurd man" in his essay "The Myth of Sisyphus," the ultimate issue for Mickey is suicide. Why should one continue
to live in a world without meaning and under an irreversible sentence of
eventual death?

As if in answer to his question (and still under the title heading of
"the abyss"), we see Elliot and Lee in a hotel room. Lee and Elliot use their
romantic fantasies about themselves and others as the ground for meaning in their lives. Both are willing to betray those whom they supposedly
love; yet, unlike Yale and Mary in *Manhattan*, both are vulnerable to the
guilt which accompanies their actions.

In the next scene, Lee breaks up with Frederick, effectively destroying his only link to the world. Frederick, like Mickey, has experienced the
meaninglessness of life and the terror of dread; however, unlike Mickey,
he has given up the search in order to inhabit a sterile abyss of his own
making, one of loneliness, bitterness, and frustration. He is filled with
hatred for the hypocrisy around him. It is in this scene that we hear his
marvelously entertaining condemnation of our culture:

FREDERICK: You missed a very dull TV show about Auschwitz. More grue-
some film clips! And more puzzled intellectuals declaring their mysti-

fication over the systematic murder of millions. The reason they can never answer the question, "How could it possibly happen?" is because it's the wrong question. Given what people are, the question is "Why doesn't it happen more often?" Of course, it does, in subtler forms.

LEE: I have a real headache from this weather.

FREDERICK: It's been ages since I just sat in front of the TV, just changing channels to find something. You see the whole culture: Nazis, deodorant salesmen, wrestlers, a beauty contest, a talk show. Can you imagine the level of the mind that watches wrestling, huh? But the worst are the fundamentalist preachers! Third-rate conmen telling the poor suckers that watch them that they speak with Jesus! And to please send in money! Money, money, money! If Jesus came back, and saw what is going on in his name, he'd never stop throwing up!

While giving this speech, Frederick is as pleased with himself as we have ever seen him. For the first time, we see him eating, enjoying a sandwich as he glances at the newspaper and smacks his lips in self-satisfied delight. Allen obviously agrees with Frederick's diagnosis of society, but he condemns Frederick for his willingness to absent himself from life in order to sit in smug judgment on the rest of us, his moral inferiors.

Yet one cannot help feeling sorry for him when he discovers that Lee has been with another man and tortures himself for not marrying her when he had the chance. Again, he refers to himself as the teacher and Lee as his pupil. Like so many of the men in Allen's films, this is the only kind of relationship he is capable of having with a woman. To her discredit, Lee is not rejecting the inauthentic nature of the Pygmalion-Galatea relationship. She has simply taken all she wants from Frederick and has now found a new teacher in Elliot.

With a quote from Tolstoy ("The only absolute knowledge attainable by man is that life is meaningless"), we return to Mickey's quest. While the quote seems as pessimistic as possible, it also prepares us for Mickey's turn to religion, since Tolstoy, as he grew older, claimed to be spiritually "resurrected" by faith.

Again we start a section with a glimpse of a work of art, this time a replication of Rodin's "The Thinker," as Mickey emerges from a library frustrated by his discovery that philosophy provides no satisfactory answers to his questions. He mocks the thought of Socrates and Nietzsche by ridiculing trivial aspects of their theories (Socrates's acceptance of the homosexual act as an appropriate metaphor for ideal love in *The Symposium*, and Nietzsche's odd theory of "Eternal Recurrence"), and he rejects Freud's approach for its failure to help him after many years of analysis. Speculating on the possibility that love might be the answer, he is led to remember his one disastrous date with Holly many years ago after the collapse of his marriage to Hannah.

The date took place during Holly's period of drug dependency. In a scene reminiscent of Alvy's terrible date with Pam in *Annie Hall*, we see them together at a punk rock concert, sitting alongside teenagers with spiked hair. Mickey writhes in agony as he is forced to listen to the loud and raucous music while he watches Holly shovel cocaine up her nose, an activity she continues even when he gets her to go hear Bobby Short sing Cole Porter. At the date's end, he describes the evening as being as much fun as the Nuremberg trials, a comment that reminds us of Frederick's claim that we engage daily in the subtle creation of our own little Auschwitzes. Yet, despite their terrible evening together, Mickey confesses that he has always had a little crush on Holly. Apparently Hannah is doomed to marry men who lust after her sisters.

IV. Afternoon
The Audition
The Leap

This section begins with Elliot and Lee drinking and dancing in a dark hotel room, then moves to Elliot at home with Hannah that evening. He is moody and curt, responding to her suggestion that they have a baby by telling her, "That's the last thing we need!" and accusing her of forcing him to fit into her preconceived notions of life. When Hannah is confused and frightened by his manner, she tries to draw him out by asking him a series of questions. Another reference to the Holocaust emerges when Elliot compares her attempt to probe his feelings to being questioned by the Gestapo, although it is clear that he's the one really doing the torturing. He tells himself just to get it over with and admit his love for Lee. Once again, however, he ignores his conscience and instead hugs Hannah, apologizing profusely, telling her that she is too good for him — words which he knows couldn't be more true.

Hannah and Holly shop for clothes as Holly tells her about her one date with David. Her depiction of David raising his daughter alone because of his wife's institutionalization is strongly reminiscent of the story of Scott and Zelda Fitzgerald — evidence that Allen is drawn to Fitzgerald's romantic aura of doomed idealism. Finding out these details of David's private life only intensifies the image already created by his love for beautiful old buildings and his habit of sitting in his private box at the Met, sipping wine and crying as he watches opera. The fact that David is played by Sam Waterston, the actor who played Nick in the 1974 film version of *The Great Gatsby* (which also featured Mia Farrow as Daisy), only reinforces the allusion to Fitzgerald. The only question is whether Holly will be able to cast herself as Sheila Graham, the gossip columnist with whom Fitzgerald spent the last years of his life.

Allen presents us with a humorous account of Mickey's turn to organized religion. His interview with a Catholic priest shows just how desperate he has become. Catholicism's appeal for him is aesthetic ("it's a beautiful religion") and practical (it will give him the strong structure that he craves), not spiritual. He concedes that he has not yet been able to make Kierkegaard's leap of faith, and he asks to join that wing of Catholicism which is "against school prayer, pro-abortion," and "anti-nuclear."

In a delightful scene, we see the reaction of Mickey's parents to the news of his planned conversion to Catholicism. His mother, whom we never see, cries loudly from a bedroom in their apartment, while his father (Leo Postrel), in his heavy accent, reacts with astonishment that his son would want to believe in Jesus Christ. They engage in debate over whether it makes sense to worry about what happens when you die.

His father argues that worrying about such things now is ridiculous. We have enough problems as it is. Either death will mean unconsciousness or it won't. If death is unconsciousness, then we won't be there to feel anything. If, on the other hand, we are conscious after death, there will be plenty of time to deal with that then. Mickey's explanation to his mother that he needs answers to big questions leads to this wonderful exchange:

> MICKEY: If there's a God, then why there is so much evil in the world, just on a simplistic level? Why were there Nazis?
>
> MOTHER: Tell him, Max!
>
> MAX: How the hell do I know why there were Nazis? I don't know how the can-opener works!

Despite the humor of this scene, ultimately Mickey will come to conclusions very similar to those of his father, whose name, Max, is the same as the nickname used by Rob and Alvy in *Annie Hall*. His father's voice is the voice of experience, the same voice that Allen honors repeatedly in *Broadway Danny Rose*. His father's attitude implies that Mickey should concentrate on living a good life, respect his Jewish heritage, and not worry about metaphysical issues that are beyond his control.

These are truths that Mickey will have to discover for himself as we see him attending Catholic services, helping the priest to put away books in his office, and staring at a holographic image of Christ on the cross in a shop window, an image whose eyes appear to open and close as Mickey shifts his position and then walks away, shrugging his shoulders. We see Mickey come home to his apartment carrying a paper bag from which he unloads a crucifix, a prayer book, a framed picture of Jesus, and, as the punchline to the gag, a loaf of Wonder Bread and a jar of Hellman's mayonnaise. This phase cannot last. Mickey will not be able to abandon his heritage for a culture of white bread and mayo.

V. Summer in New York
Autumn Chill
Lucky I Ran Into You

Elliot tells his analyst about his frustrations and indecision over his affair with Lee. Comparing himself to Hamlet in his inability to make up his mind, Elliot describes the sorry state of his on-again, off-again affair with Lee. As we hear him tell his analyst how they meet periodically to argue or make love, we see Lee on the campus of Columbia, where Elliot tells us she is taking courses randomly. She meets a young man and walks with him, talking energetically. By this means, Allen lets us see that by doing nothing Elliot has allowed the decision to be made for him, and Lee is already drifting into a relationship with a new teacher.

Having given up on Catholicism, Mickey is reduced to discussing reincarnation with a Hare Krishna in a park. In the scene with his father, when asked why he doesn't try Buddhism rather than Catholicism, he responds that it is too alien to him, a description which surely covers the followers of Krishna as well. Mickey confirms this as he asks himself who he thinks he's kidding. With a shaved head, wearing robes, and dancing in airports, he thinks he'll look more like Jerry Lewis than a man on a spiritual quest.

Time continues to fly by as we see Lee by herself reflecting on her attraction to her English professor, Doug, and her strange sense of guilt about betraying Elliot. We are reminded of Danny Rose's defense of Lou to Tina when he makes the case that cheating on only one person at a time requires some sort of moral integrity. Soon, Lee is telling Holly about her newest love, the professor, obviously delighted that at last she need not be secretive about her love life.

This year's Thanksgiving dinner shows the consequences of the events that took place at last year's dinner. Hannah and Holly continue to argue in the kitchen, this time over Holly's depiction of the problems in Hannah's marriage in her first play.

Acknowledging that perhaps he, too, sometimes uses his art cathartically to exaggerate and purge the problems of real life, Allen reveals that Holly's play relies heavily on details that she must have gotten from Lee, who must have gotten them from Elliot. Hannah feels violated by this open airing of her private life. She is also incensed by the depiction of a character clearly based on herself as distant and incapable of sharing with others. She denies that she is like this character, yet when she refuses to tell Holly about her problems with Elliot because she "doesn't want to bother" others, Holly tells her that that's just the point: people want to be bothered by the difficulties of those they love.

The extent to which Holly's characters are drawn from real life is emphasized by her mother's pleasure in being depicted as a "boozy old flirt with a filthy mouth." Later this point will be reinforced when Holly, in her second play, purges herself of her hostility towards April and David by developing a plot line in which an architect is stabbed to death by his insane ex-wife as he walks with his new girlfriend. Holly is learning how to express her emotional life through her art, just as Alvy was able to do when he wrote a revised, and more upbeat, version of his breakup with Annie into his play.

Just at the point where Hannah is dangerously close to figuring out that Lee must be having an intimate relationship with Elliot, we see Elliot and Lee in the dining room, breaking up. Lee tells him that she's met someone new, replaying the earlier breakup scene with Frederick. Lee is so lacking in self-esteem, so dependent on men for her definition of herself, that the only legitimate excuse in her mind for breaking up with a man is to tell him that she has met someone else.

Meanwhile, Hannah's parents are again holding court at the piano as Evan loudly tells everyone how Norma was once so beautiful that men used to drive their cars off the streets in their attempts to catch a glimpse of her. In this film, we're reminded that no relationship, no marriage, ever runs completely smoothly. The successful ones, like Evan and Norma's, are not the ones without problems, but the ones in which the participants stick together through the rough times in order to enjoy the good ones—which, we will see by the film's end, Elliot and Hannah are ultimately able to do.

Hannah confronts Elliot in the bathroom with her fears that he is telling Lee or Holly about their problems behind her back. Complaining of a throbbing headache, Elliot at first denies Hannah's accusations and then concedes that he does talk to her sisters because he needs "to matter to somebody." Hannah is shocked by this and declares that he matters to her. When Elliot claims that she seems to have no needs, she cries out in pain that she has enormous needs. At the end of this scene, when the camera focuses in on her stunned, beautiful face as she slowly blinks her eyes in shock and sorrow, she touches our hearts like the sight of an animal blinking in pain.

Later, desolate and alone, she stares at a photo of herself and her sisters. A second later, we see Elliot's hand as he turns off a lamp, and in darkness, we strain to hear Hannah's small, wounded voice as she tells him, "It's so pitch black tonight, I feel lost." For the first time, Elliot realizes that she really does need him. "You're not lost," he responds, and as they begin to make love, he bursts out with emotion, exclaiming, "I love you so much!"

The upbeat tone continues as Mickey meets Holly by chance in a record store. At first, she browses in the opera section, showing that she may still be thinking of David; yet, as they laugh and joke together, they move into the jazz section, an indication that she is attracted to Mickey and happy to see him. She tells him about her writing career and asks if she can read him her new play. He tells her, and us, that it's now been a year since he quit his television job and that he's been living on his savings.

In his apartment, we hear Holly reading the end of her play to an enthralled Mickey sitting on an ottoman at her feet. The play's last line tells us that we have to play the hand we're dealt in life, even when that hand, good as it may be, can't get us everything we want. Mickey is knocked out by the play; he thinks it's wonderful, and he immediately offers to help her with it. For the first time, an Allen persona is stunned speechless, not by his betrayal at the hands of those he nurtured, but instead by a woman who has made herself into something remarkable without his mentoring. The cycle of Pygmalion-Galatea relationships may at last be broken as Mickey begins a romantic and professional partnership in which he and Holly start out as equals.

Later, after we see that Mickey and Holly are becoming closer, we hear him tell her how, only a month before, he was finally able to overcome his dread. Alone in his apartment, ready to kill himself with a rifle resting against his forehead, he thinks to himself that perhaps there is a God after all. But, he tells himself, a possibility isn't good enough for him; like Descartes or Husserl, he requires certainty, absolute apodicticity. At this, the gun goes off, harmlessly breaking a mirror. He explains that in his excitement, he must have accidentally squeezed the trigger as the perspiration from his forehead allowed the gun's muzzle to slip. This "miracle" could be interpreted as God's answer to his demand for proof.

Scared to death and needing fresh air, he escapes from his apartment, walking aimlessly through the streets until, exhausted, he goes into a movie to sit down and rest. The movie theater has always been Allen's place of worship, so it is no surprise that he receives his enlightenment and salvation in one. As we see the Marx Brothers in *Duck Soup*, he describes the event this way:

> I'm watching these people up on the screen, and I started getting hooked on the film, you know, and I started to feel, "How could you even think of killing yourself, I mean, isn't it so stupid? I mean, look at all the people up there on the screen, you know, they're real funny, and what if the worst is true? What if there's no God, and you only go around once and that's it? You know, don't you want to be part of the experience? You know, it's not all a drag," and I'm thinking to myself, "Jeez! I should stop ruining my life searching for answers I'm not ever going to get, and just enjoy it while it lasts!" And, after … who knows? I mean, you know, maybe there really is something, nobody really knows! I know "maybe" is a very slim reed to hang your whole life on, but it's the best we have! And I actually began to enjoy myself!

VI. One Year Later

Back at the annual Thanksgiving dinner, we hear Lee and Hannah praise Holly's writing to their parents. As we hear a refrain of the tune from "God, she's beautiful!" we see Elliot again staring at Lee. This time, however, he is at peace with himself as he watches her happily kissing her new husband. He regrets the anguish he caused with his foolish romantic obsessions, and he happily admits to himself that Lee was right when she told him he loved Hannah more than he knew. In our last view of him, he is hugging Hannah lovingly as the camera pans to show us Evan at the piano, playing "Isn't It Romantic," with Norma, drink in hand, sitting by his side.

Holly enters the apartment and bends down to kiss the children who come to greet her. In front of a large mirror, she admires herself as a maid in the dining room finishes her preparations for the feast, dimming the lights so that the candles might be lit. In the semidarkness, we see a hand reach up behind Holly to caress her shoulder as we hear Mickey say, "Don't get nervous, it's just your husband!" We watch their reflection in the mirror as he hugs and kisses her, telling her how beautiful she is. To the strains of "I'm in Love Again" (the same song Bobby Short played on the evening of their first date), he tells her that he was just explaining to her father how ironic it is that he used to come to these gatherings with Hannah without imagining that he could love anyone else:

> MICKEY: [*kissing her neck repeatedly as he speaks*] And here it is, years later, and I'm completely in love with you! The heart is a very, very resilient little muscle! It really is! It would make a great story, I think. A guy marries one sister, it doesn't work out, and then, years later, he winds up married to the other sister. You know, how you going to top that?
>
> HOLLY: Mickey?
>
> MICKEY: Yeah, what?
>
> HOLLY: I'm pregnant!

In the end, once he accepts life for what it is (like the character in Holly's play), he is ready to receive the love of a good woman and find his salvation. Even his infertility is cured.

The Jewish theologian Martin Buber has suggested that God only enters the lives of those who wish it. If one chooses to live one's life without God, then no evidence of his existence will appear. But once one chooses to open oneself up to the possibility of God, by initiating a genuine dialogue with Him as Mickey did in the movie theater, Buber contends that a true "*Ich-Dich*" ("I-Thou") relationship is possible. Using the pronoun *dich* (the intimate form of the second person singular, like *toi* in French), Buber contends that only by allowing oneself to be completely vulnerable before God can one construct an authentic and loving relationship with another person.

Prior to his revelation, Mickey was a self-obsessed man who had chosen to maintain an "I — It" relationship with the other people in his life, talking at them about his concerns as though they were inanimate listening posts. Rather than working to obtain a genuine discourse with others, he initially engages in what Buber calls "pseudo-listening." For example, in his discussions with Gail and his father he doesn't hear a word they say. However, in his final rejection of his suicidal pessimism, Mickey moves from the role of a mere disgruntled spectator and critic of life (characteristic of the "I — It" relationship) to that of a participant in the "I-Thou" relationship. The disclosure of his deepest feelings and hidden parts allows him to fully participate in his relationship with Holly, God's gift to him as a direct result of his conversion.

For her part, Holly is Allen's most positive female character to date, and the first to stand on her own in her relationship to an Allen persona. Unlike so many of the relationships he has shown us, in which the woman's development of her own voice has signaled the end of romance, here the discovery of that voice is the mechanism that triggers it. The Allen persona has finally learned how to encourage and support a woman without dominating or suffocating her.

When Mickey asks Holly, rhetorically, how she could possibly top their story, she does just that, through her exercise of her uniquely feminine ability to become pregnant. For once, the woman has the last word, and the whole film can be seen as a celebration of love and family as a meaningful foundation for our moral and spiritual lives.

For the brief moment of this film, Allen is willing to concede that the search for meaning is a waste of time, and that true contentment comes only from an acceptance of the simple pleasures of family, love, and faith. The film begins and ends at a family Thanksgiving dinner, suggesting that we should give thanks for what we have and give up trying to uncover profound truths. The only character intent upon continuing the search, Frederick, is portrayed as a pompous intellectual doomed to a wasted life of despair. When we last see him, he is holding his head in his hands.

Thus, somewhat surprisingly, Woody Allen, the New York intellectual, has presented us with a film that condemns overintellectualization. This film embodies the kind of sentimentality and reliance on miracles (such as Holly's unlikely conception) one associates with the films of Frank Capra. In pictures like *It's a Wonderful Life*, Capra presents an optimistic view that critics have disparaged as "Capracorn."

Maurice Yacowar tells us that in a 1987 interview with the BBC, Allen, after reflection, decided to revise his own view of the film along just such critical lines when he stated that *Hannah* was "more 'up' and optimistic than I had intended, and consequently was very popular. It's only optimistic in the sections I failed" (1991, p. 252).

In his biography of Allen, Eric Lax reiterates Allen's disappointment with the film, and tells us that the film's popularity was

> for Woody, "always a very dubious sign"— but he feels it is a somewhat middlebrow picture. What disappointed him was his inability to successfully write the ending he wanted. Ideally, Hannah's husband would still be infatuated with her sister, who is now in love with someone else, but he was unable to make it work on film. The result was a movie that ended like almost every movie, with happy endings all around: Hannah and her husband are secure, and the characters played by Woody and Dianne Wiest, supposedly unable to conceive a child, find that they have. It was too neat and tidy a finish for him. Life is more ambiguous, more unpleasant than that, and life is what he wants to accurately portray [1992, p. 277].

It is as difficult to agree with Allen's rejection of *Hannah* as to agree with him that *Stardust Memories* is his greatest achievement (Shales, 1987,

p. 90). Like many great artists, he is too hard on himself, and on his audience. In this case, his self-criticism is undone by his artistry; he has been so skillful in giving us a glimpse of redemption that not even his own condemnations can stop us from experiencing the joy of his creation.

– 6 –

"Just Allow Yourself to Feel": *Another Woman* (1988)

I. If Something Seems to Be Working, Leave It Alone!

Another Woman is the first Woody Allen film to begin with a prologue prior to the credits, and only the second to begin with a voice-over narration (*Manhattan* began with a prologue but had no traditional credits). Using what has now become a familiar Allen technique, we see an empty space — this time a hallway with a door at its end — into which a character moves; in this case it is the film's protagonist, Marion Post (Gena Rowlands).

Over the sound of a clock ticking, we hear Marion describing herself as the director of undergraduate studies in philosophy at a very fine women's college. She is married to a cardiologist who, she jokingly tells us, once "examined her heart, liked what he saw, and proposed." The marriage is a second one for both of them, and her husband has a teenaged daughter to whom she has tried to be a good stepmother. She quickly mentions that she has a married brother (she tells us nothing about him), goes on to mention that her mother recently passed away, and proudly says that her father is still alive and in good health. While she is telling us all this, we see pictures of each of the characters she is describing, including a picture of herself, alone, looking into the camera with a very self-satisfied expression.

She goes on to tell us that she is in the process of starting a new book, always a difficult thing to do; and so, having taken a leave of absence from her work, she has rented a small apartment away from her home (where, she claims, nearby construction noise distracts her), so that she can shut herself off and concentrate on her writing. It is only at this point that Allen's black-and-white credits roll to the soothing music of Eric Satie's Symphony Number 3.

Separated from the rest of the film as it is, this prologue tells us a great deal about Marion. Like the prologue, Marion has set herself off from everything — both literally, by getting a solitary apartment in which she can be alone with her work, and metaphorically, by choosing to isolate herself from those around her. She shows us the important people in her life through static photographs that allow her to categorize them solely in terms of the neat little labels she has attached to each of them (husband, undisciplined stepdaughter, married brother, dead mother, alive and healthy dad).

She tells us there is "not much else to say," as though her life were so well-structured and complete that actually going about the task of living it is almost an unnecessary formality. Her life stands fulfilled ontically as one of achievement. Yet, of course, we know that if this were really the case, there would be no reason for her to be telling us about herself, and no reason to make a film about her.

Her voice-over narrative, which continues throughout the film, uses an interesting selection of tenses. Let us examine the first sentence we hear her say: "If someone had asked me when I reached my fifties to assess my life, I would have said I had achieved a decent measure of fulfillment, both personally and professionally; beyond that, I would say, I don't choose to delve." This sentence begins by referring to the past in a subjective manner ("If someone *had* asked me ... I *would have* said") implying that she is *now* speaking from some later point. Yet the sentence ends in the present ("beyond that, I would say, I don't choose to delve"). The second sentence reveals the same unusual structure. It begins in the past ("Not that I *was* afraid of uncovering some dark side of my character") and ends in the present ("but I always *feel* that if something seems to be working, leave it alone!").

This grammatical structure is sufficiently ambiguous to confuse us about the timing of the narrative we are hearing. Is Marion telling us about her current life, or is she recalling a stage in her life beyond which she has now progressed? The answer to this puzzle is not given to us until the film's ending, when we are able to conclude with some confidence that in fact the film we are watching is a visual presentation of the book Marion finally chooses to write. This interesting film structure somewhat parallels that of *Manhattan*, in which it eventually becomes clear that the film is the novel that Isaac is starting to write during the voice-over prologue.

With this revelation, it is possible to analyze this film hermeneuti-cally, that is, using a technique of reinterpretation based on all that we know by the time we have watched the film in its entirety. On the surface, the film shows us a woman who slowly and painfully comes to realize that her life is not as perfect as she initially believed. This process of introspec-tion is initiated by Marion's accidental discovery that, through a heating vent, she can clearly overhear the sessions of a psychiatrist who has an office in the apartment next to hers.

At first, when she overhears the traumas of a man struggling with his bisexuality (a problem completely foreign to Marion), this discovery seems to be merely a momentary irritation, easily resolved by placing two sofa cushions against the vent. Later, when Marion is roused from a drowsy state by the tortured musings of a woman patient (one of the cushions having slipped from its place), this aural accident becomes the catalyst that precipitates Marion's reevaluation of her life.

Returning to the prologue, we can now interpret the meaning of the strange tense structure. Knowing that the narration is Marion's voice from the end of the film examining herself as she was at the beginning of the film, it is understandable that she starts her sentences recalling how she *was*; and because she has only recently begun to change, by the end of those sentences she has reentered the way of thinking she was in at the film's beginning. In other words, this film should be viewed as Marion's thera-peutic autobiography, her attempt to recapture her own ways of being in order to transform them from the perspective of an increasingly greater self-understanding.

While such a technique is basic to many different forms of therapy, it is most closely associated with the approaches used in phenomenolog-ical schools of psychology, those most influenced by the work of such philosophers as Martin Heidegger. This makes sense because, early in the film, we learn that Marion's field of study is in fact German philosophy and that she has written some important work on Heidegger. Indeed, Yacowar (1991, p. 265) describes Marion as a "Heideggerean philosopher" who "represents self-deluding rationalization." In an end note, he remarks that "in 'Remembering Needleman,' Allen parodied Heidegger as a scan-dalously self-serving rationalizer" (p. 296).

Yet Yacowar is incorrect in claiming that Marion is presented as a Heideggerean from the film's beginning. In fact, in the one scene in which Heidegger is mentioned, just the opposite is suggested. This scene, a pain-ful memory of the engagement party for her and her current husband, Ken (Ian Holm), also shows Marion resisting the passionate advances of a nov-elist named Larry Lewis (Gene Hackman) and ends with the unpleasant appearance of Ken's first wife, Kathy (Betty Buckley). During a series of toasts from their friends, one female partygoer says, "And to Marion's new book! German philosophy will never be the same!" to which Marion answers, "Let's hope not!" This is immediately followed by a large, bearded man's declaration: "Marion, you'll go on forever. Heidegger definitely got what he deserved!"

These toasts suggest that Marion's work on German philosophy, and specifically on Heidegger, is extremely critical, not supportive as Yacowar suggests. Furthermore, as we interpret the film hermeneutically (again, understanding its earlier scenes from the perspective of its ending), it becomes increasingly clear that the "new Marion" (the one at the film's end) is critical of the "old Marion" (the one at the film's beginning) precisely because of her conversion to an acceptance of the most important claims made by Heidegger, claims about such issues as the ontic versus the ontological, the authentic versus the inauthentic, and the important role of dread and the "call." In fact, the method of hermeneutics, which seems most appropriate for understanding the film's structure, is one that was used by Heidegger and is closely associated with his work.

Heidegger claimed that too much emphasis is put on the ontic, present-at-hand approach to life and not enough on the ontological and ready-to-hand approach which is prior and more characteristic of one's human condition as being-in-the-world. Heidegger urges us to view our lives as inseparable from all that is around us, and, through the experience of dread (a realization of one's genuine mortality), he describes how one is faced with the choice of either becoming authentic or inauthentic. The authentic person chooses to fulfill her true caring nature, even though this means exposing the vulnerable parts of herself to a world of others who can sometimes treat her harshly. On the other hand, the inauthentic person chooses to fall into the *Mitsein*, in which one hides one's real nature behind a mask designed to superficially satisfy the demands of others without exposing one's true self to the inspection of the world.

Our first exposures to Marion reveal her to be just the sort of person whom Heidegger would describe as indifferent or inauthentic. She cuts herself off from the rest of the world and classifies everyone (including herself) in ontic terms which deny the genuine, ongoing connections between them. She hides her true feelings behind a mask of normalcy. Her jokey characterization of the origins of her relationship with Ken in the prologue typifies the old Marion's concealment of her true feelings and the derivative nature of her smug descriptions of her life.

Once again (hermeneutics requires a perpetual process of reinterpretation), she tells us that Ken, in his role as a cardiologist, "examined her heart, liked what he saw, and proposed." By reducing the emotional connotations of the word "heart" to their physical ones, Marion trivializes their relationship by suggesting that Ken chose her in the same way that one might choose a car, by inspecting the engine and kicking the tires.

As an expert on the present-to-hand forestructure of the heart, Ken has little interest in its more ontological activities. Marion initially hides this fact from us (and herself). Only later, in a crucial memory of the engagement party, do we discover that Ken was still married when he took Marion's heart for a test drive, and that, unfeelingly, Ken chose to be with Marion at precisely the time that his wife was in the hospital having her ovaries removed. Continuing the car metaphor, Ken was unwilling to "own" a wife who had just lost her most characteristically female parts, so he lost no time in trading her in on a model that was in better condition.

Ken's choice to live his life as an inauthentic, unfeeling person is epitomized by his reaction to Kathy's "scene" at the engagement party when she appears unexpectedly to return some of his things. Rather than becoming emotional, he retains his composure, physically forcing her out the door as she accuses him of committing "adultery with a philosophy professor in a Holiday Inn while his wife is in the hospital having her ovaries removed!" His response ("I realize that you've been hurt, and if I've done anything wrong I am sorry. I accept your condemnation") is wholly inadequate to deal with the horrendous charge she has made against him.

Later in the film, when Marion confronts Ken with her realization that he is having an affair with Lydia (Blythe Danner), one half of the married couple who are supposedly their best friends (Marion and Ken even spend their anniversary with them), Ken responds to her accusations in exactly the same polite, formal, unfeeling manner. Like Yale, Mary, and so many other inauthentic Allen characters, Ken is entirely self-involved and unwilling to concede that an apology is insufficient compensation for those whom one has thoroughly betrayed. Furthermore, like Lloyd in *September* (1987), Ken is a man of science who has accepted the claims of his intellect over those of his soul. He lives his life in a cocoon of empty formality coupled with a mechanical hedonism that drives him from one woman to another.

II. An Anguished, Heart-Wrenching Sound

Marion has no excuse for ignoring Ken's failings at the time of their marriage. At the engagement party, Larry, the novelist who loves her, tries desperately to persuade her to break off with Ken and live with him. When she upbraids him for being disloyal to his friend (she met him through Ken), we are struck by the irony of her remark, given the degree of loyalty Ken has shown to his own wife and will later show to Marion. The situation is reminiscent of Danny Rose's attempt to defend Lou to Tina by suggesting that Lou would never cheat on more than one person at a time. Larry speaks with Allen's voice when he challenges Marion's complacency in the following exchange:

> LARRY: What can I say to change your heart?
>
> MARION: I'm really amazed at you! He's your friend! He's just had an embarrassing experience.
>
> LARRY: Yes, he is my friend, and I love him, but he's a prig, he's cold and he's stuffy. Can't you see that? "I accept your condemnation," Jesus!
>
> MARION: He handled the very difficult moment quite well.
>
> LARRY: Oh, too well! Do you like that?
>
> MARION: He's a wonderful man! He's a terrific doctor! I love to be with him! I love reading books with him! Having ...
>
> LARRY: [*pointing to his head*] It's all up here! Up here!
>
> MARION: And he's sexy!

Larry ridicules Marion's attempt to convince him, and herself, that Ken is worthy of the love she pretends to feel for him. Larry is right when he characterizes their relationship as being all intellect and no emotion. In fact, Marion's memory of the scene follows her realization that she and Ken do not have the kind of passionate relationship that would allow for spontaneous acts of lovemaking like the one described by Lydia and Mark (Bruce Jay Friedman) at a party.

As the film progresses, she remembers that she and Larry did once feel such authentic passion for one another when they kissed in a tunnel in the park; however, at that time, Marion was too afraid of her genuine feelings, and too comfortable in her web of self-deception, to allow those feelings to fully emerge.

Heidegger claims that the "call" to authenticity is heard only by those who have come face-to-face with the reality of their own mortality. Initially, it is unclear that Marion's dread has resulted from such an experience; but later, when she has lunch with Hope (Mia Farrow), the pregnant woman whose therapy sessions she's overheard, Marion reveals that the experience of turning fifty was in fact just such an encounter with the awareness of her own death. She describes how she was never affected by the traumas which everyone predicted for her when she turned thirty and forty, but fifty hit her hard. While acknowledging that she wasn't *that* old, she describes how she realized that she had determined much of her life by the choices she had made, some of which she admits to regretting today. The ticking of the clock heard in the film's prologue and early scenes now makes sense: it reflects Marion's realization that her time is running out, that she can no longer afford to hide her true feelings from herself.

Hope's role in the film is ambiguous. At first, we only hear her words (we don't see her), and those words seem to accurately describe Marion's situation. Marion hears Hope only when she herself is in a disconnected mental state, most usually when she is drowsy or asleep. Marion's introduction to Hope is an evocative description of her own inner voice. Resting her head on her desk in a state of exhaustion, Marion is brought back to awareness by the intrusion of Hope's voice, a monologue that could well be the "call" of Marion's authentic self precipitated by her trauma at turning fifty and facing her own mortality:

> I just know that I woke up during the middle of the night and time passed and I began having troubling thoughts about my life, like there was something about it not real, full of deceptions, but these deceptions had become so many, and so much a part of me now, that I couldn't even tell who I really was. So I began to perspire. I sat up in bed with my heart just pounding and I looked at my husband in bed next to me and it was as if he was a stranger. And I turned on the light and woke him up, and I asked him to hold me. And, only after a long time did I finally get my bearings.

In addition to being Marion's double, her inner voice, Hope is also a flesh-and-blood person whom Marion can see and follow and, eventually, meet and talk with.

After Marion is transformed by her realizations about herself during her lunch with Hope, and by her simultaneous discovery of Ken's infidelity, Marion encounters Hope one last time. Returning to her apartment, Marion overhears Hope describing her encounter with Marion and hears herself described as a very sad woman who, Hope fears, is exactly what she herself might become if she doesn't change directions immediately. Later, when Marion approaches the psychiatrist (Michael Kirby) to reveal the problem of the vent, he tells her that Hope has left town and can no longer be reached.

An alternative interpretation of Hope's presence in the film is suggested by Allen's use of the poems of Rainer Maria Rilke. Marion's mother, who died before the film began, is eventually revealed to have been a passionate, feeling woman who liked to walk in the woods and read the poems of Rilke, a habit Marion emulated as a young girl. Rilke (1875–1926) was a German poet who devoted himself to what he viewed as the primary task of his time, the reconciliation of our deepest inner feelings with the apparent lack of any foundation for a reasoned belief in a spiritual reality. Greatly influenced by existential precursors such as Nietzsche, Rilke was a Romantic poet in a period when Romanticism was desperately in need of a basis for belief.

In response to the fundamental alienation of the contemporary life, Rilke claimed that we must commit ourselves totally to our feelings even though we know we can never prove their validity. At one point, Marion rereads one of her mother's favorite Rilke poems and discovers the stains of her mother's tears on the page near these lines:

> for there is no place therein
> that does not see you.
> You must change your life.

Through Rilke's poetry, Marion's mother's voice calls to her, just as Hope's voice did, urging her to transform herself while she still can.

Marion's father (played by John Houseman as an old man and David Ogden Stiers as a young one) is an academic historian who resembles Ken in his empty formality, his disdain for feeling, and his failure to love the ones closest to him. Like Marion herself, he values only the intellect and selectively ignores anything that might trouble him. In one memory, we learn that he forced Marion's brother, Paul (played by Stephen Mailer as a young man), to work at a monotonous job in a paper factory to earn enough money to send Marion to Bryn Mawr. Her father despises his son for valuing his emotions more than his intelligence, and makes it clear that he will not allow Marion to make the same mistake.

In his entry on Rilke in *The Encyclopedia of Philosophy*, J. P. Stern describes Rilke's image of the Angel:

> He is a messenger (*angelos*) from another sphere; hence there must be one who sent him. But the angel comes upon us with a terrible majesty and strength which to us who are weak is all his own. In many such astonishing images Rilke expresses the "pure [=necessary] contradiction" that he sees as the root of our being: only by living in total commitment to "the Earth," the here and now, can man transform it into "the heart's inner space," and thus wrest some eventual transition into a "soundless" Beyond — wrest it from he knows not whom. The most accomplished practitioner of such transformations is Orpheus, the poet-maker who, in the creative act, stills all strife by transforming it into song.... Rilke's

poetry is not necessarily esoteric, and the creative activity he extolled is closely related to the poetic; but he addressed himself to the single individual. The social sphere of modern life is branded as wholly inauthentic (Rilke either ignored or briefly satirized it); all concerted action is an escape from defective selfhood [Edwards, 1972, vol. 7, p. 201].

Echoing Rilke's concern for the individual, Allen has Hope's psychiatrist respond to her worries about the problems of the world by telling her: "Don't worry about humanity. Get your own life in order." Hope's appearance as an anguished, weeping, pregnant woman may not initially suggest "majesty and strength" in contrast with Marion's controlled, successful professor; but, from the viewpoints of Rilke, Heidegger, and Allen, it requires more strength to confront one's inner fears and feelings than to lock them away. In this sense, and in her impact upon Marion, whom she literally brings to the place where her life will be forever changed (the restaurant where she discovers Ken with Lydia), Hope acts very much like the angel of Rilke's poetry. In addition, Hope's name and her pregnancy symbolize the positive impact she has upon Marion, who ends the film filled with her own sense of hope and a rebirth of her own feelings and aspirations.

Further, Hope's pregnancy relates to Marion's greatest regret: her decision to abort the child that her first husband wanted so badly. We learn that, in traditional Allen fashion, Marion's first husband, Sam (Phillip Bosco), was her philosophy professor and mentor. In one riveting scene between Sam and Marion, she gives him a birthday present of a white mask which fits perfectly over her own face. We watch as he kisses her longingly through the mask. According to Nietzsche, Rilke, and Heidegger, too many of us hide our most powerful feelings behind a mask of indifference. Marion did just that when she had her abortion without even discussing it with Sam, who she knew longed for a child. Her excuse at the time was her commitment to her work, but in the restaurant scene, she confesses to Hope that her real reason for getting the abortion was her fear that having a child might elicit powerful feelings from within her, feelings of which she was terrified.

Her only opportunity to experience any of the emotions of parenthood has come from her relationship with Laura (Martha Plimpton), her teenaged stepdaughter. Early in the film we learn that Laura is closer to Marion than she is to her own parents. Marion is able to convince Laura to stay with her mother even when her father's words to the same effect have no influence on her. Laura is caught, just as Marion was, between an emotional mother whose feelings frighten her, and a cold, distant father whose expectations overwhelm her. To Laura, Marion seems the perfect role model, a strong, successful woman who, at least initially, seems to have a successful marriage.

Marion encourages Laura to emulate her, taking her to visit her own father, now in his eighties and living alone, in the old family house. The visit is what one would expect, with her father (John Houseman) announcing that he prefers to live alone, seeing only his housekeeper and, once a year, the other members of the board of the Smithsonian Institution. Even after all these years, he still speaks angrily about his son, Paul, and he condemns Marion for occasionally slipping him money. When Laura tries to break the gloomy atmosphere of the visit by lightly asking him if he hopes to fall in love and marry again, he demonstrates his dim view of all emotions, especially love, by saying that he hopes that at his age he has become immune to such feelings. Later, Marion rebukes Laura for asking such a frivolous question, reinforcing her attempt to mold Laura into a copy of herself.

We learn that Marion has accidentally discovered Laura making love with her boyfriend, Scott (Josh Hamilton), in a cabin before a roaring fire. Although she didn't intervene, we hear Laura tell Scott that her awareness of the fact that Marion saw them was enough to transform their lovemaking from something beautiful and romantic into something sleazy and cheap. As Marion listens, we hear Laura tell Scott that although she thinks Marion is great, she also finds her to be very judgmental, and she worries that Marion talks about her to others with the same disdain she brings to any discussion about Paul. Marion realizes that her influence is having an undesirable effect upon Laura, devaluing her sense of romance and poetry just as Marion's father devalued those feelings in herself.

At the film's end, when Marion meets Laura after her breakup with Ken, she is happy to learn that Laura has retained her own character, feelings and all. She tells Marion that she was not really shocked by the collapse of the marriage as it never seemed quite right to her. Hearing this, Marion realizes that Laura's perceptions, grounded in her emotive intuitions, are more accurate their her own, forcibly shorn of all emotion. This insight helps her to discover that she may have as much to learn from Laura as Laura has to learn from her. Marion is pleased when Laura assures her that the split with her father will not change their relationship. In fact, given Marion's new commitment to honesty, and Laura's strained relations with both of her birth parents, we suspect that their connection will now deepen rather than dissipate.

III. The Black Panther

Marion's relationship to Paul is key to her transformation into an authentic, feeling person. As already noted, their father rejected Paul as a young man, forcing him to work in his cousin Andrew's paper factory to raise enough money for Marion's college tuition. This pivotal sacrifice, made unwillingly, tainted the sibling relationship for decades. Despite Paul's crucial contribution to Marion's eventual professional success, she adopted her father's lack of respect for him, treating him horribly while pretending to herself that they were very close.

Early in the film, we see Marion meet briefly with Lynn (Frances Conroy), Paul's then-estranged wife. With her father's impatient disdain, Marion refuses to talk with Lynn because she arrived late for their meeting. Despite the fact that Marion has no pressing engagement (she is only going to her apartment to write), she forces Lynn to humiliate herself by quickly revealing her request for money. When Marion asks her why Paul didn't come to her himself with the request, Lynn tells her that Paul despises her, especially when he must degrade himself by asking for her help. Marion refuses to accept this truth, turning her head to look around her like an animal searching for a way to escape a dangerous trap.

Marion claims to hardly know Lynn, a situation for which Lynn blames Marion, who has repeatedly rebuffed Lynn's attempts to know her better. Marion is not disturbed by the impending breakup of her brother's marriage. She neither offers her sympathies nor asks if she can help. Later, we learn that Lynn and Paul were able to reconcile, while, in the interim, Marion and Ken irreversibly split. We realize, along with Marion, that a marriage based primarily on emotion may, in the long run, be more stable than one based on the supposedly firmer foundation of a shared intellectualism.

At the height of her inner turmoil, after hearing Laura describe her judgmental tone when discussing Paul, Marion finds herself unable to work and in need of fresh air. Like Mickey in *Hannah*, she wanders the streets interminably until she finds herself at Paul's office. When Paul asks her what she is doing there, she is unable to say. Paul, more in touch with her feelings than she is herself, tells her that something must be wrong, that she must need something, since she only comes to him when she needs something.

At this she acknowledges her need and asks him to tell her honestly why they have grown so far apart. He reminds her of an incident in which he showed her something he had written, and he recites the very words she used to dismiss its worth:

> This is overblown, it's too emotional, it's maudlin. This may be meaningful to you, but to the objective observer it's so embarrassing.

Understandably, Paul tells her, after this experience he avoided her presence to save her from embarrassment and himself from the pain of rejection by a sister he both idolized and feared. Confused and unsettled by this revelation, Marion is unable to stay in Paul's presence. Later, however, after her split with Ken, she returns to ask if she can spend more time with him and his family, an offer which Paul accepts by tenderly placing his hand on her shoulder.

The image of Marion as a trapped animal is explicitly raised in the film's references to Rilke's poem "The Panther." As a teenager, Marion wrote an essay in which she claimed that the caged panther was frightened by its glimpse of death outside of its cage. However, in a vision late in the film, Marion sees the caged panther followed by a shot of the white mask she wore in front of Sam. Thus the panther also represents Marion's pent-up emotions, which she is able to keep under control only by wearing the white plaster mask. In the film's final shot, Marion is shown dressed completely in black, identifying her with the panther at last released from its cage (Yacowar, 1991, p. 269).

Another of Marion's crucial relationships is with Claire (Sandy Dennis), the best friend of her youth. Immediately after thinking of Claire, Marion miraculously runs into her and her husband coming out of the theater where Claire is performing in a play. As with her brother, Marion claims to have only just realized how long they have gone without seeing one another. But Claire seems uncomfortable at Marion's appearance and claims not to have time for a drink. However, her husband, Donald (Kenneth Welsh), obviously curious about Marion, insists that they go.

Marion and Donald talk animatedly in a bar as he flatters her for her achievements, and she reciprocates by praising his recent staging of *Mother Courage*. When she gets him to agree that the play's translation was atrocious, while maintaining that his staging was wonderful, Claire, who has excluded herself from their conversation, explodes in anger. Claire accuses Marion of flirting shamelessly with her husband and tells Marion that they didn't gradually lose touch with one another; Claire purposely cut off all connections with her because Marion once seduced a man named David away from Claire, only to then reject his attentions. Like Stephanie in *September*, Marion has made a practice of betraying her best friend by competing for the attention of the men who interest her friend, even though Marion herself has no genuine desire to get involved with them.

Late in the film, but before Marion has discovered Ken's infidelity with Lydia, the two couples go out for an evening of music and food. At the restaurant, a woman at another table interrupts them to tell Marion that she was a student of hers twenty years ago and that the experience changed her life. She especially remembers a lecture Marion gave on "Ethics and Moral Responsibility." Ken beams with pride and Mark and Lydia praise her for the impact she's had on others, yet Marion is clearly more disturbed than pleased.

By this point, she is unable to sleep at night and unable to write during the day. It is in this state that she has her most important and lengthiest vision. In it, she enters the psychiatrist's office as Hope is leaving. The psychiatrist asks Marion for her diagnosis of Hope's condition and, clearly referring more to herself than Hope, she responds:

> MARION: Self-deception.
>
> PSYCHIATRIST: Good. It's a little general.
>
> MARION: But I don't think she can part with her lies.
>
> PSYCHIATRIST: No? Too bad.
>
> MARION: Not that she doesn't want to.
>
> PSYCHIATRIST: It's precisely that she doesn't want to. When she wants to, she will.
>
> MARION: It's all happening so fast.
>
> PSYCHIATRIST: I have to hurry. I'm trying to prevent her from killing herself.
>
> MARION: You don't think she would?
>
> PSYCHIATRIST: She's already begun.
>
> MARION: She has?
>
> PSYCHIATRIST: Oh, not very dramatically. That's not her style. She's doing it slowly and methodically and has been since she was very young. Now, if you'll pardon me, I have another patient.

The next patient turns out to be her father. She listens as he admits his regrets: that he didn't spend his life with the woman he loved most deeply, that he's been a bad father both to Paul and herself, and that he wasted his life pursuing an academic prominence which he now realizes was "stupid" and demanded too little from him.

She next finds herself walking down the street in front of the theater where she ran into Claire. In the theater, Marion encounters Hope, who invites her to stay. Marion discovers that she has interrupted a rehearsal of a play about her own life, a play directed by Donald (whose staging she admired), and starring Claire as herself. She watches as Claire and Ken play scenes dramatizing the shallowness of her marriage. When Ken tells Marion/Claire that she tossed and turned in her sleep repeating the name "Larry," Marion is overwhelmed with feelings of "melancholia and longing."

Larry appears and holds hands with Claire, who is now playing the role of his wife. Marion interrogates him, learning that he is happily living in Santa Fe, although his wife concedes that he expresses a longing to return to New York. When she leaves Marion and Larry to talk, he asks Marion if she's read his novel in which he based one of his characters on her, a character named Helinka. After telling her that he has a daughter whom he deeply loves—a revelation which draws the camera's attention to the face of Hope, the expectant mother — Larry leaves to join his wife, who "needs" to show him a beautiful sunset. Marion clearly wishes someone needed her in that way. She sadly realizes that Larry could have been that person once, but not anymore.

Although she wants to go home, Donald urges her to stay for their "big second-act finale," the suicide of Marion's first husband, Sam. At first she denies his death was a suicide until Sam begins to talk directly to her from a stool under a single bright spotlight. Sam explains that their marriage, like so many of Allen's Pygmalion-Galatea relationships, was one in which Sam was the teacher who molded the "dazzling" young female student. Their joy in the relationship lasted only so long as he still had things to teach her. When she had absorbed all he had to give her, then, he tells us, she felt "suffocated" and had to get away (just like Annie and so many others). Ironically, he reveals, fifteen years after their divorce, when Sam killed himself with a combination of pills and alcohol, his cause of death was listed as "suffocation."

Unable to take any more, Marion leaves, but we don't see her actually wake up from her dream. The line between fantasy and reality is as thin here as it is in *Stardust Memories*. Sandy Bates and Marion Post both view the world initially through filters of self-deception which distort their views. Unlike Bates, however, who only falls further into madness and despair as the film develops, Marion, through the intervention of Hope (pun intended), is able to regenerate herself and begin again authentically.

When Marion discovers Hope crying in the back of a musty antique store under Gustav Klimt's painting of a pregnant woman (also named "Hope"), she is led first to a gallery, where they "marvel" at more of Klimt's work, and then to the restaurant where she discovers Ken's infidelity. Klimt's art is from the same period as Rilke's poetry, and it evokes similar sensations of melancholia and a nostalgia for the spirituality of a lost romanticism in which we can no longer believe.

In the film's final scene, a rejuvenated Marion successfully works on her book — the story that we have just experienced, rather than the abstract philosophical opus she started out to write. During a break, she looks up

Larry's account of their involvement in his novel. She reads with pleasure his description of her as someone who was "capable of intense passion if she would one day just allow herself to feel." We see her sitting at her desk with the book in her hands as we hear her voice-over:

> I closed the book and felt the strange mixture of wistfulness and hope, and I wondered if a memory is something you have or something you've lost. For the first time in a long time, I felt at peace.

As the credits roll, the answer to her question is clear. She had lost her precious memory of Larry's effect upon her along with all of the other emotions she had hidden within herself. While her process of transformation has involved much anguish, at its conclusion she is sufficiently whole to regain her most valued memory, which she may now cherish. She has also gained a peace of mind which will, we suspect, allow her to respond the next time she has the opportunity to create an authentic relationship with a man.

Another Woman is Allen's most complex and subtle film to date. Although it makes heavy demands on its audience, it rewards real effort with a sophisticated portrait of the process by which someone chooses to become inauthentic, and the corresponding suffering required for that person to retrieve her soul. Rather than simply attacking inauthenticity blindly, with no attempt to understand how it comes about (as he might be accused of doing in earlier films), here Allen empathetically reveals its origins and points to the possibility of redemption even for those who at first glance appear to have fallen farthest. In his next full-length film, *Crimes and Misdemeanors*, Allen will move even more deeply into inauthenticity's abyss.

– 7 –

TRADITION:
New York Stories,
"Oedipus Wrecks" (1989)

Unlike the mythical story of the king who kills his father and marries his mother, "Oedipus Wrecks" is the tale of a man who wishes to kill his mother to hide his ancestry. In it, Allen once again demonstrates that family, heritage, and traditional values are essential ingredients in the creation of an authentic life.

I. Mills or Millstein?

After the seriousness of *Another Woman*, Allen's excursion back into broad farce for his segment of the trilogy *New York Stories* comes as a refreshing change of pace. For the first time since *Broadway Danny Rose*, Allen himself plays the leading role in a story with strong comic overtones. In fact, "Oedipus Wrecks" (hereafter referred to as *OW*) owes its plot to a situation briefly mentioned in the earlier film.

At the beginning of that film, we see Danny attempting to comfort a man whose elderly wife remains mesmerized in a trance induced by Danny's client, a hypnotist. Danny promises him that his wife will soon snap out of it, simultaneously offering him a free dinner if she doesn't, hedging his bets by asking him if he likes Chinese.

In *OW*, Sheldon Mills (Woody Allen) is the victim of such a mix-up rather than an agent for its perpetrator. Engaged to a beautiful blonde named Lisa (Mia Farrow), Sheldon is attempting to restart his life after a failed marriage for which he is still paying alimony. Lisa, also making a new start, brings three children to their proposed union. On the face of things, Sheldon should be happy, but he isn't. He still has one problem, a problem hinted at by the music accompanying the segment's credits: "I Want a Girl Just Like the Girl That Married Dear Old Dad."

When we first see Sheldon, he is talking to the camera:

> I'm fifty years old. I'm a partner in a big law firm. You know, I'm very successful. And I still haven't resolved my relationship with my mother.

At this admission, the camera shows us a shot of a man listening to him, and we realize that Sheldon is speaking not to us but to his psychiatrist (Marvin Chatinover). Once again, as in *Annie Hall*, a story is presented in the form of a therapy session.

Sheldon tells him about a recent dream in which his mother, Sadie (Mae Questal), dies. As he is taking her coffin to the cemetery, he hears her voice criticizing his driving and giving him directions. By starting the segment in this way, Allen sets the tone for the dreamlike scenario to come. We hear Sheldon complain about his mother's constant criticisms of him. He ends his session by confessing, "I love her, but I wish she would disappear." The story to follow will confirm the old saying, "Be careful what you wish for because you might get it."

The primary conflict between Sheldon and Sadie is her contention that Sheldon is turning his back on his heritage. All of her complaints are attempts to force Sheldon to face up to the facts about himself, to accept the role he's inherited by virtue of his background and ethnicity. She never tires of telling others that his real name is Millstein, not Mills. By changing it, she implies, he is denying his Jewishness and trying to pass as something he's not.

She wants him to accept the truth about himself, like the fact that he's losing his hair and that he was a bedwetter. Most of all, she wants him to accept *her*, to accept the fact that his mother is a pushy old Jewish lady whose goal in life is to make sure that he passes his heritage on to a new generation. The first time he brings Lisa to her apartment for dinner, Sadie criticizes everything about him, including his eating habits. She complains to Lisa that Sheldon thinks she's too loud in public and that he claims she is always embarrassing him. She insists on showing Lisa endless pictures of Sheldon as a baby as she reveals humiliating details about his childhood.

Sheldon's response to all of this is to become self-conscious and ashamed. Lisa, clearly uncomfortable, rightly fears that Mrs. Millstein doesn't approve of her. During Lisa's brief trip to the bathroom, Sadie seizes the opportunity to tell Sheldon:

> SADIE: Look, look! Listen, Sheldon, don't get married!
>
> SHELDON: I don't want to discuss it!
>
> SADIE: I want to discuss it! What do you know about that? After all, where do you come to a blonde with three children? What are you, an astronaut?

This last comment implies that Sheldon is losing sight of his proper place in society. His aspiration to marry "a blonde with three children" is like "shooting for the moon or the stars"—it simply isn't appropriate for a man of his background.

Sheldon next tells his psychiatrist how Sadie embarrassed him by interrupting an important meeting when she appeared uninvited with his Aunt Ceil (Jessie Keosian) after a matinée of *Cats*. We see his horror as the two women come towards him down the long hallway. He tries, as always, to shush her before she embarrasses him again, but his mission fails. One of his senior partners, Bates (Ira Wheeler), urges Sheldon to rejoin the meeting, and Sadie loudly exclaims to Ceil (who is hard of hearing), "This is Bates, the one with the mistress."

Sheldon's agony is relieved by an event that occurs on a Sunday outing with Lisa, her children, and, at Lisa's insistence, his mother. Sadie ceaselessly complains as the group is led to an outdoor table for lunch. While her complaints are humorous, we do wonder why Sheldon can't give in for once and eat indoors as she demands.

It is during the following magic show that Sheldon's wish comes true. Once again, magic plays an important role by symbolizing a character's desire to control his environment. The magician (George Schindler) uses the name Shandu the Great, the name of the escape artist who taught Danny Rose how to wriggle free of ropes. Shandu calls Sadie out of the audience to be the subject of his "Chinese box trick," in which he places her in a large box, sticks swords through it, and then reopens it to show that she has mysteriously vanished. Even though Sadie states clearly that she doesn't want to take part in the trick, no one pays any attention, and she is forced into the act.

The trick goes smoothly until it is time for her to "magically reappear." This she fails to do, amazing not only the audience but Shandu and his crew as well. At first, Sheldon reacts to this "miracle" hysterically, threatening to sue the theater and hiring a sleazy private investigator, although he rejects the suggestion that the police be called because, as usual, he is afraid the publicity will embarrass him. Echoing the gag from *Broadway Danny Rose*, Shandu offers Sheldon free tickets to a future show to make up for the loss of his mother.

II. Sadie in the Sky

As three weeks pass without Sadie's reappearance, Sheldon tells his therapist that he's never been so relaxed and happy. With his mother gone, all the stress has left his life. He is more productive at work, and best of all, his sex life has never been better. Overcoming his guilt, he calls off the search, happily accepting his good luck that Sadie disappeared without anything terrible having happened. He didn't even have to attend her funeral!

Sheldon's bliss is powerfully disrupted, however, when he hears loud noises coming from the street as he is shopping in a grocery store. When he emerges from the store, he is horrified to find his mother up in the sky, larger than life and telling all of New York about his shortcomings and her frustrations. This is his worst nightmare come to life. Now everyone in the city knows everything about him. Strangers on the street call him a "mama's boy" or demand that he treat his mother better. Initially, Lisa tries to be supportive of Sheldon in his time of need, but when Mom calls her a *kurveh* (a prostitute) in front of millions of people, she is humiliated and warns Sheldon that she's not sure how long she can take it.

At the advice of his psychiatrist, who acknowledges that science and rational thought stand helpless before this inexplicable phenomenon, Sheldon goes for help to a psychic named Treva (Julie Kavner). Treva claims to have mystical powers, rejecting Sheldon's skepticism with assurances that if only he does what she tells him, she will be able to return Sadie to earth.

Over a period of another three weeks, we are shown a variety of humorous scenes in which Treva and Sheldon try one outrageous mystical stratagem after another. They humiliate themselves by wearing ridiculous masks and costumes as they dance, chant, and sprinkle various magic powders. Comic as they are, their efforts seem hopelessly artificial and contrived. The only authentic moment comes when Treva interrupts her attempts to bewitch Sadie's apartment by playing a beautiful piece on her piano.

As time progresses, television newscasters tell us that New Yorkers have become accustomed to Sadie's presence. We even see Ed Koch argue that she has a right to remain airborne; after all, she's a help to the police in spotting crime. Only Sheldon and Lisa can not adjust to Sadie's ongoing presence. When he sneaks out of his apartment one morning to avoid reporters, Sadie calls down to him, "Why are you running? They only want to ask you some questions."

III. Tradition

Eventually, Sheldon interrupts an absurd dancing ritual involving monk's habits, candles, and chanting, to tell Treva that he thinks she's a fraud and that he wants to give up. Crying, she confesses that she has never really had any occult powers. She also reveals that she *wanted* to believe:

> TREVA: I always have hopes! I always think that there's more to the world than meets your eye, hidden meanings, special mysteries. Nothing ever works! Ever!
>
> SHELDON: Look, maybe you're right. Don't get so upset, you know, after all, my mother is floating around up there!

Treva goes on to admit that she started out to become an actress, but when she couldn't get any work, she became a waitress, until some astrologer told her that there was a fortune to be made in the occult field, "that people flock to it because their lives are so empty."

Sheldon comforts her and tells her it isn't her fault that they failed. With his usual contempt for the West Coast lifestyle, he tells her that if she had moved to California, by now she would probably have "a swimming pool and your own church!" As he consoles her, he starts to realize how much he likes her. He agrees to stay for a typically Jewish meal of boiled chicken and potato pancakes. After dinner, Sheldon praises Treva as "a marvelous storyteller," and we begin to see that without the artificial trappings of the psychic, she is a sweet Jewish girl who loves nothing better than taking care of a man in the traditional way. Their mutual attraction is palpable as Sheldon excuses himself to go home. Entranced by one another, Sheldon and Treva have great difficulty saying goodnight. Treva reinforces her image as the traditional Jewish woman by giving him some chicken and pancakes to take home with him for a snack later.

When Sheldon returns to his apartment, he finds a letter from Lisa telling him that it's all over between them, that she just can't take it any more. "It's funny," she writes, "you wake up one day and suddenly you're out of love! Life is odd. All the best to you, Lisa." Sheldon throws down the letter, disgusted that Lisa did not even have the courage to break up with him in person (whereas, on the other hand, Treva is able to admit her failings honestly and to his face). Sheldon finds himself unwrapping a drumstick and holding it up to his nose to smell, as rich broth drips from it and romantic music swells loudly on the soundtrack. He looks around him with an expression of awakening realization, concluding with a small smile (Isaac's smile from the end of *Manhattan*), as he finally discovers his true destiny.

The film's last scene begins one morning as Sadie calls down from the sky to awaken him, only to discover that, for once, he has anticipated her desires by coming onto his balcony to see her. Leading Treva by the hand, he introduces her as his new fiancée. When Sadie sees Treva (dressed attractively for the first time) and hears her voice, she realizes that Sheldon has finally accepted his heritage and found a nice Jewish girl. Having at last achieved her goal, Sadie leaves the sky and reappears on a sofa, back to her normal self and complete with photo album. Sheldon watches with a smile of happy resignation as Sadie tells Treva all of Sheldon's failings, and Treva responds by playing the game as it should be played, clucking appropriately and glancing at Sheldon in mock outrage.

In "Oedipus Wrecks," as in *Radio Days*, Allen asserts the value of maintaining the ties of family and heritage. At its outset, Sheldon disguises his identity behind a phony name, hides his mother out of fear of rejection, and pursues a shallow relationship with a woman capable of abandoning him when he needs her most. In the course of the tale, a miracle forces Sheldon to realize that he can find happiness only by unashamedly returning to the values and customs of his heritage.

When we first see her, Treva has disguised herself even more thoroughly than Sheldon. Wanting to be an actress, she plays the part of the screwy psychic, trying to tap into the mysteries of the universe by means of rituals and disguises totally alien to her own culture. Only at the end, when she fully explores her identity as a Jewish woman, is she able to bring Sadie back down to earth.

As for Sadie, with all her *mishegoss* (wackiness), she is the most honest and the wisest of them all. Having assured the continuity of her heritage, she will now be able to fulfill the role she was truly born to play: a loving Jewish grandmother!

Despite its sincerity and good humor, *OW* paints too simplistic a solution to the problems of contemporary life. With its fatalistic determinism, *OW* denies the freedom and creativity which Allen has valued so highly in other films (e.g., *Manhattan*). We will have to turn to his next effort, *Crimes and Misdemeanors*, for a serious examination of this conflict between freedom and tradition.

– 8 –

"IF NECESSARY, I WILL ALWAYS CHOOSE GOD OVER TRUTH!": *Crimes and Misdemeanors* (1989)

To this point in his career, Allen's investigation of the moral decline of society had been limited to acts which, while clearly immoral, were rarely illegal. In *Crimes and Misdemeanors*, his best film to date, the main character, Judah Rosenthal (Martin Landau), comes to "see" that in a world devoid of a divine presence, all acts are permissible, even murder.

The apparent philosophical despair of this film, in which the most moral individual, Ben (a rabbi), is shown gradually going blind, has been taken by many to symbolize Allen's ultimate sense of hopelessness. All of the supposedly virtuous characters are shown wearing glasses because of their inability to see the true nature of the world. As the film progresses, one character, Halley (Mia Farrow), is apparently able to discard her glasses only after she has also discarded her values by agreeing to marry the arrogant, pompous but successful TV producer Lester (Alan Alda). Allen's character, Cliff Stern, is punished for his commitment to his beliefs as we see him lose everything he cared for: his love, his work, and even his spiritual mentor, the philosophy professor Louis Levy (Martin Bergmann), who, like Primo Levi, survived the Holocaust but responds to the petty immoralities of everyday life by killing himself.

Most ominously, Judah, who bears the name of one of the greatest fighters for traditional Jewish values and heritage, betrays the faith of his father Sol (David Howard) by not only committing a murder; but also renouncing the consequences of his guilt in a universe which he declares to be indifferent to our actions.

I. Judah's Crime

These themes are introduced at the very beginning of the film when we hear Judah address the audience at a banquet given in his honor:

> JUDAH: That the new ophthalmology wing has become a reality is not just a tribute to me, but to a spirit of community, generosity, mutual caring, and answered prayers. Now it's funny I use the term answered prayers, you see, I'm a man of science, I've always been a skeptic, but I was raised quite religiously, and while I challenged it, even as a child, some of that feeling must have stuck with me. I remember my father telling me, "the eyes of God are on us always!" The eyes of God! What a phrase to a young boy! And what were God's eyes like? Unimaginatively penetrating and intense eyes I assumed. And I wonder if it was just a coincidence that I made my specialty ophthalmology?

At the words "even as a child," we are shown two Orthodox Jewish men sitting in the front of a synagogue reading sacred texts as they sway back and forth in the traditional fashion.

In these first scenes, Allen establishes the conflicting elements which will dominate his starkest investigation yet into the increasing moral and religious paralysis which grips contemporary American society. By giving his protagonist the first name of "Judah," and so explicitly showing us his Orthodox Jewish upbringing, Allen makes clear his intention to explore the role of religion, specifically the role of Judaism, in the story he is about to tell. The name Judah reminds us of one of the scriptural names for a part of ancient Israel (Judea), as well as, most obviously, the famous and successful Jewish leader Judah Maccabee, whose story is the historical focus of the Jewish holiday called Hanukkah ("dedication").

In the second century B.C.E., Syria and Judea were ruled by a Greek king named Antiochus IV (ruled 175–163 B.C.E.). Within Judea a conflict developed between some upper-class Jews who were drawn to the sophistication of their Greek rulers and those Jews, both affluent and lower-class, who rejected the Hellenizing influences and demanded a rigid adherence to ancient Jewish culture. Eventually, the Greek king directly involved himself in the conflict by forbidding the "observance of the Sabbath, circumcision, and Torah study" (Hein, 1993, p. 309). According to the authors of *Religions of the World*:

> When his officials demanded that Israel sacrifice to Zeus, the people were outraged. The Book of Maccabees tells how an elderly priest, Mattahias of Modin, openly defied this order, instead killing the Syrian official who had made the demand. Mattahias led his five sons and their followers in the ensuing battle against the Greek regime, and one son, Judah Maccabee, emerged as the leader of the successful resistance. The Hellenizers' retreat inspired the Maccabees to cleanse and rededicate the temple in 165 B.C.E. That occasion served as the historical basis for the Jewish festival of Hanukkah [Hein, 1993, p. 309].

Thus, the festival of Hanukkah instructs Jews to reject the sophisticated — and admittedly appealing — ideas of secular society in favor of a strict adherence to traditional values. It further seems to make a divine promise to those Jews who follow God's word: If they will reject the easy temptations of a corrupt and morally weak society, then God will miraculously intervene to support their struggle to maintain their integrity. This promise does require commitment and faith on the part of the devout Jews. God did not intervene until after the rebellion was in full swing, and, even then, His intervention was one more of moral support than actual involvement in the battle. In fact, the story suggests, Jews themselves have the force of will, courage, and physical strength necessary to defeat immorality if only they choose to use it openly.

Although we see in his speech at the testimonial dinner that he still carries with him a sense of obligation towards his Jewish heritage and the values it epitomizes, Judah can not bring himself to resist the temptation to follow his reason alone and deny the objective existence of all values.

The conflict between reason and faith is presented explicitly in many of the film's relationships. Here, for example, is a dialogue between Judah and Ben (Sam Waterston):

> JUDAH: Our entire adult lives you and I have been having this conversation in one form or another.
>
> BEN: Yes, I know. It's a fundamental difference in the way we view the world. You see it as harsh and empty of values and pitiless, and I couldn't go on living if I didn't feel it with all my heart a moral structure, with real meaning, and forgiveness, and some kind of higher power, otherwise there's no basis to know how to live! And I know you well enough to know that a spark of that notion is inside you somewhere too.

JUDAH: Now you're talking to me like your congregation.

BEN: It's true, we went from a small infidelity to the meaning of existence.

In this exchange, the fundamental conflict present in all of Allen's films is laid bare for our inspection. This conflict, which I have called "the existential dilemma," pits our recognition of the claim that there can be no rational basis for grounding values against our need to conduct our lives in accordance with a set of just such standards. Returning to our discussion of Soloveitchik, again we see the dialectic between the hedonism of Adam the first (represented here by Judah) and the redemptive spirit of Adam the second (Ben). This conversation has indeed gone on within Allen's work throughout his entire career, just as it has gone on between Judah and Ben throughout their whole lives.

While Ben and Judah are in one sense presented as the two extremes on these issues, in another sense, as Ben has just told us, this conflict is really taking place within Judah. Judah does have a spark of Ben's faith within him and the film's primary drama turns on the way he decides to resolve this crisis and the consequences of that decision. When Ben says that they have moved "from a small infidelity to the meaning of existence," he suggests an interpretation of both the film's title and the interrelationship between its two plotlines. How one acts to deal with "a small infidelity" determines one's position on the very "meaning of existence." The distance between such small misdemeanors and unforgivable crimes is much shorter than normally thought, once one has rejected all notions of values and responsibility.

This point is strikingly similar to the one made in the novel whose title most resembles that of this film, namely Dostoyevsky's *Crime and Punishment*. In that book, an author who (like Kierkegaard or Soloveitchik) has made the leap of faith while acknowledging the apparent fundamental absurdity of the world, shows us how the failure to make that leap leads a student named Raskolnikov, overcome by existential dread, to murder an elderly woman. Through his dialogue with his pursuer, and his own corresponding internal debate, Raskolnikov is led by the novel's end to a genuine acceptance of the possibility of religious redemption.

Interestingly, Judah's situation requires that, in order to accept Ben's challenge, he must choose to have faith not directly in God, but (like Buber) in the redemptive power of an authentic "I-Thou" relationship with his wife Miriam (Claire Bloom). Judah must decide if he can trust Miriam sufficiently to chance the possibility that the revelation of his sin will destroy both of their lives. If he decides that he does not trust her enough to take this risk, then one must wonder at his reasons for wishing to maintain his marriage with her.

At a surprise birthday celebration at home with his family, Judah is given a treadmill. Confirming the hint that his family represents a form of staid boredom while his mistress Dolores (Anjelica Huston) brings with her excitement and melodrama, Judah is called to the phone to hear Dolores' threat to be at his house in five minutes if he doesn't meet her at the gas station down the road. Ominous sounds of thunder accompany her threats, and by the time Judah arrives to meet her, a full-fledged storm is in progress.

Sitting in a car, Dolores demands that they go away together and that, when they return, Judah must "bring things with Miriam to a conclusion." She also gives him a birthday present, an album of Schubert's music. Her choice of birthday present, a gift of the music she knows he loves, suggests that she represents the desires of his soul while Miriam's treadmill symbolizes the dullness of his respectable married life. Nonetheless, her ultimatum brings him to the point of crisis.

When he returns home, the sound of thunder accompanied by a brilliant flash of lightning announces Judah's appearance as he descends the stairs with Ben's words about morality and forgiveness racing through his mind. Images of hellfire surround him as he stares into the burning fireplace and ignites a cigarette with his lighter. Ben's voice expands into a fantasy of his actual presence as he tries to persuade Judah to give up the murderous schemes of his brother Jack (Jerry Orbach) in order to ask the world, and God, for forgiveness. Judah rejects Ben's arguments, and when Ben mentions God, Judah reveals that Jack has at last convinced him to become a hedonistic nihilist:

> JUDAH: God is a luxury I can't afford.
>
> BEN: Now you're talking like your brother Jack.
>
> JUDAH: Jack lives in the real world. You live in the kingdom of heaven. I managed to keep free of that real world, but suddenly it's found me.
>
> BEN: You fool around with her for your pleasure, and when you think it's enough, you want to sweep her under the rug?
>
> JUDAH: There's no other solution but Jack's, Ben! I push one button and I can sleep again nights.
>
> BEN: Is that who you really are?
>
> JUDAH: I will not be destroyed by this neurotic woman!
>
> BEN: Come on Judah! Without the law it's all darkness!
>
> JUDAH: You sound like my father! What good is the law if it prevents me from receiving justice? Is what she's doing to me just? Is this what I deserve?

At this Judah picks up the phone, calls Jack, and tells him "to move ahead with what we discussed. How much will you need?" Judah has now resolved to place his own selfish interests over the law, morality, and God. In doing so, he explicitly abandons the faith of his fathers and places himself outside of God's realm. His self-deception is massive: he refuses to take any responsibility for creating his predicament (he claims that the real world "found him" as though he did nothing to bring that about), and he refuses to consider the possibility that he may truly deserve what is happening to him.

Judah's namesake, the Maccabee, gave up his life to fight for his father's faith against the superior military forces of his people's oppressors. The original Judah did nothing to "deserve" his fate, yet he never questioned his obligation to sacrifice everything in this cause. The contemporary Judah expects to be handed a life of wealth and comfort without sacrifice. Like Dr. Faustus, Judah is willing to sell his soul in exchange for the satisfaction of his desires. In his fantasized dialogue with Ben, he is so mired in lies that he won't even allow Ben to use his strongest argument (that Judah is cold-bloodedly plotting a murder), restricting him to "sweeping her under the rug" instead. As a result of this betrayal of his heritage and the best part of himself, we expect to see him punished both by society, and, if we believe, by God.

After the murder has taken place and Judah has visited the scene to remove incriminating documents, we see him back at home, sitting alone in the bathroom with the lights on while an unaware Miriam sleeps soundly in the bedroom. Suddenly, the phone begins to ring. Judah rushes to answer it only to find there is no one on the other end of the line, suggesting that God is calling Judah to task for his crime, yet refusing to speak to him directly.

II. The Seder

Driving in his car, Judah again thinks of the synagogue his family attended in his childhood. Finally, unable to stop himself, he goes to the home of his youth and asks the current owner if he may look around. He tells her of his memories of playing with Jack there and of the high expectations they all had of him, expectations that were never fulfilled. Suddenly, he hears the sound of a Passover seder emanating from the dining room. Standing in the doorway, he watches as his imagination creates a seder from his youth.

The first sounds he hears are those of the Hebrew prayers over the eating of the bitter herbs. The seder is a dinner service performed at home with the head of the family, in this case Judah's father Sol (David Howard), leading the service and explaining its meaning as he sits at the table's head. The eating of the bitter herbs represents the suffering of the Jews when they were slaves in Egypt until Moses came, with God's help, to lead his people into freedom in the promised land.

We listen as Judah's Aunt May (Anna Berger), challenges Sol by questioning the legitimacy of the "mumbo-jumbo" of the religious service. Calling her a "Leninist," Sol acts offended by the tone of her comments as she questions the existence of any objective set of moral values and argues that "might makes right" even when it comes to the Holocaust.

This scene contains the most complete discussion of morality and faith to be found in any of Allen's films. In fact, it is so powerful that it could stand alone as a superb discussion of philosophical issues, comparable to the famous "Legend of the Grand Inquisitor" section from Dostoevsky's *The Brothers Karamazov*. Like that passage, this scene contains a dialogue between those who favor a nihilistic view of the universe as a meaningless, mechanical environment in which we are completely free to create the meaning of our lives however we wish, and the believer who uses the same freedom to choose to have faith in God and morality while acknowledging that there is no rational basis for that faith. Thus, in this debate, we revisit the distinction made by Soloveitchik in his discussion of the conflict between Adam the first and Adam the second.

The "nihilists" (Aunt May and her supporters among the sederquests) take a position resembling not only that of the Grand Inquisitor, but also that of a variety of philosophers throughout Western history, including the Sartrean existentialists. Like Soloveitchik's "majestic man," they favor the evidence of the senses and the scientific use of reason over the desires and beliefs of the so-called "soul." The "believer" (Sol), on the other hand, takes a position resembling the more mystical religious traditions which culminate in the existential theories of theists such as Kierkegaard, Marcel, Buber, and Soloveitchik.

The dialogue also reminds us of Socrates' debate with the Sophist Thrasymachus in one section of Plato's best known dialogue, *The Republic*. Like Thrasymachus, May argues that what is just is "whatever is in the interest of the stronger party." For Thrasymachus, what was important was to appear to the world at large as a just, honorable person while simultaneously acting unjustly so as to get away with as much as possible. While Socrates is able to defeat the Sophist's arguments in the context of this dialogue, Plato's opponents have always contended that this was made possible only because Plato purposely did not allow Thrasymachus to give the best possible arguments.

Allen does not similarly handcuff the nihilists in his scene. Their arguments are presented so compellingly that it is made clear that this incident from his youth contributed greatly to Judah's later choice of the rational life of the man of science over that of the believer which his father wanted so much for him. May's use of the fact of the Holocaust adds to the potency of her position and is worth a more detailed examination. For the sake of this discussion, I will temporarily play devil's advocate by expanding her arguments.

For May, one of the most striking moral implications of the Holocaust lies in the fact that it vividly demonstrates that human beings can violently disagree concerning the moral principles which they adopt. The fundamental assumption underlying natural law theory (the position for which the Man in the Hat appears to argue) states that, while people of good intent might legitimately disagree over many normative issues, ultimately there exists a universal set of underlying basic principles on which we all can and should agree.

But, May would counter, in the twentieth century if we have learned anything, it is that people do not agree on many fundamental principles of value. Debates and disagreements over such issues have characterized numerous international conflicts and matters of dispute. Thus, perhaps the most difficult problem facing natural law theorists is not just to decide what these natural laws are, but also to persuade others to adopt them or to forcibly impose them upon people who disagree, which would only result in the confirmation of May's contention that "might makes right."

Thus, May contends, the role of morality in each individual's life is only what they choose it to be. If one wishes to uphold "morality," however one defines it, then one may do so. If, on the other hand, one wishes to ignore the issues of morality altogether, and commit a crime, even murder, then there is nothing to prevent it other than one's own conscience ("And I say, if he can do it, and get away with it, and he chooses not to be bothered by the ethics, then he's home free.") There is no question that the arguments of the nihilists in this scene overwhelm the naturalist claims of the Man in the Hat that we are all basically "decent," and, it is implied, that all agree on the most important fundamental values.

Even more compelling for the nihilists' position is the question of how God could have allowed the Holocaust to take place. How could an all-powerful caring God have stood by and allowed millions of innocent people to die without intervening as He is claimed to have done during the story of the original Passover, the Exodus from Egypt?

Yet, in its own way, Allen's presentation of Sol's position is also compelling. While acknowledging that his position is based on faith rather than logic and reason, Sol ultimately claims that the life of the man of faith, Soloveitchik's Adam the second, is more fulfilling than that of the nihilists' Adam the first. As we discussed earlier, Adam the second makes the Kierkegaardian leap of faith into belief without the safety net of logic or evidence. Given the fact that he feels that a life without morality or God is a meaningless one which can only end in bitterness and despair, he chooses to believe, precisely because there is no reason to do so, in a sacrificial act analogous to that of Abraham in choosing to obey God's command to sacrifice Isaac despite the dictates of both his desires and his reason.

Even if there is no God, if one's faith is a denial of the "truth," it is better to believe than not to believe because only through belief can the spiritual life, the only one capable of fulfilling our deepest human needs, be attained. For Sol, the existential human condition is such that each of us *must* choose the values by which we will live. Even those, like the nihilists, who claim to have chosen to deny all values are making a choice which implies its own set of values. The nihilists' choice ultimately implies the acceptance of the ethic of hedonism, the belief that one is justified in doing whatever one wishes. This is itself a value system which posits the worth of individual pleasure over the demands of a traditional morality and religion.

It is impossible to avoid responsibility for choosing some values; every act in which one engages represents a favoring of the worth of that action over all the others available to one at that moment. Therefore, since one must choose to believe in something, and that choice must be made without any objective knowledge of right and wrong, one should choose those values which best correspond to one's vision of how the universe *ought to be*. For Sol, this means that one should choose to believe in a universe governed by a caring and moral God who may not directly intervene in human affairs or manifest His presence in any concrete fashion. One should choose to do this not because one can know with certainty that such a God exists, but, rather because without such a belief life would not be worth living.

In this sense, the woman at the seder table is right in comparing Sol's choice to have faith to the aesthetic activity of an artist, but wrong in suggesting that only those born with "a gift" have the capacity to do this. For, according to existentialists like Sartre, the human condition is such that *all of us* are condemned to create the meaning of our lives on the basis of our freedom. Thus, Sol is not unusual in his *ability* to have faith, but only in the *strength of his commitment* to that faith. Sartre makes a similar point about the relationship between art and morality in his essay, *Existentialism and Humanism*:

Rather let us say that the moral choice is comparable to the construction of a work of art.

But here I must at once digress to make it quite clear that we {existentialists} are not propounding an aesthetic morality, for our adversaries are disingenuous enough to reproach us even with that.... There is this in common between art and morality, that in both we have to do with creation and invention. We can not decide a priori what it is that should be done.... Man makes himself; he is not found ready-made; he makes himself by the choice of his morality, and he can not but choose a morality, such is the pressure of circumstances upon him. We define man only in relation to his commitments; it is therefore absurd to reproach us for irresponsibility in our choice [Sartre quoted in Kaufmann, 1975, pp. 364–365].

Returning to our discussion of Dostoyevsky, in his passage on the author in *The Encyclopedia of Philosophy*, Edward Wasiolek describes the dilemma raised by Dostoyevsky's acceptance of the notion of radical freedom and the meaninglessness of our experience in this way:

The total freedom of the underground man brought Dostoyevsky to the total terror of a universe without truth or principle, good or evil, virtue or vice. This nihilist vision of the universe was to send philosophers like L.I. Shestov and Nietzsche into dark ecstasy over the naked power of the will, and it was also to bring Dostoyevsky to what seemed to be an irresolvable dilemma: Freedom is the supreme good because man is not man unless he is free, but freedom is also a supreme evil because man is free to do anything, including illimitable destruction.... These two kinds of freedom are most fully embodied and brought into conflict in the persons of Christ and the Grand Inquisitor in "The Legend of the Grand Inquisitor."... Christ's freedom is that of conditionless faith, given by man in fearful and lonely anxiety and without the reassurance of rational proof, miracles, or the support of the crowd. The freedom of the Grand Inquisitor is the freedom of the superior will, presented in its most attractive form.... So powerfully did Dostoyevsky dramatize the Grand Inquisitor's argument against Christ and his freedom that critical opinion has split since that time in choosing Christ or the Grand Inquisitor as the bearer of truth. Dostoyevsky was without doubt on the side of Christ, but he meant to have each reader decide in free and lonely anxiety where to place his own belief [Edwards, 1972, Vol. 2, p. 412].

In the same manner, Allen presents the views of both the nihilist and the believer so powerfully that it is possible to claim that he himself favors either side. Indeed, it is for this reason that Allen has so often been accused of favoring narcissism or moral relativity. While it is clear that this debate rages within Allen as fiercely as it did within Dostoyevsky, ultimately, in my view, Allen's own position is in accord with the believer. We have seen Allen's indictment of those who have forgotten the values of their heritage too often to conclude otherwise.

Finally, it is in this scene, for the first time, that Judah is forced, by the most powerful moral voice within him (that of his father), to face up to the true nature of his crime by giving it the name it deserves, that of *murder*!

When we next see Judah, he is in his office lying to a police detective about his knowledge of and involvement with Dolores. While his lies seem persuasive to us, Judah expresses his terror that he may have made a slip as he talks over the incident with Jack. When he then reveals that he has an overpowering urge to just confess and get the whole thing over with, Jack explodes in anger, urging him "to be a man," and saying that he's not going to go to jail to satisfy Judah's sense of guilt. Judah demands to know if Jack is threatening him. While Jack denies it, Judah realizes that his father was right in his claim that "one sin leads to deeper sin, adultery, fornication, lies, killing...." Judah now sees that the way he thought about Dolores, as a problem that could be solved by just one push of a button, could also be applied by Jack to him. In a sense, Judah's intellect leads him to use the golden rule to see the ultimate wrongness of his act. By acting to murder Dolores when she became a problem for him, he intellectually gave his permission to Jack to do the same if he, Judah, were to become a similar obstacle.

Judah becomes riddled with guilt. We see him sitting in his car in front of Dolores's apartment house, almost wishing for the police to see him there and question him. At a meal in a restaurant with Miriam and Sharon, we learn that Judah has been drinking heavily and acting irritably. We hear him say in a whisper, "I believe in God, Miriam, because, without God, the world is a cesspool." He pounds the table in anger when Sharon suggests they should leave, and finally goes for a walk by himself outside, "to get some air."

III. Cliff Stern and Louis Levy

The second plotline in *Crimes and Misdemeanors* is the story of Cliff Stern (Allen) and his attempt to maintain his moral integrity in the face of the nihilism represented by his wife Wendy (Joanna Gleason), her brother Lester (Alan Alda) and Halley Reed (Mia Farrow). While Wendy and Lester are Ben's siblings, they share none of his spiritual commitment. Wendy urges Cliff to make a flattering documentary of Lester, a successful but shallow TV producer. Halley works for public television, which has commissioned the show. Cliff reluctantly agrees only because he needs the money to finance his much more serious project, a film profile of the philosopher Louis Levy. As the film progresses, we learn that Cliff's marriage to Wendy is close to ending and we watch as Cliff competes with Lester for Halley's affection.

Cliff initially approaches Halley to ask her why PBS is wasting its time with a profile of an idiot like Lester. Halley agrees with Cliff and tells him that she argued against it but that they "like to mix it up." She notes that Lester "is an American phenomenon." When Cliff responds, "So is acid rain!" Halley asks him why he agreed to film the documentary if he hates its subject so much. Cliff confesses that he's just doing it for the money so that he can finance his real project, a film on the philosopher Louis Levy. He then asks her if he can show her some of his footage of Levy in order to convince her that a show on Levy would be much more appropriate for her series.

Cliff shows her a clip of one of his interviews with Levy in his office. Levy (Martin Bergmann) is a white-haired, older man with glasses who speaks with a European accent. In a return to scriptural metaphor (initially evident in connection with Judah's name and its reference to the story of the Maccabees), Levy speaks of another biblical reference, this time the ancient Israelites' notion of a fierce but caring God.

While Allen has shown us a number of philosophers in his films (for example, Leopold in *A Midsummer Night's Sex Comedy* and Marion in *Another Woman*), this is the first time that a philosopher has been portrayed from the beginning as a voice of wisdom — almost, in a sense, as the voice of God. Like God, Levy is never encountered directly; we experience him only in Cliff's videotapes and, finally, in his last note. Levy speaks to Cliff, who wishes to spread Levy's message to the rest of society through his art (the documentary he hopes will be shown on PBS).

In the excerpt that Cliff shows Halley, Allen returns to the theme of sacrifice that has played so large a role in his earlier films. While God cares for us, He also demands that we make the Kierkegaardian leap of faith by following a strict moral code of behavior despite the fact that this code might require us to act contrary to our interest or even our reason. By the same token, however, Levy speaks of God and morality as the "creations" of the Israelites. They "conceived a God that cares." This use of language suggests that we have no proof either of God's existence or of the validity of the moral code, yet we "conceive" of them in a way which has been historically compelling. Here again, Allen is presenting us with the existential dilemma — our desire to ground our lives in a set of traditional ethical values derived from a supernatural presence, even as we acknowledge sadly that no ontological foundation exists to justify such a belief.

The theme of vision is emphasized by the fact that four of the major characters (Cliff, Ben, Halley, and Louis Levy) wear glasses, while Judah (not in need of vision correction himself) is an ophthalmologist. Judah has already told us about "the eyes of God," which his father claimed always to be upon us. The four bespectacled characters are the ones who seem most open to Levy's descriptions of the obligations incumbent upon those who choose to follow God, yet they are shown as suffering from impaired vision, and perhaps the most saintly of them, Ben, is in the process of going blind. This suggests that those of us who retain an interest in God and morality have simply failed to see that such concerns have lost their relevance in these corrupt times.

Removing her glasses (a gesture which might indicate insincerity), Halley tells Cliff that, while the show on Lester cannot be cancelled at this point (as Cliff had hoped), she is really impressed with Levy and will fight to get financing and support from PBS to include Cliff's documentary in the fall schedule. When Cliff responds by telling Halley that even though they have only just met, he has "taken an instant liking to her," Halley responds, "And I to him," pointing to the screen where she has just watched Levy. The expression on Cliff's face indicates his disappointment in Halley's response. While Cliff is confessing an attraction to Halley not only as a professional but as a person, Halley will only admit to liking Cliff's work.

Cliff brings a present to the apartment of his niece Jenny (Jenny Nichols). The present is a book of old photographs of New York from the twenties. Once again, Allen's persona reveals a nostalgia for earlier, presumably more moral times; however, when Cliff mentions that the book has a chapter on speakeasies, we wonder just how much better things were back then. His sister Barbara (Caroline Aaron) starts to cry uncontrollably as soon as Jenny leaves the room. She tells Cliff about a horrible experience she has had with a man she met through a personal ad she placed in the newspaper. While this man initially appeared to be a gentleman, late one night, after an evening of dancing and drinking, he insisted that she allow herself to be bound to her bed, after which he got over her and "went to the bathroom" on her. Following this humiliation, he took his clothes and left.

Cliff responds to Barbara's story with disgust and tries to get Barbara to promise never to place such an ad again. She tells him of the immensity of her loneliness as a widow, saying he could never understand what that's like, given his successful marriage to a woman he loves. Cliff disillusions her about the success of his marriage, confessing that "neither of us has the energy to do anything about it, but it's not so great."

Barbara's pathetic story reinforces the film's sense that all standards have disappeared in contemporary society. In the past, a young widowed woman with a child would have been a part of an extended family that would have helped her and eased her grief and loneliness. For example, although Aunt Bea in *Radio Days* remained unmarried, she was part of the family and never lonely, a point emphasized when Joey's father discovers her playing solitaire on New Year's Eve. Instead of teasing her, he says, "No date tonight? Well, it's all right. We're all together, you know."

Given the disintegration of our collective sense of family and community, it never occurs to Cliff to tell Barbara to call him whenever she feels lonely. Instead, he responds by comparing his own loneliness and misery to hers. Don't feel so bad, his comments suggest; marriage is no picnic these days either.

As if to confirm Cliff's point, we see Wendy in bed reading as a discouraged Cliff comes in, sits on the edge of the bed, and tells Wendy about Barbara's horrendous experience. When an unsurprised, and apparently uninterested, Wendy asks why the man defecated on Barbara, Cliff responds, "I don't know. Is there any, is there any reason I could give you that would answer that question satisfactorily?" He goes on to ponder the mysteries of human sexuality, as Wendy matter-of-factly puts down her magazine, sets her watch alarm, and then announces that she's going to sleep. Their marriage has deteriorated to such an extent that Wendy does not feel an obligation to express even the most superficial kind of concern for Cliff or the members of his family. Her lack of response to his revelation shocks us. She doesn't ask how this came to happen to Barbara, nor does she ask how Barbara is doing now. We wonder what could have happened between them for her to treat Cliff so callously, and we can't understand why they remain in such an apparently loveless union.

Cliff's plans are destroyed when he learns that Louis Levy has committed suicide. Shocked, Cliff sits in his office watching a videotape in which Levy expresses his views on suicide:

> LEVY: But we must always remember that we, when we are born, we need a great deal of love in order to persuade us to stay in life. Once we get that love, it usually lasts us. But the universe is a pretty cold place, it's we who invest it with our feelings, and, under certain conditions, we feel that it isn't worth it anymore!

At this, the video screen goes all white, almost as though an explosion had suddenly engulfed Levy.

Halley appears to offer her condolences. Cliff tells her, and us, the following:

CLIFF: Oh, God, it's been terrible, you know? I called, the guy was not sick at all, and he left a note, he left a simple little note that said "I've gone out the window," and this is a major intellectual and this is his note, "I've gone out the window." What the hell does that mean, you know? This guy was a role model, you'd think he'd leave a decent note!

HALLEY: Well, what? Did he have family or anything?

CLIFF: No, you know, they were all killed in the war. That's what so strange about this. He's seen the worst side of life his whole life, he always was affirmative, he always said "yes" to life, "yes, yes," now today he said "no!"

HALLEY: Imagine his students, imagine how shattered they're going to be?

CLIFF: Listen, I don't know from suicide, you know, where I grew up, in Brooklyn, nobody committed suicide, you know, everyone was too unhappy!

HALLEY: Boy, you know, this will put a damper on the show!

CLIFF: Well, I've got six hundred thousand feet of film on this guy, and he's telling how great life is and now, you know, you know, what am I going to do? I'll cut it up into guitar picks!

HALLEY: I was just thinking that no matter how elaborate a philosophical system you work out, in the end, it's got to be incomplete.

    This pessimistic, and unquestionably accurate, appraisal of all philosophical systems, including those to come, leaves us with apparently few options. On the one hand, like Judah, Jack, or Lester, we can choose to base our lives solely on hedonistic principles seeking to get as much as we can for ourselves and destroying those who get in the way. Or, like Aunt May, we can become permanent cynics, attacking everything and everyone around us while hypocritically pinning all our hopes on some utopian ideology (like Marxism) which promises us salvation, either here on earth or in some mystical heaven. Or, we can take Sol's approach and choose to commit ourselves to a set of values while simultaneously acknowledging that such a choice can only be based on faith, never on knowledge. Finally, we can follow Louis Levy's path and escape all of life's woes and contradictions by simply ending life.

    In the last videotape we watch of Levy, he begins by echoing Camus in his suggestion that we all need to be given a reason not to commit suicide, "to persuade us to stay in life." Yet, as Cliff tells us, Levy was able to construct such a reason through the creation of his philosophy of affirmation. This positive outlook on life was enough to get him through horrendous experiences. Cliff hints, but does not actually say, that Levy's family was killed in the Holocaust, and that Levy just barely escaped with his life. Given May's earlier reference to the Holocaust as the ultimate horror, one can understand Cliff's incredulity that Levy could make it through such an experience, survive, go on to live for over forty more years, and then, suddenly, decide to take his own life.

The answer to this puzzle, like that surrounding the death of Primo Levi, the real-life figure whose story it recalls, is never revealed; but we can speculate. Despite its overwhelming horror, in some ways the Holocaust can be dealt with intellectually if it is viewed as an aberration, a unique event perpetuated by a nation cowed by economic collapse and international humiliation, and led by a madman who ruled with an iron fist. If the Holocaust was such an aberration, detested and abhorred by all sane, right-thinking, decent people, then we can be shocked by the enormity of its evil while still remaining basically optimistic about the human condition and its future.

After all, one could argue, the world did eventually crush Nazism, and when the true scope of the Holocaust became known, the international community agreed to hold war crimes trials at Nuremberg at which the remaining architects of the killing were tried, convicted, and executed. Today, only a very small number of crackpots, with no real clout, continue to defend the Nazis; and even most of those fanatics base their defense on the obviously erroneous claim that the Holocaust did not actually occur. By making such a claim, no matter how hypocritically, they admit openly that had the Holocaust in fact taken place, even they would be forced to admit that it was wrong.

Addressing May's other implicit point, namely the question of how God could have stood by and allowed the Holocaust to take place without intervening, theologians have had an answer to this kind of question for centuries. Because it is essential to God that we humans possess the free will to choose between good and evil, He leaves it to us to decide when to resist the evil of others. It was only after the Jewish people agreed to follow Moses and make the many sacrifices required to reach the promised land that God sent the miracles which helped pave their way to the Exodus. And, even with God's miracles, the Egyptians were not convinced to allow the Jews to go; right until the end they pursued their former slaves until finally, with the miracle of the parting of the waves, they were destroyed.

In a similar fashion, a theologian could argue that the Holocaust was perpetuated by free individuals who chose to obey the immoral commands of their leaders when they could have done otherwise. Eventually, because so many around the world freely chose to risk their lives to oppose this evil, it was destroyed. Such a theologian could even argue that God may in fact have intervened miraculously in the conflict in ways that are clear for those who wish to see them. Again and again, one could argue, the Allies were helped by accidents, discoveries, and mistakes in strategy on the other side which some could call miracles. Indeed, if, at the beginning of the Battle of Britain, you had told most people that in a mere five years the Axis would be completely defeated and Hitler dead, they would have be willing to call such an outcome a miracle.

But none of this answers our question. If in fact Levy was able to survive the Holocaust with his optimism intact, then what could have occurred in the intervening years to destroy his spirit and lead him to suicide? The answer to this question is hinted at in Allen's portrayal of the character Frederick in his 1984 film *Hannah and Her Sisters*. Frederick is a man who has experienced the meaninglessness of life and the terror of dread. Rather than persevere, he has given up the search in order to inhabit a sterile abyss of his own making, one of loneliness, bitterness, and frustration. He is filled with hatred for the hypocrisy around him and he expresses it in this compelling soliloquy:

> FREDERICK: You missed a very dull TV show about Auschwitz. More gruesome film clips! And more puzzled intellectuals declaring their mystification over the systematic murder of millions. The reason they can never answer the question, "How could it possibly happen?" is because it's the wrong question. Given what people are, the question is "Why doesn't it happen more often?" Of course, it does, in subtler forms.... It's been ages since I just sat in front of the TV, just changing channels to find something. You see the whole culture: Nazis, deodorant salesmen, wrestlers, a beauty contest, a talk show. Can you imagine the level of the mind that watches wrestling, huh? But the worst are the fundamentalist preachers! Third-rate conmen telling the poor suckers that watch them that they speak with Jesus! And to please send in money! Money, money, money! If Jesus came back, and saw what is going on in his name, he'd never stop throwing up!

For Frederick, the Holocaust is not the unique aberration of which we spoke, but instead simply an exaggeration of the way we regularly treat each other more and more in our contemporary world. Like Allen himself, Frederick is convinced that the evil of the Holocaust is symptomatic of a fundamental degradation of the human spirit which is progressing at a frighteningly rapid pace in a world in which everyone is increasingly motivated by hedonistic self-interest, and all references to morality are taken to be either the ravings of pompous frauds or the sighs of hopelessly naive innocents who have blinded themselves to the operation of the "real world" all around them.

Louis Levy finally realized this truth, the ultimate extension of Hannah Arendt's famous description of "the banality of evil," and, being a fundamentally honest person, concluded both that nothing he could say or do would stop this degradation and, further, that he no longer wished to live in such a world. Given the complete pessimism of such a conclusion, he had nothing more to say, so in his note he simply reported his decision.

IV. You've Seen Too Many Movies

Cliff tries to cheer himself up by finally making his move on Halley. After he kisses her, she tells him he shouldn't have done that, and he responds in virtually the same words used by Isaac in *Manhattan* when he finally kissed Mary: "It's something I've wanted to do now for weeks, you must know that!" However, unlike Mary (and all other previous objects of the romantic interests of an Allen persona), Halley says no. She claims not to be ready for a new romance because of the breakup of her marriage, and she denies Cliff's concern that she may be interested in Lester. She does let Cliff kiss her again, however, and when she leaves, she claims to be confused, allowing us to hope with Cliff that a relationship will still materialize between them.

We see Lester walking down the hallway at his office. In just a few seconds, he manages to demonstrate just how much of a horse's ass he really is. First, he demands that a script on the homeless be cut by five minutes (presumably for more commercials), and he warns his staff not to let its author trick them by typing it over in a more compressed form. Then, he tells them to fire a writer from a show because he's just not funny enough — "he has cancer, I'm sorry, I'll send him flowers."

We then see Lester and Cliff sitting (not together) in the audience of a screening room, and we realize we are watching Cliff's finished documentary. In it, Lester is portrayed as more and more of a bully and a tyrant, one finally compared visually to Mussolini, as Cliff sits in the audience with a broad grin on his face.

Outraged, Lester leaps up from his seat and tells Cliff that he's fired. While acknowledging that he's no saint, Lester denies Cliff's characterization of him as someone who has "deadened the sensibility of a great democracy." Lester will now finish the film himself, Cliff tells Halley as they walk together in the park, and will probably portray himself as a hero. Halley tells Cliff that he never should have made such a negative film, that she could have told him PBS would never have shown it that way because, she tells us once more, they are only interested in "upbeat" films.

Throughout the film, we have been told repeatedly that even public television, which is supposedly more serious and honest than commercial television, has fallen into the inauthenticity of an American culture which demands sterility from its media, here in the form of doctored documentaries with upbeat messages. Allen's antagonism to commercial television has been quite clear from his comic pokes at it as far back in his career as *Bananas*. *Crimes* marks the first occasion on which he has satirized PBS, although his antipathy to the publicly funded network probably dates back to 1971, when PBS refused to carry a program they had commissioned (eventually called *The Politics of Woody Allen*); as Eric Lax tells it:

> "The commercial networks offer you no freedom at all," Woody explained when he agreed to do the show. PBS offered freedom but ultimately withdrew it. Privately, PBS felt the program was potentially too offensive at a time when they were the subject of intense criticism from conservatives and their funding was under consideration…. "It was an honest disagreement," he (Allen) said during the controversy over the show's cancellation…. "It was all so silly. It wasn't Jonathan Swift. If the show had gone on as scheduled, it would have passed unnoticed." Which is why Woody makes films [1992, pp. 118-120].

During their walk, Cliff asks Halley to marry him once he can free himself from Wendy. Halley tells him that they have to talk, and then reveals that (like Tracy in *Manhattan*) she must go to London for a few months to work. While Tracy went for six months, Halley claims to be going for only three or four. When she tells him it's for the best, Cliff probably concludes that he is being given this time to wrap up the loose ends of his marriage so that he can greet her as a free man on her return. While he is disappointed by this news ("I feel like, you know, I feel like I've been handed a prison sentence"), we still can hope that things might work out between them.

Back in the movies with Cliff and Jenny, we watch an old prison film, *The Last Gangster* (1937), in which Edward G. Robinson serves out a term as stylized titles show the months passing. Allen then cleverly uses a similar title to tell us that Cliff's sentence has now passed as he shows us the exterior of the hotel where the wedding reception for Ben's daughter is being held. Thus the film is given a certain symmetry in that it begins and ends at public celebrations.

Ben, wearing dark sunglasses which suggest that he is now completely blind, is surrounded by guests who must be identified for him by his wife. We see Cliff and Wendy making their way through the guests. Cliff complains that everything he's wearing is rented, and Wendy responds by asking him if they can get along at this, the last event connected to her family that they will have to attend together. Clearly, Cliff has accomplished his goal and is on the verge of being free to pursue his romance with Halley. Judah and Miriam are also present. We see Judah pat Ben reassuringly on the arm as he tells Judah how happy he is that he is there.

Cliff tells his sister how his breakup with Wendy has saddened him despite its inevitability, and he jokes about how long he's gone without sex. Judah, on the other hand, seems to have overcome his depression. We see him celebrating with Miriam as Sharon tells Chris that she expects him to get drunk and then argue with Ben about God. She also jokingly points out the similarities between Judah's attitudes and those of his Aunt May.

We see Cliff standing uncomfortably as two women praise Lester for paying for his niece's wedding because, we assume, the now-blind Ben is out of work and without an income. Suddenly, Cliff, a look of shock on his face, begins to move slowly away from the talking women and towards the entrance of the reception hall. Cliff is horrified to see Halley, all dressed up (and without her glasses), standing with an exuberant Lester. As Cliff stares at her grimly, Halley and then Lester greet him happily, and we over-hear Lester introducing Halley as his fiancée.

Cliff, completely ignoring Lester, asks Halley when she returned (in the same stunned voice that he has used so often when confronted by betrayal). She says she returned just that morning and claims to have been trying to call him all day (an obvious fabrication). We overhear Lester telling the story of how he pursued her relentlessly in London, sending her white roses every day (just as Lou did to Tina in *Broadway Danny Rose*). Giving Halley a squeeze, he adds that he thinks it was the caviar that finally got her. The man listening to Lester remarks that he used to envy Lester for his harem of young, pretty starlets, but now he envies him even more.

Halley's betrayal tops all of the past betrayals in Allen's earlier films. Her lack of glasses suggests that she has overcome whatever earlier moral standards she might have had, and Lester's comments about the caviar confirm our suspicion that Halley is marrying Lester primarily for his wealth and fame, as well as the career opportunities he can create for her. In this sense, Halley's betrayal is most offensive because she betrays not only Cliff but herself. If we assume that she ultimately shares Cliff's opinion of Lester, and that she was starting to fall for Cliff when she left for London, then she has chosen to sell her soul (just as Judah did) for the sake of material success. Earlier, Judah quoted Sol as saying that each little sin leads to deeper ones. Halley's misdemeanors are different from Judah's crime only in degree, not in kind.

The wedding ceremony now seems to mock Cliff as we see him sitting in the same row as Lester, Halley, and Wendy. Still shocked, he glances towards Halley in dismay, but she ignores him.

The scene shifts, and we see a woman telling Cliff's sister Barbara that she knows the perfect man for her. When a suspicious Barbara asks what the hitch is, she learns that the guy will be in jail for the next few years serving a sentence for insider trading. In today's society, with its lack of respect for the law and morality, his legal problems are actually considered an asset because they show that he knows how to work the system and "make a bundle."

Halley approaches Cliff as he drinks alone in an alcove. She tries to convince Cliff that Lester is really a wonderful man, but Cliff refuses to listen. When Halley asks him to give her a little credit, he responds, "I always did before today." She then returns his one love letter to her. Like Louis Levy, Cliff realizes that he really doesn't have any more to say. By her actions, Halley has demonstrated what kind of person she is, and Cliff now has no interest in her. He shows his disdain by slipping into his impersonal comic persona, joking about the contents of his letter. When Halley says she hopes that they will always remain friends, we don't have to see Cliff's face to know his reaction; his silence speaks volumes.

A unidentified man dances Russian-style to the band's loud music until he pulls a muscle in his leg. Two children steal bits of icing from the uncut wedding cake. Feeling the need to escape these antics, Judah slips down a hallway for a cigarette and encounters Cliff, sitting alone and drinking on a piano bench in near-darkness. Judah immediately starts talking to Cliff as though they were old acquaintances, even though there has never been any indication that they even know each other.

With the protagonists of the film's two stories now together, Allen presents us with this dialogue:

> JUDAH: I have a great murder story.
>
> CLIFF: Yeah?
>
> JUDAH: A great plot! {pause} Hey, I've had too many to drink, I mean, forgive me, I know you want your privacy.
>
> CLIFF: No, it's OK, you know, I'm not doing anything special.
>
> JUDAH: Except my murder story has a very strange twist.
>
> CLIFF: Yeah?
>
> JUDAH: Let's say there was this man who was very successful, he has everything…

As Judah tells Cliff his story, the scene shifts and we see Lester and Wendy happily discussing the fact that she's met someone new and the irritating Cliff will soon be out of both of their lives. We then return to the dialogue between Judah and Cliff:

> JUDAH: And, after the awful deed is done, he finds that he's plagued by deep-rooted guilt. Little sparks of his religious background, which he'd rejected, are suddenly stirred up. He hears his father's voice, he imagines that God is watching his every move. Suddenly, it's not an empty universe at all, but a just and moral one, and he's violated it. Now, he's panic-stricken, he's on the verge of a mental collapse, an inch away from confessing the whole thing to the police. And then, one morning, he awakens. The sun is shining and his family is around him, and, mysteriously, the crisis is lifted. He takes his family on a vacation to Europe and, as the months pass, he finds he's not punished; in fact, he prospers. The killing gets attributed to another person, a drifter who has a number of other murders to his credit so, I mean, what the hell, one more doesn't even matter. Now he's scot-free, his life is completely back to normal, back to his protected world of wealth and privilege.... People carry awful deeds around with them. What do you expect him to do? Turn himself in? I mean this is reality! In reality we rationalize, we deny, or we couldn't go on living!
>
> CLIFF: Here's what I would do. I would have him turn himself in because then, you see, then your story assumes tragic proportions because, in the absence of a God, or something, he is forced to assume that responsibility himself, then you have tragedy!
>
> JUDAH: But that's fiction, that's movies, I mean, I mean, you've seen too many movies. I'm talking about reality! I mean, if you want a happy ending, you should go see a Hollywood movie. [*chuckles*]

At this point, Miriam comes upon them and tells Judah that they ought to be getting home. Judah jumps up and says goodbye to Cliff ("Nice talking to you, good luck to you!"). Happily, Judah puts his arm around Miriam's shoulder as he tells her that they must plan a wedding like this for Sharon. Miriam tells him how happy he has made her tonight, and we see them stop and kiss as the romantic song "I'll Be Seeing You" begins to swell up around them.

V. And Yet...

For many filmgoers, this pessimistic exchange is the end of the film. When Allen shows a blind Ben dancing with his daughter, followed by a montage of earlier scenes from the film, many in the audience probably start rustling in their seats and preparing to leave the theater. However, those willing to stay are presented with an audio excerpt from Louis Levy that was not heard earlier in the film, an excerpt that is considerably more optimistic about the future than the film's apparent first ending:

> We are all faced throughout our lives with agonizing decisions, moral choices. Some are on a grand scale, most of these choices are on lesser points, but, we define ourselves by the choices we have made. We are, in fact, the sum total of our choices. We wince and fall so unpredictably, so unfairly, human happiness does not seem to have been included in the design of creation. It is only we, with our capacity to love, that give meaning to the indifferent universe. And yet, most human beings seem to have the ability to keep trying, and even to find joy, from simple things like the family, their work, and from the hope that future generations might understand more.

At these last lines, Allen returns us to the scene of Ben dancing sweetly with his daughter. As Levy's voice fades out, so does the quiet music accompanying it. Ben and his daughter stop dancing, and she kisses his cheek as the crowd applauds approvingly. She is clearly the symbol of the future generation to which Levy refers. In her adoration for her saintly father, and the approval of the crowd, lives the suggestion that there are real reasons to hope for the future.

Levy's soliloquy contains all the elements of a Sartrean existential analysis of the possibilities for authentic moral projects in an indifferent universe in which all meaning springs from the ways in which we exercise our ontological freedom and take responsibility for our acts. We can no longer expect an all-powerful God to intervene in human affairs to right our wrongs or cure the evils of society. If we wish to live authentically in accordance with moral principles which we construct for ourselves, then we must take the responsibility for creating the meaning for our own lives, and commit ourselves to act in accordance with those principles, even when this means making material sacrifices. Thus, at the film's conclusion, Cliff may be down, but he is not out. He has maintained his integrity, and in this sense, Cliff still has a genuine chance to construct a fulfilling life by pursuing the very goals (family and work) which, Levy tells us, are the fundamental ingredients for a joyous life.

As for Judah, on the other hand, despite his assertions to the contrary, it is not at all clear that he has really escaped from his deep sense of guilt. If he had, then why would he have indiscreetly told Cliff, a virtual stranger, so accurate a version of his story? Obviously, if Cliff thinks about what he was told, he might very well come to realize the significance of Judah's "murder story." The details of what Judah told him would be easy enough to check: the trip to Europe with his family, the recent murder of one of his patients about which Judah was questioned by the police, the conviction of another man who had also been found guilty of other murders. While it may be unlikely that Cliff will be the one to investigate Judah's "story," there is no reason for us to think that Judah won't repeat this incident again and again, telling strangers his murder plot every time he's had too much to drink, until eventually he is taken seriously.

Even if this doesn't happen (Judah would tell us we've seen too many movies), it is clear that Judah is lying, especially to himself, when he claims to have overcome his guilt. His life will always be tainted by his crime. While he might be able to force himself to pretend to enjoy his wealth and security, he admitted to Cliff that he is just rationalizing. Given what we have seen of his character, it is more likely that his high spirits at the film's end are temporary, and that, in the long run, he will secretly torment himself for the rest of his life. In addition, we know that Judah cannot truly take pleasure from the primary source of human joy which Levy mentions, that of family. He can't find joy in his family because he ultimately realizes, no matter how hard he tries to hide the truth from himself, that with them he wears a mask, he inauthentically hides his true nature.

How could he find joy in a relationship with a woman who bores him, whose idea of a birthday present is a treadmill? We know now that Judah is a sensitive and passionate person. How long will it be before he tires of the endless empty chatter of his home life and his wife's desire to entertain guests he finds shallow and frivolous? Like Marion Post, he is trapped in a loveless marriage to a person who, like Ken, doesn't realize how lonely he really is. However, unlike Marion, he is doomed to remain trapped for a lifetime. When he arranged to have Dolores killed, he destroyed any chance of beginning again authentically. His fate will now be more like that of the characters in Sartre's No Exit, doomed to spend eternity in relationships with those who can only serve as tormentors.

In the end, Judah has failed to fulfill the obligations imposed on him when Sol named him after the great Jewish leader. Instead of defending the values of his heritage against the pagan hedonism of those who wished to oppress his people, this latter-day Judah has betrayed all for the sake of a material wealth which, in the long run, means very little to him.

Interestingly, Allen himself denies this interpretation. In response to a question I posed to him (see Appendix), Allen said, "You are wrong about Judah; he feels no guilt and the extremely rare time the events occur to him, his mild uneasiness (which sometimes doesn't come at all) is negligible." While the reader is free to accept Allen's response as the final word on this point, I would argue that the film's text gives stronger support to my interpretation. How could I possibly claim to have greater insight into Judah's character than his creator? I would contend that in many instances artists do not possess privileged access to all of the nuances of their creations. Ernest Hemingway was famous for denying symbolic meanings in his novels, meanings that were obvious to his readers. Allen acknowledged that his audience may on occasion understand his work even better than he does when he told me in our interview that "Louis Levy was related to Primo Levi only unconsciously. I wasn't aware of the similarity in name 'til long after the picture was out and someone pointed it out to me. I'm very aware of Levi's writing, and he is probably present on an unconscious level" ("Questions and Answers with Woody Allen").

Ultimately, I think Allen wants each of us to make our own decisions about the film's meaning. He wants to affect us, to shock us, so that we will leave the theater thinking seriously about these issues, something we would be less likely to do if he had provided us with Cliff's more traditional Hollywood ending.

It is appropriate that the film should end with a shot of Ben. Only by blinding ourselves to the so-called "truth" of the "real world" can one create a meaningful and fulfilling life. If the universe is fundamentally indifferent to our human capacity to love and create meaning for our lives, then we have absolutely no reason for choosing a truth that destroys life's joy over the fulfilling subjective values we can create for ourselves. In this sense, Sol is right when he proclaims, "If necessary, I will always choose God over truth!"

– 9 –

LOVE'S LABOR'S LOST:
Husbands and Wives (1992)

Fifteen years after *Annie Hall*, Woody Allen presented us with an even more pessimistic view of romance. Where *Annie Hall* is a bittersweet reflection on the pains and joys of love, the tone of *Husbands and Wives* is dark from beginning to end. This pessimistic view mirrors that of Jean-Paul Sartre in his essay from the 1930s, *The Emotions: Outline of a Theory*, and in *Being and Nothingness*, written during the Nazi occupation of France in the 1940s. As in his other films, Allen drops lots of clues that help us identify the theory he is using. The first clue comes at the film's beginning, when we see Judy Roth (Mia Farrow) holding a book with Sartre's name emblazoned on its cover. Later, Jack (Sydney Pollack) mentions Simone de Beauvoir, Sartre's lifelong companion and collaborator. In addition, at two points in the film, there is explicit discussion of the desire of Allen's character, Gabe Roth, to move to Paris, where he would like to live in a small apartment and spend his days writing at a table in a cafe — precisely the lifestyle associated with Sartre. While these clues may initially seem trivial, they grow in significance as one comes to discover the many similarities in the positions of Allen and Sartre on the issues of love and marriage.

It is in his films of hopelessness, such as this one, that Allen's perspective appears to be most in accordance with Sartre's. In order to demonstrate how Sartre's account of love parallels the relationships examined in this film, I will first summarize Sartre's theory of the emotions and show why he claims that love and sexual desire are characterized by elements of inauthenticity.

I. Sartre's Theory of the Emotions

In his theory of the emotions, Sartre's contrast between the emotions and rationality seems as stark as Jane Austen's view in her novel *Sense and Sensibility*. However, while Austen makes the distinction in a classical Aristotelian manner, Sartre claims to be offering us a description based on the method of phenomenology. Some critics have suggested that Sartre simply perpetuates the rationalist position of Descartes, a position that sharply distinguishes between rationality and "the passions of the soul."

Sartre describes emotional consciousness as an unreflective way of apprehending the world. Like all consciousness for Sartre, emotional consciousness is intentional; its object is rooted in the world. However, unlike reflective consciousness "in which the for-itself (consciousness) *is* in order to be to itself what it is," unreflective consciousness is spontaneous (Sartre, 1971, p. 806). Unreflective consciousness is not unconsciousness (a state whose existence Sartre denies), but a way of acting in which one is not conscious of acting at all.

According to Sartre, we enter into this unreflective behavior in order to transform the world from that of seemingly irresolvable difficulty into a realm of "magical" facility. In other words, when the usual methods for resolving problems seem too difficult to apply, or when it appears to consciousness that no practical method for resolution even exists, consciousness unreflectively chooses to radically transform its view of the world to one in which magic is the reigning force.

In such situations, consciousness denies the rational, reflective view of the world as controlled by deterministic processes. These processes can be altered through the manipulation of instruments or tools, in order to enter a realm where consciousness truly believes that the world can be changed simply through the overwhelming desire to change it. Sartre gives many examples of this process. A hunter charged by a raging lion responds by fainting. Here the hunter is faced with a situation in which there appears reflectively to be no escape. The hunter thus chooses to magically transform the world into a realm in which danger can be avoided by eliminating consciousness of that danger. Sartre refers to this process as passive fear.

Fear can also be active. Should the hunter drop his gun and start running away from the lion, he would be engaging in an active denial of the reality of the danger in which he finds himself, a danger he is unwilling to accept.

In another of Sartre's example, a man strains to reach some grapes hanging overhead. When he realizes that the practical difficulty of reaching the grapes cannot be resolved, he responds by muttering, "They were too green." Here, when tension ensues from his inability to achieve his goal, he resolves that tension by projecting onto the world the inadequacy he feels within himself.

Sartre discusses sadness and joy in similar terms. Sadness results from reflective spontaneous choice to deny the reality of a situation in order to retreat into a realm either where the object of sorrow is denied ("My God, I can't believe she's dead!") or where consciousness denies the possibility of constructively facing its new circumstances ("I just can't go on without her.") Joy, on the other hand, is a magical attempt to instantaneously possess the totality of what one desires, rather than engaging in the prudent, often difficult process that would actually bring about such possession. A woman tells a man that she loves him, and he responds by singing and dancing for joy, rather than engaging in "the difficult behavior which he would have to practice to deserve this love and make it grow, to realize slowly and through a thousand little details (smiles, little acts of attentiveness, etc.) that he possesses it" (Sartre, 1948, p. 70). The man grants himself a respite from the prudent endeavor of seeking to achieve his goal in order to symbolically act out that achievement by incantations and gyrations.

Sartre does admit the existence of false emotions, feigned role-playing which one occasionally engages in at socially appropriate times. One might pretend to be sad at the funeral of a relative one disliked, or feign pleasure at the reception of an unwanted gift. However, Sartre's theory relates to genuine emotion, which is only present when consciousness truly believes in, and freely chooses to enter, the magic realm. Once one chooses to initiate an emotional response, it is often very difficult, if not impossible, to disengage oneself from that emotion until it has run its course. The process of undergoing an emotion is a physical one that should be taken seriously as a commitment from which consciousness cannot easily retreat.

In this sense, emotion is a "phenomenon of belief." Consciousness lives in the new world it has created through the mediating presence of the body. Emotional consciousness is analogous for Sartre to sleeping consciousness in that both modes create new worlds, transforming the body so that consciousness can experience these new worlds through "synthetic totalities."

Thus, concludes Sartre, "the origin of emotion is a spontaneous and lived degradation of consciousness in the face of the world" (1948, p. 77). Emotional consciousness is not aware of itself as a degradation of consciousness, however. Emotional consciousness is its own captive; it is absorbed in itself and tends to be self-perpetuating. The more emotional one becomes, the more emotional one is likely to become. Such an escalating emotional cycle can be broken only through either a purifying reflection or removal of the affecting situation. Only by such means can consciousness be released and returned to freedom.

Admittedly, Sartre states, the world itself sometimes appears magical rather than determined. An earthquake, a solar eclipse, an erupting volcano can all be viewed as introducing magical qualities into the appearance of the world. However, if consciousness chooses to accept the magical interpretation of such events, it does so at the expense of reflective consciousness, which is capable of interpreting such phenomena in a nonemotional context.

Finally, Sartre points out that pure reflective consciousness can direct itself to emotion by way of a phenomenological reduction which reveals consciousness in the process of constituting the world in terms of a magical realm. Through such a reduction, one can come to realize that "I find it hateful because I am angry," rather than believing that "I am angry because it is hateful."

We can extend Sartre's account of emotional consciousness as described in both *The Emotions: Outline of a Theory* and sections of *Being and Nothingness* in order to briefly summarize his ontological basis for claiming that emotional consciousness is a degradation of consciousness. When consciousness unreflectively chooses to try to magically transform the world, it is attempting to deny just what it is; it is attempting to pretend that consciousness is not capable of pure reflection (akin to rationality). When the man who fails to reach the grapes tells himself that "they were too green," he is attempting to lie to himself, to escape his own condition as reflective consciousness capable of making calculated choices on the basis of a pure activity of freedom.

Emotional consciousness is just as much in bad faith as is Sartre's famous example of the waiter in a restaurant who is only pretending to be a waiter, only role-playing (Sartre, 1971, pp. 101–104). Emotional consciousness, once entered into, is sincere; it is truly believed in; but it is not authentic. Emotional consciousness is by its very unreflectiveness a conscious denial of itself and the freedom which it is. This is why Sartre can claim that emotional consciousness "is its own captive in the sense that it does not dominate its belief" (1948, p. 78). It denies its own freedom so that "freedom has to come from a purifying reflection or a total disappearance of the affecting situation" (1948, p. 79).

Emotional consciousness is an attempt to deny one's own condition. It is always an attempt to be what one is not. Anguish is the common emotional response to the realization of one's total ontological freedom and responsibility. By fleeing into anguish, one refuses this newly discovered responsibility. Anguish, then, is itself in bad faith as a denial of one's true condition.

As one form of emotional consciousness, love is also in bad faith. In his description of love in Part III, Chapter Three of *Being and Nothingness*, Sartre states that in love, consciousness attempts to possess the consciousness of the person loved without reducing this consciousness to an object. Consciousness wishes to merge with the other person into a unified whole. According to Sartre:

> we have seen that this contingency (of otherness) is insurmountable; it is the fact of my relations with the other, just as my body is the fact of my being in the world. Unity with the other is therefore in fact unrealizable in theory, for the assimilation of the for-itself and the other in a single transcendence would necessarily involve the disappearance of the characteristic of otherness in the other [1971, p. 477].

In other words, the choice to love is an unreflective attempt to become just what consciousness knows in fact that it is not — a unified whole with the other. Thus, for Jean-Paul Sartre, both love and sexual desire are necessarily doomed to failure because they are emotional realms entered in bad faith.

There are two other reasons, according to Sartre, that love must fail. First, at any point it is possible that the beloved might suddenly see the lover as only one object in a world of objects. The magic spell of love is very fragile. The strands of its web may be broken at any time. The lover is constantly aware of the possibility of the "awakening" of his beloved; hence the lover is tormented by a "perpetual insecurity" which itself leads to love's destruction.

Second, love is constantly threatened by the look of a third person. When the lovers become aware that they are objectified by someone else, the spell is again broken, and each of the lovers is forced to see the other no longer as an absolute transcendence, but merely as a mundane object. In other words, the spell of love is constantly under pressure because of the awareness of each of the lovers that others view them differently from the way they view each other. According to Sartre:

> Such is the true reason why lovers seek solitude. It is because the appearance of a third person, whoever he may be, is the destruction of their love.... even if nobody sees us, we exist for all consciousness and we are conscious of existing for all. The result is that love as a fundamental mode of being-for-others holds in its being-for-others the seed of its own destruction [1971, p. 491].

The inevitable failure of love leads Sartre into a description of sexual desire, which has as its goal the incarnation of the flesh of the other. Where love seeks to possess the freedom of the other, sexual desire seeks "to possess the other's body, to possess it in so far as it is itself a 'possessed'; that is, in so far as the other's consciousness is identified with his body" (1971, p. 512).

Sartre sees sexual desire as a primary attitude which characterizes our being-for-others and not just as a "psycho-physiological reaction." He points out that young children, elderly persons, and even eunuchs experience sexual desire. This desire is not contingent on the physiological possibility of achieving satisfaction; it is a fundamental structure of the way in which we relate to others.

In sexual desire, "I make myself flesh in the presence of the other in order to appropriate the other's flesh" (Sartre, 1971, p. 506). Where usually I experience my body as merely an extension of my consciousness which I utilize as an instrument to achieve everyday goals (for example, fixing my car or writing with my pen), in sexual desire I experience my body as a tingling mass of sensations, sensations which I savor the way a gourmet savors fine food. Continuing the analogy, which Sartre himself suggests (and which Allen often uses), sexual desire is a kind of hunger, a hunger which results from a troubled consciousness, a hunger which we try to satisfy initially by experiencing our bodies not as an instrument but as "pure facticity," the feeling of my skin and muscles, etc. (Sartre, 1971, p. 505).

For Sartre, "the being which desires is consciousness making itself body." But what is it that consciousness seeks in sexual desire? What is its goal? Sartre states that consciousness wishes to persuade the other to also transform her/his experience of her/his body from instrumentality into "pure facticity." I want the other to feel her/his own body as flesh, to submerge her/his own consciousness into an identity with her/his body as felt experience.

The caress is the means by which this incarnation of the body of the other is attempted. In caressing the body of the other, I bring her/his flesh alive under my fingers, not just part of her/his body but all of it as an organic whole experience. The caress is a shaping, a communicating between my body and that of the other. The caress is to desire as language is to thought.

Thus, the possession that is sought in sexual desire "appears as a double reciprocal incarnation" (Sartre, 1971, p. 508). It is not enough that I experience my own body as flesh. (S)he must also experience both her/his own and my body as flesh for the possession to occur.

Yet we still have not described the "motive" of desire, its meaning. Sartre resolves this issue by first identifying desire with emotion, by pointing out that desire also results from a choice to magically transform the world. This transformation comes about when I encounter the other but do not know how to react to the other's look. I am aware of being-looked-at, and this sparks in me a desire to reach into the subjectivity of the other; it draws out of me some "vague memory of a certain *Beyond*" (Sartre, 1971, p. 511). This is when I start to make myself desire. I want to appropriate that special magical quality that I believe exists in the subjectivity of the other. I want to become enchanted. I want to grasp the freedom of the other within the facticity of her/his body.

It is at this point that sexual desire becomes doomed to failure because of the impossibility of the ideal of desire, which is

> to possess the other's transcendence as pure transcendence and at the same time as body, to reduce the other to his simple facticity because he is then in the midst of my world but to bring it about that this facticity is a perpetual appresentation of his nihilating transcendence [Sartre, 1971, p. 512].

I cannot actually come to possess the transcendence of the other. As a matter of fact, Sartre points out, at the height of the sexual experience, I lose my awareness of the other altogether. At this point, I am aware only of the pleasure in myself; I lose touch with the incarnation of the other. This pleasure is "both the death and the failure of desire" (Sartre, 1971, p. 515). With this pleasure comes the end of desire, and in this pleasure I forget the very incarnation of the other that I had hoped to possess.

We can conclude that for Sartre, both love and sexual desire fail for basically the same reason: because they attempt to simultaneously capture the other-as-subject and the other-as-object. This cannot be done. I can never possess another person in any sense. Thus Sartre claims that emotional consciousness is a degradation of consciousness because it is in bad faith. And it is always ineffectual because it is attempting to be something it knows it cannot be. Sartre would not deny that many people value emotional goals in their lives very highly. However, Sartre would state that to the extent a person chooses to devote himself or herself to an emotional goal, that person can accurately be said to be in bad faith.

Thus, for Sartre, relationships of love and sex are always battlegrounds in which the two combatants vie for dominance. In fact, he contends that in every such relationship, one person ends up controlling the other. Using the disagreeable terminology of bondage, Sartre says that in every relationship, one person plays the role of the "sadist," while the other is the "masochist." The relationships likely to endure for the longest time are those in which the roles of the participants have long ago been defined and accepted.

In societies where separation or divorce is virtually unthinkable, either for religious or cultural reasons (or both), couples tend to define the power structure of their relationship early on and maintain that structure throughout their life together. This was the usual practice for most French (and, to a slightly lesser extent, American) marriages until the relaxation of societal attitudes towards divorce which began after World War II. As we all know, until divorce began to become socially acceptable in the sixties, it was not at all uncommon to find married couples who despised and tortured one other another for years rather than face the loss of social standing that came with separation.

This of course is what Sally (Judy Davis) means when she tells Judy (Mia Farrow) that staying in an unhappy marriage only out of fear carries the risk of becoming one's own parents. From this pessimistic perspective, the dramatic rise in the divorce rate (now up to 50 percent) is not due to a contemporary unwillingness to stick by one's commitment even when the going gets tough. Rather it is the natural result of a cultural environment that no longer coerces people to stay in marriages that have become loveless. In fact, according to Sartre's theory, at least as it is expressed in *Being and Nothingness*, if people were really honest in their relations with one another, then *every* marriage would end in divorce, for no two people could honestly pretend to love one another for a lifetime. It was because of this belief, and because of Sartre's opposition to taking an oath which by its very nature must be hypocritical, that Sartre and his partner, Simone de Beauvoir, never married.

If Allen is indeed basing his portrayal of love, sex, and marriage on this aspect of Sartre's theory, then *Husbands and Wives* should show us a group of people hypocritically battling one another for dominance in their relationships, while also pursuing the "magical fantasy" of possessing, either romantically or sexually (or both), the partners of their dreams.

And, in fact, that is exactly what we see. In the film, two married couples go through the traumas of separation. The relationships within each couple are characterized by vicious power struggles in which each person fights to impose his or her interpretation of reality on the other. All four individuals experiment with outside lovers in the attempt to create new romantic ties that would allow each to pursue the goal of complete domination over another person. Eventually, Judy destroys her relationship with her husband, Gabe Roth (Woody Allen), a successful and self-confident writer, so that she may marry Michael (Liam Neeson), a weaker and needier person, because she can more easily dominate him.

The other couple, Sally and Jack (Sydney Pollack), reconcile even though they acknowledge that they have not resolved their many problems. They admit that they have reunited primarily because they both fear loneliness in their old age and are willing to choose security over romantic fulfillment.

Gabe, ultimately the saddest of the characters, writes a novel in which he portrays love and marriage as a choice between "chronic dissatisfaction and suburban drudgery." Although he flirts throughout the film with one of the students in his writing class, a twenty-year-old woman named Rain (Juliette Lewis) with a history of failed affairs with older men, by the film's end he refuses to become involved with her because of his realization of the doomed nature of the relationship (and, indeed, of *all* relationships, from the Sartrean perspective which Allen adopts in this film).

II. Love's Labor's Lost

When Jack and Sally reveal at the film's beginning that they have decided to split up, Gabe and Judy react with horror (Judy says she "just feels shattered"). Soon, Judy is shown talking directly to the camera, answering the questions of an off-camera interviewer (Jeffrey Kurland). He asks her why she was so upset by Jack and Sally's announcement. She responds that they did not seem appropriately upset given the magnitude of their decision. When he asks if she's also angry because Sally didn't confide in her earlier about the problems in her marriage, she says that now, in retrospect, she realizes that Sally did occasionally wonder aloud what it would be like to be single again given all that she's experienced and all she now knows.

The film establishes that lies and petty deceits intrude regularly into the friendships and marriages of its main characters. With its pseudo-documentary structure and its scenes of intimacy which we know could not be real, the film superficially resembles Jean Resnais's 1980 *Mon oncle d'Amerique*, in which the director uses a similar technique to illustrate the theories of human behavior developed by French research scientist Henri Laborit. That film also follows a group of characters into intimate situations in order to empirically convince us of the validity of the deterministic theory of human behavior which it appears to embrace. In one hilarious scene in the Resnais film, we hear a narrator explaining the causes of the characters' behavior as we see white rats reenacting scenes that originally had human characters.

However, Allen's film differs from Resnais's in that Allen's documentary makers never reveal the theory, if any, upon which they are basing their study; nor does their understanding or expertise (they can't even videotape properly without jerking the camera around) seem sufficient to handle the behavior of the very complex individuals they have chosen to study. From the beginning, we have no confidence in their ability to explain everything to us; and so, at the film's conclusion, we are not especially surprised when their project seems to have been abandoned because of their lack of insight and their inability to deal effectively with the pain they are recording.

When we see Gabe talking to the interviewer about the widespread occurrence of professor-student relationships, he denies that he has ever acted on such opportunities, even though he admits to having daydreams. In fact, Gabe claims, he has never cheated in any of his relationships, including his marriage to Judy, because it "is not my style." He reminisces about his most passionate relationship, with a woman named Harriet Harman (Galaxy Craze), as we see her combing her hair enticingly. Gabe tells us about Harriet's unquenchable hunger for sensual experiences of all sorts, including sex in a variety of unusual locations, with multiple partners (including other women), and under the influence of various drugs. Finally, he tells us, Harriet, like Dorrie in *Stardust Memories*, or Fitzgerald's Zelda, ended up in a mental institution. He admits to a weakness for women like Harriet:

> See, I've always had this penchant for what I call "kamikaze women," I call them kamikazes because they crash their plane, they're self-destructive, but they crash it into you, and you die along with them. As soon as there's a challenge, as soon as there's very little chance of it working out, or no chance, or there's going to be hurdles or obstacles, something clicks into my mind, maybe that's because I'm a writer, but some dramatic, or aesthetic, component becomes right, and I, I go after that person and there's a certain dramatic ambience that, that, it's almost as though I fall in love with the person, in love with the situation in some way, and, of course, it has not worked out well for me, it has not been great....

Given this revelation of Gabe's deepest yearnings, we wonder what he is doing with a woman like Judy, someone who is nothing like his "kamikaze woman." After all, by definition, no relationship with a kamikaze woman could ever become something permanent. If it did, then it would no longer have the "dramatic, or aesthetic, component" which he finds so attractive.

The structure of the movie, as in so many of Allen's serious films, follows more than one story while exploring the common theme that holds them together. We see what happens to two marriages that have grown stale when they are externally challenged by the introduction of tempting new romantic possibilities. In one marriage, Jack and Sally's, the couple agrees to separate as the film begins, while in the other, the Roths', separation does not officially take place until the film is almost over. Within this structure, Allen is able to draw a portrait of contemporary marriage that exposes its deficiencies and makes clear the conditions and compromises necessary for success. All the characters use relationships of love, sex, and marriage both to protect themselves from life's pain and to satisfy their personal needs and desires. As in Sartre's theory, relationships are nothing but a deceptive game they play in order to get what they want. Each character carefully creates a set of masks, personas presented differently to each acquaintance and calculated to bring whatever the person is after. Usually, the maintenance of these masks requires a certain degree of self-deception as well, because those most likely to succeed in seducing and manipulating others are those who have first succeeded in fooling themselves. Thus the characters who make the greatest attempt to deal honestly with both themselves and others are at the greatest disadvantage in playing "the game," and are most vulnerable to exploitation and hurt. In this film, that person is Michael, the one character who, as far as we can see, honestly wears his heart on his sleeve.

Walking with Sally as they commiserate with her over her loneliness and her fear of crime now that she is living by herself in her suburban house, the Roths are shocked when they run into Jack with his arm draped around a beautiful young blond (Lysette Anthony). Humiliated, Sally suddenly remembers an appointment and hurriedly hails a cab. Jack proposes that the Roths stay with him and his girlfriend for dinner. We learn that her name is Sam; she's a vegetarian, an aerobics instructor, and a fan of televised awards shows like the Grammys. In other words, she is the typical "trophy girlfriend" whose values represent everything that Allen has always ridiculed and despised.

While the women are shopping, Jack and Gabe argue. Gabe expresses his shock and dismay at Jack's decision to leave the woman with whom he's raised a family to take up with a "cocktail waitress." Jack resents Gabe's tone and defends Sam as a warm, wonderful woman with a degree in psychology who is inspiring him with her mania for fitness.

Jack praises Sally and at first denies that what he is doing has anything to do with her. Soon, however, he is telling Gabe how much he hated her Radcliffe friends, her interior decorating (like Eve in *Interiors*), and her passion for opera. After decades of feeling controlled by a dominating, brilliant, and cold woman, it is clear that Jack feels he's earned a vacation with an empty-headed, beautiful blond with whom he can enjoy great sex. Jack makes clear his resentment of Gabe's judgmental attitudes and his willingness to lie to avoid what Jack feels are the responsibilities of friendship ("Your mother is not in town, Gabe, she's in Florida").

Much later in the film, at a party, we see Jack bragging about how much better he's felt since he broke up with Sally, until a friend tells him that he saw Sally recently at a party with Michael and she looked great too. All at once, Jack is overwhelmed with jealousy. He peppers his friend with questions about Sally and Michael.

At the mention of Sam's name, Jack leaps up to look for her. When he discovers her arguing in her naive way about the provability of astrology, he humiliates them both by dragging her out of the party. In the driveway, his behavior towards her becomes abusive and violent. Once in the car, like Alvy, he acts out his frustrations by crashing into the cars parked in front and behind. At this, Sam jumps from the car, and when Jack grabs her and drags her back kicking and screaming, we can see the party's guests watching them from the doors and windows.

Jack wants to have his cake and eat it, too. He wants his "cocktail waitress," and at the same time he wants to imagine Sally alone, properly chastised and humiliated. While we have no way of knowing if Jack would have wanted Sally back if he hadn't heard about Michael, it is clear that Sam was just a symbol to him, a "toy" that he felt he deserved in recognition of his many years of service. He treats her like a personal possession, and he would probably be shocked if he were told that his actions could be construed as criminal assault and kidnapping. Although Sam accuses him of being drunk, his alcohol consumption didn't seem to be bothering him until he was told about Sally and Michael.

Jack drives to his old house and uses his key to enter, surprising Sally and Michael, who are upstairs in bed. Enraged by Michael's presence (even though he's left Sam in the car outside), he begs Sally to let him come home. Sally tells him that too much has happened for them to start over. However, we can sense her delight at this turn of events. Seeing Jack and Sally together with no one else present for the first time, we can tell how perfectly suited they are for one another. Both are extremely emotional people who get satisfaction from yelling and cursing at the top of their lungs while they work off their energy pacing around the room. Jack tells Sally that all relationships have problems, that theirs are no worse than other people's.

When Sally informs Jack that she has met someone she likes, Jack hypocritically asks her how she can throw away all the years they've spent together. When Sally accurately points out that those years didn't seem to bother him when he had his affair, Jack begins to sound like a child, repeating over and over again that he didn't know what else to do. Although we never find out exactly what he means by this, we can guess.

It is clear, both from what we've seen of the two of them and from remarks made by Jack, that Sally has always been the strong, dominant one in their relationship, what Sartre would call the "sadist." Like Eve in *Interiors*, she decorated their home, dictated their activities together (like going to the opera), and acted as judge and jury for all of Jack's actions. Feeling victimized and hopelessly stifled by this situation (like all the "suffocated" women in past Allen films), Jack, usually the "masochist," declared his independence in the only way he could think of, by having an affair with someone whom *he* could dominate.

With Sally, we now realize that from the beginning Jack's ultimate goal was retaliation, and that he always intended to get back together with Sally when the time was right. His fantasy probably included having Sally beg him to come back, but when he heard that Sally was with someone else, he became terrified of really losing her and reverted to his usual subservient position.

The narrator tells us that less than two weeks later, Jack and Sally got back together. We see the film's two original couples clinking glasses in a toast of celebration. Jack and Sally attempt to give Gabe and Judy lessons on the importance of maturity in recognizing that the roots of many years of marriage grow quite deep and the real test of a relationship is how the participants react in a crisis.

III. The Beginning of the End

In their apartment, we watch over a period of one long night as Gabe and Judy's marriage finally and completely disintegrates. Like Jack, Gabe refers to Michael unfairly as "that character" in her office, and when he asks her if she's in love with Michael, she lies (as she later admits to the interviewer) and denies it. Their conversation continues to go downhill as they argue about her decision to return to therapy with a female analyst whom Gabe doesn't trust (shades of *Annie Hall*); whether he flirts with other women at parties ("Of course you flirt, you put on a whole other personality"); whether she lied to him when she initially said she didn't want any more children; and, abstractly, whether change implies death (Gabe) or life (Judy).

Gabe's attempts at sexual advances are rebuffed by Judy as she accuses him of using sex "to express every emotion except love." In the last throes of their relationship, Gabe reminds Judy of some of their happy memories together as he tries to patch things up with nostalgic affection. But this doesn't work. As she admits to the interviewer (but not to Gabe), she is, by this point, so obsessed by her infatuation for Michael that all she wants to do is get Gabe out of her life as quickly as possible. Thus, using all the weapons in her potent arsenal, she attacks Gabe at all of his vulnerable points in order to force him to agree with her that things are really over between them. As her first husband told us, Judy always gets her way, and so we are told that soon after that evening, Gabe moved out of their apartment and into a hotel.

We see Sally at home receiving what we learn is yet another phone call from Michael begging her to reconsider her decision to go back with Jack. She puts him off brutally, refusing to meet with him and demanding that he stop calling her. We have already learned, from Judy, that Michael was initially so devastated by the news of Sally's decision that he called in sick to work. We then see Judy pretending to comfort Michael and help him get over his feelings for Sally, when in fact, she is really moving in for the kill.

We see Gabe at Rain's birthday party. The atmosphere lets us know that we are in for an exciting evening, what with all the people chattering happily and someone playing the song "Top Hat" on the piano. When Rain's mother asks Gabe about his wife, he admits he's separated. Rain looks smugly satisfied, and her mother responds, "Oh, you writers!" as though she still lives in the culture of the fifties when separations were considered avant-garde. A few moments later we see Rain's parents alone in front of their refrigerator, lovingly discussing their astonishment at how quickly the years have passed. Although we see them for only a moment, this glimpse suggests that positive, permanent relationships may be possible after all.

Meanwhile, tremendous bursts of lightning and thunder further confirm our feeling that something dramatic is about to happen, as Carl (Rain's boyfriend) tags along behind Gabe and Rain like a chaperon, telling Gabe about the most recent weather reports on the storm. Rain, obviously toying with her power to arouse the men watching her, opens the door to bare her face to the rain. Gabe mutters the word "dangerous," and we can't tell if he's referring to the storm or to her.

When the electricity goes out, the party crowd titters excitedly to one another as they walk around with lighted candles in their hands. Alone with Rain in the kitchen, Gabe gives her a birthday present. When she then asks him for a "birthday kiss," he pretends not to know what she means, giving her a little peck on the cheek. Apparently a bit tipsy, she demands a real kiss. He lists all the reasons why their getting involved would not be a good idea.

She tells him how disappointed she is that he won't kiss her since all the elements (the storm, the candlelight, her mood at turning twenty-one) have all conspired to create a "magical" setting. Finally, he gives in, and they kiss passionately as the thunder and lightning burst behind them in cinematic glory to rival all the great movie kisses of the past. To the interviewer, Gabe acknowledges that during the kiss all he could think about was whether the lightning was somehow going to break through the window and get him. He also confesses that he couldn't resist kissing her as the scene was crying out to be played, even though he knew it was crazy.

We switch to Michael and Judy, who, at precisely the same moment in the storm, are arguing about whether she is pushing herself upon him. In his last gasp of rebellion before finally giving in, Michael accuses her of giving him no space for himself as she forces him into a relationship with her that he doesn't really want. He even admits honestly that he will never feel towards her what he felt towards Sally. At this revelation, she goes running out into the rain, saying that she never wants to see him again. Allowing his fear of loneliness, his desire for the security of marriage, and his ultimate weakness to overcome his honesty, he chases after her, begging for forgiveness and swearing never to say anything that might cause her pain again. He accepts her charges that he's selfish and self-centered, when in fact we have seen that those labels much more accurately describe her.

Meanwhile, still during the storm, we see Jack and Sally together in bed as they admit to one another how much nicer it is to be at home rather than out in the storm trying to use theater tickets. Sally confesses how much thunder, or any loud noise, still frightens her and expresses her happiness that they are back together again so she need not be scared and lonely. The obvious subtext here is that it is much more pleasant, secure, and relaxing to be in a comfortable marriage than to be in the tempestuous world of unstable relationships where you have to work so hard all the time to try to get what you want.

The narrator now tells us that a year and a half have passed and that Judy and Michael have married. In response to a question about whether they are happy, Judy beams with pleasure as she responds that things are going well. When she jokingly says that Michael puts up with her idiosyncrasies, she glances over to him, knowing that he is now sufficiently well trained that he will immediately undercut the remark, switching its onus onto himself.

We then see a quick shot of Judy's first husband, reminding us of his analysis of Judy's passive-aggressive strategies for getting what she wants as he points out her track record in working her way through himself and Gabe. Michael politely attempts to refute this accusation by claiming that it was he who pursued Judy, and not the other way around. Judy innocently says that she hoped she didn't push, as though she is just considering this possibility for the very first time.

Jack and Sally are the next ones to give an exit interview to the narrator. Their descriptions of love place all the emphasis on the security that the companionship of a marriage partner can provide as one looks ahead to old age, as opposed to notions of passion or excitement. For them, tolerance of each other's foibles is the key to success in marriage, even when those foibles include sexual problems—which they now acknowledge they will probably never overcome. This view of marriage as a "buffer against loneliness" may seem boring or depressing, but to Jack, this criticism comes from "unreal expectations," which can only lead to greater unhappiness and disillusionment in the long run. Ultimately, they endorse a pragmatic view of love and marriage in which they deny the importance of living up to some societal fantasy of romantic bliss, in favor of doing "whatever works." They conclude by pointing out the irony of the fact that, with all their problems, they are the ones who managed to stay together while Gabe and Judy did not.

Finally, we return to Gabe, who tells us the rest of the story of his "romantic moment" with Rain. It turns out, despite all of our expectations, that this time Gabe somehow found the strength to allow his reason to overcome his desires. We see him explaining to Rain that they should not follow up on their wonderful moment because it is so clear that an impossible relationship like theirs could only end badly. Disappointed, Rain accepts his decision sadly, toying with the music box he gave her as she regretfully leaves the room.

Gabe describes leaving the party, going out into the rainy night, and instinctively directing his steps back towards his old apartment and the security of Judy's arms. He tells us that, when he remembered that he could never go back to Judy, and in fact had nowhere to go, he realized that he "really blew it!" In this last dialogue, he describes his current pessimistic mood:

> INTERVIEWER: So, what's your life like now?
>
> GABE: Ah, you know, I'm out of the race at the moment. I don't want to get involved with anybody, I don't want to hurt anyone, I don't want to get hurt, I just, you know, I just don't mind, you know, living by myself

and working, you know, it's temporary, I mean the feelings will pass, and then I'll have the urge to get back into the swing of things, but, that seems to be how it goes, and, and, but, I'm writing, I'm working on a novel, a new novel, not the old one anymore, and, it's fine, it's really fine!

INTERVIEWER: Is it different?

GABE: My novel? Yes, it's less, less confessional, more political.... Can I go? Is this over?

In this depressing fashion, the film ends in a freeze-frame of Gabe's face. We see the credits and hear again the rendition of "What Is This Thing Called Love?" that opened the film. We never do learn who the narrator was, or what purpose he hoped to serve by intruding on the privacy of so many people to make his documentary. The shoddy technical work and the lack of apparent insight into his subject matter have from the beginning suggested that he was not competent to deal effectively with the delicate issues into which he delved. But, in fact, Allen clearly believes that no social scientists, no matter how efficient or well trained, can effectively reduce the mysteries of love and marriage to statistical data yielding objective answers.

Such answers as we do get are in accordance with Sartre's pessimistic views. At one point, we see Rain lying in bed reading Gabe's manuscript as Gabe speaks passages from it in a voice-over. In the clinical style of Resnais's film, we are shown scenes which dramatize the passages Gabe speaks. First, Gabe explains the male's ceaseless desire for sexual intercourse in purely physiological terms, somewhat reminiscent of the comic episode on ejaculation in *Everything You Always Wanted to Know About Sex*. Actual footage of wriggling sperm cells accompanies Gabe's explanation that men are constantly bombarded by the demands of millions of sperm cells to be released, while women are dramatically less troubled by the call of only a few eggs.

Gabe then makes fun of personal ads, showing us a doctor named Feldman who wants a partner just like himself in all respects:

> a quick sense of humor equal to his, a love of sports equal to his, a love of classical music equal to his with a particular fondness for Bach and balmy climates. In short, he wanted himself, but as a pretty woman.

We move to two men with adjoining apartments, Pepkin and Knapp, who have chosen very different solutions to the problems of love, marriage, and sex. Pepkin has married and raised a large family. He lives a life of warm affection and dull security. Knapp is a swinger, bedding five different women a week. His life is filled with excitement and insecurity. Naturally, each envies the other.

As we watch newlyweds leaving a church, Gabe asks:

> What happened after the honeymoon was over? Did desire really grow with the years, or did familiarity cause partners to long for other lovers? Was the notion of ever-deepening romance a myth we had grown up on along with simultaneous orgasm? The only time Rifkin and his wife experienced a simultaneous orgasm was when the judge handed them their divorce. Maybe, in the end, the idea was not to expect too much out of life.

Following this pessimistic account, we see Rain praising the manuscript highly as she and Gabe get coffee. Gabe at first encourages her to be critical; then he expresses delight at her positive reaction, much as she did when he praised her story at the film's beginning. The power relationship between them has now clearly shifted as Gabe reveals his more masochistic tendencies.

Suddenly, Rain realizes that she left the only copy of the manuscript in the cab she had taken to meet him. Stunned, they rush to the cab company in a desperate attempt to retrieve it.

Speaking to the interviewer, Gabe acknowledges how upset he was about the manuscript's loss and how important Rain's approbation was to him. He admits that the novel was much more important to him than he let on, yet he has nothing to say when the narrator points out that Judy's approval of the book had meant nothing to him. His silence speaks volumes about the collapse of his marriage as it validates Judy's own claims, earlier in the film, that he no longer values her views.

Back at the cab company, just as Gabe and Rain are leaving, they are told that one of the drivers has just called in to say that he found the manuscript and has it at his home. On their way to retrieve it, Rain says that what just happened was very Freudian. She suggests that she must have voluntarily, but subconsciously, left the book behind because she felt threatened by some of his "attitudes towards women" and his "ideas on life." After further questioning, Rain presents the very criticisms Allen knows will be made of the film we are watching:

> RAIN: I was a little disappointed, I guess, with some of your attitudes.
>
> GABE: Like what? What attitudes? With what?
>
> RAIN: The way your people just casually have affairs like that, that's...
>
> GABE: Well, the book doesn't condone affairs, you know, I'm exaggerating for comic purposes!

RAIN: Yeah, but are our choices really between chronic dissatisfaction and suburban drudgery?

GABE: No, that's how I'm deliberately distorting it, you know, 'cause I'm trying to show how hard it is to be married.

RAIN: Well, you have to be careful not to trivialize with things like that.

GABE: Well, Jesus, I hope I haven't!

RAIN: Well, the way your lead character views women is so retrograde, it's so shallow, you know?

GABE: What are you talking ... you told me it was a great book!

RAIN: Yeah, it's wonderful! And I never said great, I said it's brilliant and it's alive, and, you know, that's not what I'm, you know, we're not arguing about it's brilliant or not, you know, *Triumph of the Will* was a great movie, but you despise the ideas behind it!

GABE: What are you saying now! You despise my ideas?

RAIN: No, I don't despise them. That example was ... okay! Isn't it beneath you as a mature thinker, I mean, to allow your lead character to waste so much of his emotional energy obsessing over this psychotic relationship with a woman that you fantasize as powerfully sexual and inspired, when in fact she was pitiably sick?

GABE: Look, let's stop this right now because I don't need a lecture on maturity or writing from a twenty-year-old twit! You asked me if you could read my book, I said okay, you told me that you loved it....

In this scene, and in Gabe's final statements, Allen acknowledges he may be trivializing dilemmas that in fact offer us much more complex choices than he shows us, and he concedes that his perspective may justifiably offend feminists. He even tells us, through Gabe, that he knows he is probably just going through a bad period in his life, and that, eventually, he will feel the old juices flowing again and his attitudes towards love will swing back in a more positive direction.

Interestingly, many of these same qualifications can be ascribed to Sartre's own theories on love and sex. As we have mentioned, all of Sartre's positions on these issues are to be found in two early works, specifically *The Emotions: Outline of a Theory*, and in sections of *Being and Nothingness*. Many have made the case that in these works Sartre was describing not the full range of human possibilities, but only the common patterns of behavior of those who have chosen to operate in bad faith.

In fact, unless one comes to this conclusion, one is compelled to view Sartre as an unrelenting pessimist not only on the issues of love and sex, but also on the fundamental questions of morality and political responsibility; for in these works he never actually describes what authentic moral or political actions would be like, leaving some detractors to conclude that Sartre believed all of us are condemned to be in bad faith all of the time, no matter what our intentions or behavior.

But such a deterministic scenario would belie Sartre's entire enterprise, in which he stresses the fundamental ontological freedom characterizing the human condition and our individual responsibility for the choices we make. If all choices were equally inauthentic from a Sartrean perspective, then life on earth would be no different from the hell Sartre portrays in his play *No Exit*. While some of his critics might be glad to come to just such a conclusion, there are ample reasons not to do so. Without going into lengthy arguments based on the entirety of Sartre's work, in which he frequently exhorts his readers to seek authenticity by becoming *engaged*— that is, committed to a set of values and projects for which one should be willing to sacrifice all — we will examine one bit of the evidence that refutes the claims of such critics.

At the end of his section on bad faith in Part I of *Being and Nothingness*, in which he demonstrates the ontological identity of many aspects of good and bad faith, as well as the important differences between this distinction and that which opposes morality to immorality, Sartre presents a footnote containing an essential clue concerning his position on this issue:

> If it is indifferent whether one is in good or in bad faith, because bad faith reapprehends good faith and slides to the very origin of the project of good faith, that does not mean that we can not radically escape bad faith. But this supposes a self-recovery of being which was previously corrupted. This self-recovery we shall call authenticity, the description of which has no place here [1971, p. 116].

In this note, Sartre suggests both that authenticity is possible and that this work is not, in his view, the appropriate place to discuss it. The only plausible reason for excluding the obviously crucial discussion of the characteristics of authenticity "here" (in that particular work) would be that Sartre considered *Being and Nothingness* a description exclusively of inauthentic modes of existence. In his notorious, and brief, conclusion to the book, in which he examines the metaphysical and ethical implications of his work, Sartre confirms that he has not yet explored these issues in the detail which they deserve, and he promises to do so in "a future work"— a work he never published.

In other words, if we take Sartre's early works to be accounts of love and sex only as they are practiced inauthentically, then the possibility of more positive, and authentic, Sartrean models for such activities remains.

Furthermore, although they may have disagreed on numerous issues, it is significant that Simone de Beauvoir clearly expressed her view, in *The Second Sex*, for example, that what she calls "genuine love" can exist, and she describes it this way:

> Genuine love ought to be founded on mutual recognition of two liberties; the lovers would then experience themselves both as self and as other; neither would give up transcendence, neither would be mutilated; together they would manifest values and aims in the world. For the one and the other, love would be a revelation of self by the gift of self and enrichment of the world [1974, p. 667].

Given all these qualifications to the views of both Sartre and Allen, there seems no point in presenting arguments here to challenge Sartre's gloomy approach as it is presented in this film, although many exist to be made. Instead, we will briefly explore one apparent contradiction between Allen's views as they have been expressed repeatedly in other films, and the position he seems to take here.

In his other films, Allen has always seemed to assert that in the internal battle between reason and emotion, emotion is of the greater significance. There exists a common misperception of Allen as someone who insists on over-intellectualizing life's concerns. Yet those characters with whom he most clearly identifies are always to be found arguing against too great a reliance on the demands of reason over to those of the heart.

Again and again, Allen pokes fun at those (like Mary in *Manhattan*, Leopold in *A Midsummer Night's Sex Comedy*, Frederick in *Hannah and Her Sisters*, Lloyd in *September*, or the doctor in *Shadows and Fog*) who insist on endlessly intellectualizing life's concerns while, for the most part, ignoring the power of their strongest emotional intuitions. Perhaps Isaac Davis in *Manhattan* expresses this point best when he tells Mary in the planetarium that "nothing worth knowing can be understood with the mind. Everything valuable has to enter you through a different opening."

Thus it is surprising to find Allen in *Husbands and Wives* apparently agreeing with a Sartrean approach on love and sex that is, as we have seen, grounded in Sartre's claim that the choice to enter the magical realm of the emotions is always in bad faith. This is particularly surprising when you consider that the greatest flaw in Sartre's published position is exactly the point Allen has made so often in the past, namely that the structure of the universe as understood through human reason does not seem compatible with the goals of human happiness.

Therefore, Allen has always contended that if we choose to favor the demands of logic over our emotions, we resign ourselves to lives of mean-inglessness and futility.

IV. The Hedgehog and the Fox

Of all of the characters in *Husbands and Wives*, Sally stands out as the most fascinating, complex, and real. This is partly because of the brilliant performance given by Judy Davis; but it is also because, in writing and directing her character, Allen has gone further than ever before in presenting a woman with a full identity of her own, one who cannot be construed simply as a female version of himself.

This is why it is particularly interesting to find Allen introducing Isaiah Berlin's analogy of the hedgehog and the fox in Sally's voice. In an interview scene, the inept narrator demonstrates his lack of understanding of what his subjects are really feeling by asking Sally why she thinks she was able to have an orgasm with Michael but not with Jack. Sally corrects him, saying she didn't have an orgasm with Michael either. When he asks her why not, she says that, although she enjoyed Michael's love-making more than Jack's, she couldn't relax sufficiently because her mind was racing. In response to the question of what she was thinking about, she says that he would laugh if she told him. When he insists on knowing, she says:

> I thought that I liked what Michael was doing to me and it felt different from Jack, and more exciting. And I thought how different Michael was from Jack, how much deeper his vision of life was. And I thought Michael was a hedgehog and Jack was a fox. And I thought Judy was a fox and Gabe was a hedgehog. And I thought of all the people I knew and which were hedgehogs and which were foxes ...

She goes on to categorize all of her friends and acquaintances using Isaiah Berlin's famous distinction between those who believe in one grand unifying truth (hedgehogs) and those who pursue many, and sometimes even contradictory, ends (foxes). As she lies in Michael's arms afterward, he honestly tells her he could feel that she was a bit distant. Rather than acknowledging what we know to be the truth, she at first pretends to have enjoyed every second of it, and then becomes very defensive as she reminds him of her problems in bed with Jack. He attempts to soothe her and says how wonderful everything was, but she now feels it necessary to torture both of them over the separateness of their respective experiences. Michael admits he can see why Jack was driven a bit crazy, a comment which only upsets Sally even more. Here we see the downside of Michael's honesty from Sally's perspective. Because of his commitment to revealing all of his feelings, he makes no attempt to pretend that everything is all right when he knows it isn't. While this attitude may be admirable, his expectations are more than Sally, in her extreme vulnerability, can take.

By her unwillingness to allow herself to become submerged in the magical spell of sexual desire, as Sartre has described it, Sally chooses (at some level of her consciousness) to retain not only her ontological separateness, but her power over herself. While this means giving up the pleasure of sex, it also allows her to retain her authority over herself and her domination of all the events in which she engages. Yet she is clearly in internal conflict over her decision and no doubt consciously wishes to reverse it. Ideally, she would prefer to be able to have it all, to enjoy the pleasures of sex while simultaneously retaining her sense of complete control and her critical faculties.

However, for Sartre, this desire, which all of us share, is like our common yearning to become God (to become an all-powerful being that is both complete and free at the same time). While we all share these desires, none of us can ever achieve them because they are ontologically incompatible. By its very nature, according to Sartre, successful sexual activity requires the willingness to engage in spontaneous activity in which one sacrifices one's godlike rational control. One's pleasure, or lack of pleasure, is for Sartre exactly proportional to one's willingness to give up such control and enter this magical emotional realm. Thus, to the extent one refuses to do this, as Sally does, one will be unable to achieve pleasure.

Allen's use of Berlin's distinction here also emphasizes another point. Berlin most concerned himself with the views of those thinkers who cannot easily be fit into either camp — thinkers like Tolstoy (and Allen) who appear to be foxes, willing to accept the myriad variety of experience as it appears to us empirically in its vastly diversified fashion, while at the same time desperately wishing for some grand scheme of life, some underlying spiritual meaning lying just out of reach, a meaning of which we occasionally catch a glimpse, but which forever remains beyond our grasp.

Thus, in exploring the reason that Gabe found it necessary to finally reject Rain's romantic overtures, and his justification for concluding that in making this decision, "I really blew it," we can do no better than to reflect upon the implications of Berlin's description of Tolstoy's ultimate fate:

> Tolstoy was the least superficial of men: he could not swim with the tide without being drawn irresistibly beneath the surface to investigate the

darker depths below; and he could not avoid seeing what he saw and doubting even that; he could close his eyes but could not forget that he was doing so; his appalling, destructive sense of what was false frustrated this final effort at self-deception as it did all the earlier ones; and he died in agony, oppressed by the burden of his intellectual infallibility and his sense of perpetual moral error, the greatest of those who can neither reconcile, nor leave unreconciled, the conflict of what there is and what there ought to be [1957, p. 123].

– 10 –

"DON'T SPEAK!":
Bullets Over Broadway
(1994)

Given the lack of positive critical and commercial attention to his previous four films, and the negative impact of the enormous publicity simultaneously generated by his personal life, Woody Allen was no doubt aware that, for the sake of his ongoing career, he badly needed to create a film which would be perceived as a success. This he achieved with *Bullets Over Broadway*, his greatest public triumph since *Crimes and Misdemeanors*. Furthermore, he accomplished this goal by creating, with co-writer Douglas McGrath, a vastly entertaining film that grounds its comedic facade in a serious exploration of the very nature of art.

I. Where Does Talent Come From?

The film's primary philosophical tension results from the growing realization of playwright David Shayne (John Cusack) that despite his years of training, hard work, and sacrifice, he possesses no genuine artistic talent, especially when compared to Cheech (Chazz Palminteri), an uneducated gangster blessed with an intuitive gift for writing, whose devotion to his art eventually overrides even his love of life.

Early in *Bullets Over Broadway* (hereafter referred to as *Bullets*), David's friend Sheldon Flender (Rob Reiner) raises many of the film's concerns in the following exchange:

> SHELDON: It's irrelevant, it's irrelevant! The point I'm making is that no truly great artist has been appreciated in his lifetime. No! No! No! Take

Van Gogh or Edgar Allan Poe. Poe died poor and freezing with his cat curled on his feet!

WOMAN: David, don't give up on it, maybe [your play] will be produced posthumously!

SHELDON: No, I have never had a play produced, that's right, and I've written one play every year for the past twenty years!

DAVID: Yes, but that's because you're a genius! And the proof is that both common people and intellectuals find your work completely incoherent! It means you're a genius!

MAN: We all have that problem. I paint a canvas every week, take one look at it, and slash it with a razor.

SHELDON: In your case that's a good idea.

ELLEN: I have faith in your plays.

DAVID: She has faith in my plays because she loves me.

ELLEN: No, it's because you're a genius!

DAVID: Ten years ago, I kidnapped this woman from a very beautiful, middle-class life in Pittsburgh, and I've made her life miserable ever since.

WOMAN: Hey, Ellen, as long as he is a good man, keep him! You know, I think the mistake we women make is we fall in love with the artist.... Hey, you guys are listening? We fall in love with the artist, not the man.

SHELDON: I don't think that's a mistake!... Look, look, look! Let's say there was a burning building, and you could rush in and you could save only one thing, either the last known copy of Shakespeare's plays, or some anonymous human being.

WOMAN: It's an inanimate object!

SHELDON: It's not an inanimate object! It's art! Art is life! It lives!

Like Nietzsche, Sheldon believes that in a world devoid of God or any ultimate, objectively valid source of moral values, aesthetic creativity is the only self-justifying principle. For Sheldon, the vision of a great artist bestows upon that person the right to create "his own moral universe," in which virtually any act is permissible if it serves the needs of the authentic artist. Sheldon and David also express the view that most people, and especially most critics, do not have sufficient aesthetic judgment to recognize great art; indeed, as David states, the fact that both common people and intellectuals find one's work "incoherent" is in itself proof that an artist is a "genius."

Like everything else in this film, Allen's presentation of these views takes the form of hilarious parody. Nevertheless, it would be a mistake to assume that for this reason the issues raised are not to be viewed seriously.

In a written exchange with me (see Appendix), Allen praised Friedrich Nietzsche as "the Michael Jordan of philosophers, fun, charismatic, dramatic, great all-around game." While Sheldon, David, and their friends are themselves examples of the untalented "anonymous human beings" to which Sheldon unreflectively referred in his Shakespeare scenario, Cheech is unquestionably a genuine artist acting out Sheldon's notion of the Nietzschean *Übermensch* (overman), a creative colossus among a population of insignificant sheep.*

In his epic poem *Thus Spake Zarathustra*, Nietzsche describes his ideal artist this way:

> I teach you the overman. Man is something that shall be overcome. What have you done to overcome him?
> All beings so far have created something beyond themselves; and do you want to be the ebb of this great flood and even go back to the beasts rather than overcome man? What is the ape to man? A laughingstock or a painful embarrassment. And man shall be just that for the overman: a laughingstock or a painful embarrassment [1978, p. 12].

Like Sandy Bates in *Stardust Memories*, Cheech resides in a moral universe of his own making in which he views virtually everyone else as a grotesque inferior. However, unlike the untalented Bates, Cheech possesses a creative gift that is spontaneous and genuine. While everyone in the film acknowledges that David Shayne's plays have always reflected his ideas, his training, and his hard work, once he starts passing off Cheech's writing as his own, everyone — including Ellen (Mary-Louise Parker) and Helen Sinclair (Dianne Wiest), the women who supposedly love him — confesses that his earlier work had always seemed lifeless and artificial. Helen puts this difference in sexual terms when she tells David that his new work shows he has "balls," while his earlier writing was done by a "eunuch."

Allen's views here parallel his earlier claim in many of his films that talent resides only in those who are born with it. In *Interiors*, Joey angrily tells her mother, "You worship talent. Well, what happens to those of us who can't create? What do we do, what do I do when I'm overwhelmed with feelings about life? How do I get them out?" In *Hannah and Her Sisters*, Holly is presented as a klutz at everything until she discovers her gift for writing, a native ability that astonishes Mickey by its unexpectedness. In "Oepidus Wrecks," Treva compares psychic ability to acting talent, telling Sheldon that neither can be acquired; you must be born with it. In the seder scene in *Crimes and Misdemeanors*, a woman says that "Sol's kind

---

*The passages from Nietzsche quoted in this chapter were suggested by John Vitale.

of faith is a gift! It's like an ear for music or the talent to draw." Finally, at the beginning of *Husbands and Wives*, Gabe Roth, an English professor, denies that writing can be taught; one either has talent or one doesn't.

II. Art Has Its Price

There is no question that Cheech is the most genuine person in the film, even if he is also its most frightening. All the other characters are parodies of types that could be found in any number of "showbiz" or "gangster" genre films of the 1930s, films like *42nd Street* or *Public Enemy*. With its clichéd plot of the naive playwright seduced by the allure of fame and celebrity, *Bullets* would be no more than a superficial light comedy were it not for Cheech's presence. Indeed, with its sumptuous period touches and its stock characters (including even a wisecracking Hattie McDaniel–type black maid played by Annie-Joe Edwards), *Bullets* at first resembles the trivial film from which Tom Baxter emerged in *The Purple Rose of Cairo*. It is Cheech's story that gives *Bullets* its weight by delving into serious issues even as it entertains with some of the funniest scenes Allen has given us in years.

Perhaps excluding Ellen, all of the film's other major characters are phonies or crooks. Allen superbly ridicules the artificial world of the theater in which everyone is always overacting as they use their claims to talent as justification for their self-indulgent eccentricities. Sheldon's theory of the artistic genius allows him to betray his best friend, as so many of Allen's characters (e.g., Yale in *Manhattan* or Lou in *Broadway Danny Rose*) have engaged in betrayal in the past. Sheldon claims to be a Marxist, and his preposterous attempt at the film's end to justify his actions by reducing love and sex to economic issues mirrors the willingness of David's agent, Julian Marx (Jack Warden), to reduce David's art to a matter of economics by accepting the financial support of the gangster Nick Valenti (Joe Viterelli).

While Valenti's demand that his untalented and obnoxious girlfriend Olive Neal (Jennifer Tilly) be cast in an important role in the play obviously compromises its integrity, the real joke is that once Olive meets with the other members of the cast, her uneducated crudeness doesn't seem that out of place among the oddities of the other cast members. Eden Brent (Tracey Ullman) with her love of her little dog, Warner Purcell (Jim Broadbent) with his need to eat constantly when he's anxious, and Helen Sinclair with her self-promoting, overdramatic prose, as well as her drinking, are presented in such a ludicrous fashion that Olive, with all her flaws, seems to fit right in.

On the other hand, Allen lets us know that the actors do have some talent. When Olive must miss a performance because of a minor injury, everyone can see that the play comes into its own as a true aesthetic creation. Perhaps the eccentricities of the actors are the price that each must pay for his talent, limited as it may be; for the film makes clear that art has its price, a price which expands exponentially in proportion to the artist's talent. Thus Cheech, the most talented artist in the film, sacrifices Olive's life, and eventually his own, out of his obsessive devotion to his art.

The choice of the relatively unknown actor Chazz Palminteri to play the part of Cheech displays once more Allen's brilliant ability to add weight to his characters by blurring the line between fiction and reality. Just as Allen has invited his audiences again and again to mistake the characters he creates for the actors who play them (e.g., Diane Keaton in *Annie Hall*, Mia Farrow in *Hannah and Her Sisters*, or himself in innumerable films from *Annie Hall* to *Husbands and Wives*), for the part of Cheech he chooses an actor whose own life mirrors the part he is playing. Palminteri's renown derives primarily from his play *A Bronx Life*, which was released as a film in 1993 with Palminteri reprising his role as Sonny, a gangster who acts as a mentor to a boy who witnesses a gangland killing. The primary moral of that story, repeated often by the boy's father, is that there is nothing in life as sad as "wasted talent." At the film's conclusion, the father makes it clear that Sonny, a talented man living his life as a petty hood, epitomizes such waste.

In interviews, Palminteri acknowledges that his play is autobiographical; that he witnessed just such a killing when he was a boy; and that, like the character in his play, he decided against informing on the killer. Thus, like Cheech, Palminteri is a product of the streets whose gift for writing allows him to create honest characters with dialogue and concerns that ring true. Furthermore, unlike Sonny, Cheech will get the chance to explore his talent rather than waste it.

The relationship between David and Cheech defines the film's most important issues. Cheech is David's opposite in every area. Where David has toiled for years to develop his talent by reading and studying the works of the world's greatest writers, Cheech has no formal education in the theater, nor does he care what others may have done in the past. Where David worships at the throne of celebrity and fame, overwhelmed by Helen's ability to introduce him to a world populated by "Max Anderson," "Gene O'Neill," and Cole Porter, Cheech cares nothing for fame. Indeed, where David allows his desire for celebrity and success to overcome his sense of moral obligation, Cheech has no need to have his talent recognized by others;

nor does it seem to occur to him that he could leave his life as a gangster to become a full-time artist.

Once Cheech discovers his gift, his art becomes a burden to him, something he just has to do, although he never understands why. In their many discussions at Cheech's pool-hall hangout, David discovers that Cheech is completely unreflective about both his art and his work. He kills because it's his job; he takes no joy in it, nor does he feel any sense of guilt. When David asks him what it was like to kill his first man, Cheech mistakes David's morbid curiosity for a professional inquiry, warning him of the inconveniences of killing someone with an ice pick.

Cheech is no Raskolnikov. He doesn't kill to test the bounds of morality; he quite simply has no moral scruples to restrain his actions. The limit of his moral reflection comes when he announces to David that everyone he has killed "deserved it," something we suspect he determined simply by reasoning that Nick would never order him to kill anyone who didn't deserve it.

Thus, when Cheech comes to realize that Olive's performance is ruining the perfection of his play, he has no qualms about killing her. Despite his creative gift, Cheech is not smart, not even about the rules of the gangland world in which he operates. When he concludes both that Olive must be removed from her part, and that David can't (or won't) fire her because of his fear of Nick, Cheech comes to what he views as the only possible conclusion: Olive must be killed by him.

Yet he develops no plan for pulling this off without implicating himself to Nick. Even though Allen's script has provided Cheech with a plausible way to do this by allowing him to discover Olive's infidelity with Walter Purcell, it never occurs to Cheech to take advantage of this opportunity. If he had simply allowed Nick to discover Olive's betrayal, as Nick almost does accidentally at one point when he visits her dressing room unannounced (forcing Purcell to hide in her closet), then Nick most certainly would have removed her from the play.

However, not only does this not occur to Cheech, he even goes out of his way to warn Purcell to stay away from Olive because of his respect for Purcell's talent as an actor. Instead, Cheech allows himself to be seen taking Olive away, and, amazingly, he kills Olive at his favorite pier, an M.O. so well known to his fellow hoods that they recognize it immediately as his personal signature. When confronted by Nick, he is remarkably unconcerned with his own well-being. Obsessed by his need to see the audience's reaction to his play on opening night on Broadway, he presents only the flimsiest of alibis, when, even at this late date, revelation of Olive's affair with Purcell might have saved his life.

The backstage shootout which closes *Bullets* is reminiscent of the ending of Allen's previous film, *Manhattan Murder Mystery*, in which the action backstage mimics that taking place on the movie screen in front of it. However, where that scene seemed contrived and stagy (some unkind audience members might have preferred to be watching Orson Welles's original over Allen's copy), here the action backstage is in perfect harmony with the play going on in front. We are even told that one reviewer of Shayne's play mistook the gunshots of Cheech's fatal shootout for intended special effects which added an "evocative" resonance to the play. Even facing death, Cheech's only concern is with the perfection of his art. His last words to David instruct him to add a line to the play's ending which will strengthen its dramatic structure. When David tries to respond, Cheech mimics Helen Sinclair's comic tagline throughout the film by covering David's mouth and saying, "Don't speak!"

In his willingness to sacrifice his life for his art, and for an audience unworthy of receiving his talent, Cheech further reflects the notion of the genuine artist as limned by Nietzsche:

> Of all that is written I love only what a man has written with his blood. Write with blood, and you will experience that blood in spirit.
>
> It is not easily possible to understand the blood of another: I hate reading idlers. Whoever knows the reader will henceforth do nothing for the reader. Another generation of readers—and the spirit itself will sink.
>
> That everyone may learn to read, in the long run corrupts not only writing but also thinking [1978, p. 40].

III. Is Morality Available Only to the Talentless?

The reason Helen and finally Cheech tell David to keep quiet is that they both realize that David has nothing to say. He is no artist, just one of Nietzsche's "readers." Throughout *Bullets*, David has been tortured by the choices he must make. He agonizes over whether he should compromise his art in order to see it produced, or, like Sheldon, write plays specifically intended to go unproduced. We strongly suspect, however, that Sheldon has even less talent than David, so that Sheldon's "sacrifice" is no sacrifice at all. If anyone were to offer Sheldon the same deal that Nick presents to David, no doubt Sheldon's principles would go out the window immediately.

David's play is called "God of Our Fathers," and there is at least one suggestion that David, despite his name, may be Jewish. But from what we see and hear of it, his play has nothing to do with its title. The characters and situations depicted are not authentic representations of David's own life or heritage. Instead, he has written a play inhabited by characters from other plays he has admired, characters who speak in an artificially theatrical manner which doesn't sound, as Cheech points out, "like people talk."

Thus, when David accepts Nick's deal at the film's beginning, it is just one more compromise of his art rather than the first. Further, when he throws open his window in the middle of the night to shout out to the world that he is a "whore" for allowing his work to be demeaned, it is no more than a theatrical gesture for Ellen's benefit. He soon assuages his conscience by calling his agent to insist on a seemingly minor demand, namely that Walter Purcell be hired for the play despite his proclivity for overeating.

As the film progresses, we see David continue to compromise his supposed integrity in other ways, as he changes his play to satisfy the egotistical demands of Helen Sinclair, then betrays Ellen by having an affair with the much older Helen simply in order to reside more fully in the world of fame. There is no question that neither David nor Helen feels anything like love in their affair. Early in the film, Helen shows us how much she really cares for her lovers when she refers to one of her past husbands as "the one with the mustache."

All Helen wants from David is the chance to regain her faded professional status by starring in successful plays written especially for her somewhat limited talents. Helen fully realizes the emptiness of the glamorous life for which David hungers. She bribes him with castoff presents that have nothing to do with him, like the cigarette case she gives him (although he doesn't smoke) whose value lies in the fact that Cole Porter gave it to her with an engraved invitation to fool around ("Let's Do It!"). One suspects that this gift had no special significance even when it was firsthand, given Porter's well-known homosexuality. Later, Allen contrasts David's starstruck excitement at a celebrity party with Helen's more experienced recognition that such parties are boring. She seduces David in the bathroom by bribing him again, this time with a promise to meet Eugene O'Neill.

David's bad faith is most perfectly exemplified by his inability to let others know of Cheech's contributions to his play despite his obvious feelings of guilt. He allows Helen to stop him with a "Don't speak!" when he finally tries to tell her the truth, even though she makes it clear that it is the artist, not the man, who attracts her. In his duplicitous condition, he lies to Helen by telling her that he will reveal their affair to Ellen, and then he lies to Ellen by denying the affair in the face of her accusations.

Unlike Cheech, David is willing to diminish the aesthetic value of the play by allowing Olive to continue in her role even after he is fully able to see the damage she is doing. By this point in the film, David has begun to realize that he has no art to compromise. Everything worthwhile in his play comes from Cheech. He knows he can no longer argue when Cheech refers to the work as "my play." Thus, when David sees that Cheech has murdered Olive to preserve the play's aesthetic worth, he is at last ready to face up to his situation honestly.

David has no trouble resolving Sheldon's earlier dilemma about whether to rescue Shakespeare's plays or the person from the burning building. For him, the life of one person, no matter how unimportant, must always take precedence over the demands of art. Showing unexpected courage, David challenges Cheech repeatedly, condemning him for his act even though he must know that Cheech could easily kill him, too, to keep him quiet. At the film's end, with Cheech dead, David could choose to enjoy the celebrity, wealth, and prestige that the success of the play would no doubt bring him. Instead, David chooses to abandon this path in favor of returning to a more honest life based on an acceptance of traditional moral values and the importance of love and family, values to which Allen has returned again and again in his films.

When David goes to the street in front of Sheldon's apartment, he publicly humiliates himself by begging Ellen to come back to him as he admits that he is no artist:

ELLEN: Congratulations on your hit, David. I always knew you had it in you.

DAVID: Yeah, well you were wrong. I have to ask you a question.

ELLEN: What?

DAVID: Did you love me as the artist or the man?

ELLEN: Both!

DAVID: What if it turned out I wasn't really an artist?

ELLEN: I could love a man if he wasn't an artist, but I couldn't love an artist if he's not a real man....

DAVID: I'm finished with it, living in the garrets, eating cheese and wine, analyzing art in coffeehouses. It's over. I love you. I want us to get married. Go back to Pittsburgh. I'll teach, we'll have kids.

ELLEN: But you're a success. You have a hit. Why the sudden change?

DAVID: Because I've wasted too much time already. I love you!

ELLEN: But you're an artist!

DAVID: No, I'm not. I'm not. I'll explain it all to you on the train back to Pittsburgh. There's two things of which I'm certain. One is that I love you, and two is that I'm not an artist. There, I've said it and I feel free! I'm not an artist! Will you marry me?

ELLEN: Yes!

David is freed by his admission because he no longer feels torn between his art and his conscience. In this film, the true artist, Cheech, has no freedom because his gift impels him to transcend traditional morality for the sake of his almost Platonic ideal of aesthetic beauty. Just as Plato could be accused of valuing perfection over conventional moral concerns (e.g., the Noble Lie), Cheech will do anything for his art. Like Howard Roark, Ayn Rand's single-minded architect in her novel *The Fountainhead* (1943), Cheech must do whatever is necessary for his art, even when it means his own destruction. He has no choice. The aesthetic impulse, Allen seems to be claiming, has a momentum of its own, which deprives the artist of the conventional pleasures of life available to the rest of us. Once he realizes that he is truly no artist, David can stop wasting his time and get on with the real pleasures of life, the ones that come from marriage and family.

The one remaining question is how Allen sees himself in relation to this dichotomy. In *Bullets*, one is either a tortured artist doomed by one's gift to suffer, or a normal person free to choose an authentic life based on traditional values. There appears to be no third option, no possibility for the existence of a morally responsible artist who fulfills both his aesthetic and his human duties.

Yet which is Allen himself? Is he telling us that he no longer considers himself an artist, that this return to comedy marks the end of his "serious phase," the phase of his career that began with *Annie Hall* and *Interiors*? Or, on the other hand, is this film an attempt to justify his past excesses, both professional and personal, by painting them as unavoidable byproducts of his enormous talent? Whatever the answer — and I for one hope that neither is correct — in his next film, questions of artistry will give way to hints of predestination.

– 11 –

"WHEN YOU'RE SMILING":
Mighty Aphrodite
(1995)

Mighty Aphrodite tries to fool us. It begins in the traditional form of a tragedy, yet, by its end, it has unmistakably transformed itself into comedy. Using the ancient Greek device of a masked chorus that comments on the action, Allen initially makes it appear that we are about to be told a story as tragic and morally instructive as those of Oedipus, Antigone, and Achilles.

Even though this device is made humorous by the introduction of contemporary situations and language, one still has the impression that the story of Lenny Weinrib (Woody Allen) will follow the traditional path in displaying a noble character whose inevitable downfall is triggered by an unfortunate surplus of overweening *hubris*, or pride. Indeed, throughout the film, we are returned repeatedly to an amphitheater in which a variety of classical Greek figures (including Cassandra) bemoan the destruction sure to befall the characters because of Lenny's arrogant disregard for the forces of destiny and morality.

I. Lenny and Linda

The story revolves around Lenny's attempt to find and then rehabilitate the mother of his adopted son. When we first see them, Lenny and his wife, Amanda Sloane (Helena Bonham Carter), are out to dinner with another married couple when they get into an argument about whether they should adopt. Lenny doesn't want a child, but Amanda does, although she isn't willing to take a year off from her work in an art gallery to have one the biological way.

Lenny opposes her plan, not on the basis of its obvious self-centered narcissism (Amanda talks of adopting a child the way others might speak of getting a cat), but instead because adoption would deprive the world of a biological replica of himself ("Adopt, what, I don't want to adopt. Not with my genes."). Eventually, Lenny gives in, and the couple almost immediately receive a healthy white male infant, whom they name Max (the nickname shared by Alvy and Rob in *Annie Hall*).

As the child grows, Amanda becomes more wrapped up in her attempts to procure her own art gallery and her interest in the romantic advances of a business associate named Jerry Bender (Peter Weller). Vaguely aware that his wife is drifting away from him, Lenny uses his growing obsession with Max's biological mother to distract him from his true problems.

Lenny's troubled marriage to Amanda is a familiar retelling of a story Allen has presented to us again and again. Once more, we have a younger woman involved with an older man who once served as her mentor but who is now regarded as a suffocating presence, especially when contrasted with the exciting opportunities represented by a new suitor who can help her professionally. The relationship of Lenny and Amanda is cut from the same cloth that produced Annie and Alvy, while Jerry Bender is just another version of Tony Lacy.

The only difference here is that Lenny, unlike Alvy, Isaac, Mickey, or Cliff, is not an artist but a sportswriter. As such, he is a man more comfortable with the characters he meets in a gym or a bar than with the artsy, well-off crowd forced on him by Amanda. Like Alvy, Lenny would rather watch a basketball game than hobnob with intellectuals. In many ways, Lenny inhabits a world comparable to that of Danny Rose, although his position in it is much more secure and his motives much less honorable.

As the film progresses, Lenny is consumed by a growing curiosity to learn more about his son's natural mother. Eventually, he illicitly obtains her name and address from the records of the adoption agency, despite the dire warnings of the leader of the Greek chorus (F. Murray Abraham), who is able to appear to Lenny much as the Bogart persona appears to Allan Felix in *Sam*, although with considerably less impact.

Now fully embarked on a quest in which he relies on the underworld connections afforded to him by his profession, Lenny eventually discovers that Max's mother (Mira Sorvino) is a woman of many names who is a bit player in the sleazy world of porno films and retail sex. Posing as a john, Lenny arranges a meeting. When he finally meets her in person,

Lenny is appalled to discover that the real mother of his child, now going under the name of Linda Ash, is a well-endowed, statuesque bleached blond with a Mickey Mouse voice and little in the way of intellect, talent, or class.

Apparently believing that his son's future is somehow dependent on the condition of his true mother — a person whose identity Max will never learn — Lenny devotes himself to the task of transforming Linda into a respectable person. While the theme of Pygmalion has dominated many of Allen's other films, the relation between Lenny and Linda contains a number of new elements. Unlike earlier Galateas (such as her namesake Linda in *Sam*), Linda Ash apparently possesses no hidden talents for her mentor to uncover and cultivate. In a parody of the various scenes in which an admiring Allen persona appreciates the raw talents of his newest discovery (e.g., Annie singing for Alvy or Holly reading her play to Mickey), here we see Lenny forced to recognize that Linda has absolutely no talent as an actress and would do better to obtain a practical skill such as hairdressing.

In addition, for the first time Allen's character is not primarily motivated by his romantic or sexual desires and fantasies. Although Lenny and Linda do end up spending a single night lustily comforting one another, his feelings towards her are more openly paternal and platonic than in Allen's earlier films. Indeed, much of the film's middle is taken up with Lenny's attempt to arrange a romantic match between Linda and Kevin (Michael Rapaport), a slow-witted young boxer searching for a traditional girl just like his mom with whom he can retire to a farm. While initially promising, the match is destroyed when Kevin accidentally spots Linda in a porno film shown to him by some of his boxing buddies.

Lenny is more successful in his attempt to change Linda's profession. Although the Greek chorus predicts that he will be killed or maimed, Lenny courageously confronts Linda's bald-headed, homicidal pimp and convinces him to release her in exchange for bench passes to Knicks games. By the film's end, Linda is sufficiently rehabilitated to be acceptable to a more serious suitor, a helicopter pilot awarded to her by the gods, *deus ex machina*, when his machine breaks down and descends on her in rural Pennsylvania. By this time, for reasons which are sketchy at best, Amanda has decided to reject Jerry Bender in order to return to Lenny, a development he supposedly welcomes, although his prior concern for his marital troubles has been minimal.

In the film's closing scene, which takes place much later, Lenny runs into Linda in a suburban shopping mall. Both are now comfortably married and are accompanied by their offspring. The final joke here is that while Linda is unaware of the fact that she is the biological mother of Lenny's son, he is equally unaware of the fact that he is the biological father of her child. The film concludes with a return to the amphitheater, where the chorus performs a farcical rendition of "When You're Smiling."

II. Destiny Takes a Hand

Although a decidedly minor effort, *Mighty Aphrodite* does touch on an interesting theme: the issue of free will versus determinism. The use of the Greek chorus and other devices of classical tragedy suggests that the tale will follow a predetermined path in which the gods, or destiny, will punish those who have dared to violate sacred principles of morality and decorum. After all, even though presented humorously, Lenny's story involves arrogant and prideful actions by a character who presumes to take upon himself the authority supposedly reserved for the fates.

There is no real justification for his immoral, and illegal, violation of rules intended to protect the privacy of adults who have chosen to hide their identity from those who adopt their biological offspring. Indeed, we are never given any plausible reason for Lenny's obsession. If he believes that Max's character is genetically determined by that of his mother, then how does it help to wean Linda away from a life of debauchery for which she seems particularly suited? Given the fact that Lenny intends to keep Linda's relationship to Max a secret from them both, what difference does it make that her life is now more respectable?

Even if we accept that Lenny is somehow motivated by his concern for his son, his actions still seem strange, since the film shows us little evidence to suggest that Lenny actually cares for Max in any serious way. As we have mentioned, Lenny was initially reluctant to have a child at all, and in his scenes with Max we are given no indication that his experiences as a father have fostered any particular bond of affection. In a rare family scene at an early birthday party for Max, Lenny is shown giving his son a variety of sophisticated toys obviously inappropriate for a child his age, which appear to have been purchased more for Lenny's amusement than Max's.

Thus Lenny's obsession with molding Linda's life appears to spring more from Lenny's frustration with his growing lack of control over Amanda than from any genuine need to help Max. Recognizing Amanda's drift from his sphere of control, Lenny feels a desire to explore new realms, to take this opportunity to escape Amanda's world of sophisticated pretense for a down-to-earth realm where he can indulge his proletarian interests and play a more important role. Lenny is by no means sure that he is unhappy to be losing Amanda. Like Alvy on the plane back to New York with Annie, Lenny has little desire to compete for Amanda's affections in the glitzy world in which she now moves. He welcomes the opportunity to return to his roots, the Damon Runyonesque world of honest crooks, whores, and pugs, a world in which he, by virtue of his position as an established sportswriter, will always be a big man.

Thus Lenny's quest to remold Linda into his own image of respectability is motivated solely by his desire to regain control of his world by dominating the life of someone inferior to him in so many arenas (intellectual, social, economic, etc.) that he need have no fear that she will be able to challenge his inherent superiority. As the clincher, Lenny starts off knowing Linda's most cherished secret, a knowledge which allows him to possess almost mystical powers in her eyes. Therefore, in this battle for control of Linda's life, all the advantages seem to be on Lenny's side; yet, somehow, by the film's end, she has achieved an equality of status and power which is quite surprising.

Even though Linda will never be able to compete with Lenny intellectually, she possesses qualities forever withheld from Lenny, leveling the playing field on which the terms of their relationship are fought out. For Linda, unlike Lenny, possesses a spontaneous genuineness, an authenticity, which defines her personhood in ways that Lenny can never affect. As the film's title suggests, Linda is the embodiment of female sensuality, a woman who relishes her sexual allure with no sense of shame or regret.

Much of the film's humor derives from Linda's unabashed celebration of the joys of human sexuality. It never occurs to her to be embarrassed by her profession or her honest enjoyment of all manner of sensual experience. She proudly shows off the sexual toys in her apartment as she brags of her roles in porno flicks and bursts with excitement at the possibility of playing a lesbian scene with a noted porno star. This is a woman who peppers her everyday conversation with references to "blowjobs" and who announces proudly that she holds the exclusive rights to the stage name "Julie Cum."

While Lenny's efforts do make Linda's life better, they are allowed to do so only on terms acceptable to her own inner nature. Thus Lenny's efforts to match Linda with Kevin are indeed doomed to failure from the beginning because Kevin's need for a "respectable girl" could never be fulfilled by anyone as inherently ebullient as Linda. Lenny's role in altering Linda's life, a role which he initiates entirely for his own selfish purposes, is predetermined by forces of which he knows nothing. The gods or forces of destiny discussed by the Greek chorus have indeed controlled all the elements of the story in ways that have been masked, just as the chorus is masked, in order to shield their machinations both from Lenny and from the audience.

It is Linda who is the film's primary protagonist, just as Annie Hall is the primary protagonist of the film that bears her name. Despite his arrogance, Lenny's sole function in this story is to serve as the unwitting agent of the fates, a bit like Clarence, the aspiring angel in Frank Capra's *It's a Wonderful Life*. This is the reason that Lenny's own story seems so superficial. Lenny's marital problems and his relationship to his son are merely the McGuffins that force Lenny into his assignment as the catalyst who will push Linda to fulfill her own destiny.

From this perspective, the concerns and predictions of the chorus—to which Lenny is apparently privy, given his interactions with two of their members (F. Murray Abraham as the chorus leader and Jack Warden as the blind prophet)—are a pretense to induce Lenny to do his part in the plot. That the concerns of the chorus are intentionally misleading is confirmed by the fact that they profess no surprise at the film's end, but instead regale us with a humorous rendition of a happy tune.

Some theorists have held that in classical tragedy we are morally instructed by witnessing the dire consequences that befall an initially noble person when a fatal flaw of character causes him to overstep the limits of propriety. In classical comedy, however, the audience is instructed by the plight of flawed characters who succeed through a series of apparent accidents by which morally desirable results are allowed to occur. In many such plays, a disreputable and rascally narrator, often a wily slave, serves the purposes of morality by plotting to aid more virtuous characters. Such a narrator is usually allowed to succeed not because of his own worthiness, but because of the worth of the characters he chooses to aid.

In this sense, *Mighty Aphrodite* is truly a comedy. Although undeserving in his own right, Lenny is chosen by fate, without his understanding, to serve as the agent who makes possible Linda's success. By literally dropping Linda's mate from the sky without Lenny's help and by giving Linda secret knowledge about Lenny equal to his own, the creator really in charge of this tale, that is, Woody Allen, lets us know that for once in his films everything was predestined from the beginning to work out for the best.

– 12 –

DISTORTED LIVES:
Deconstructing Harry
(1997)

Watching *Deconstructing Harry* is not a pleasant experience. The characters are totally unsympathetic and the plot is a confusing mix of fantasy and reality. The film's look suffers from choppy editing and overly dark lighting. Worst of all, from the perspective of many audience members and critics, the film simply isn't very funny. Most of the jokes are tired retreads of old Allen material which serve only to make us wish we were watching the films in which they originally appeared. Further, in the worst Allen tradition, a marvelous cast (including such notables as Billy Crystal, Judy Davis, Demi Moore, Elizabeth Shue, Stanley Tucci, and Robin Williams) is wasted in a series of brief sketches which are neither entertaining nor, apparently, connected to the rest of the film.

Nonetheless, I contend that a plausible interpretation of *Deconstructing Harry* can be given which illuminates more of its meaning and its place in relation to Allen's other films, especially in terms of the philosophical issue with which Allen has long been concerned, namely the relationship between art and morality. This is an area explored by Allen in many of his previous efforts, most notably *Annie Hall, Interiors, Manhattan, Stardust Memories,* and *Bullets Over Broadway.*

To make this interpretation, I must first examine a common assumption about this film, namely that in Harry Block Allen is playing a character intended to be both sympathetic and a not very well-disguised stand-in for himself. Commentators have remarked that Block appears, on the surface, to be a character very much like Allen. Yet I would contend that Block most closely resembles not Allen himself but Sandy Bates,

Allen's protagonist in the 1980 film *Stardust Memories*. This was probably Allen's least popular film with both critics and audiences; nevertheless, Allen told Tom Shales in 1987 that:

> "The best film I ever did, really, was *Stardust Memories*. It was my least popular film. That may automatically mean it was my best film. It was the closest that I came to achieving what I set out to achieve" [Shales, 1987, p.90].

It appears to me that *Deconstructing Harry* is virtually a remake of *Stardust Memories*, an attempt to revisit the themes of that film from the perspective of an older, and even more corrupt, protagonist. In *Stardust Memories*, Bates, a film auteur like Allen himself, reluctantly attends a weekend retrospective of his work arranged by a noted critic (Judith Crist). Over the course of the weekend, we watch as Bates struggles to come to terms with his desire to move away from the comedic films for which he is popularly known, in order to create a serious film which deals with life's more profound and pessimistic concerns. Bates also must deal with the contradictions in his romantic life. In the end, Bates suffers what Allen himself has described as a nervous breakdown.

Bates, like Harry Block, is a negative exaggeration of all of Allen's worst tendencies. While other Allen personas, such as Alvy Singer (*Annie Hall*), Isaac Davis (*Manhattan*), or Gabe Roth (*Husbands and Wives*), are attractive and talented characters striving desperately to overcome their bad faith, Sandy Bates is a thoroughly inauthentic and untalented dilettante who appears to be going through a richly deserved emotional crackup. It is as though Allen decided to combine his own least attractive qualities with those of his characters and turn them into a nightmare version of himself, a kind of Frankenstein's monster.

In *Stardust Memories*, and now again in *Deconstructing Harry*, Allen presents us with portraits of men who are actually as depraved as some of Allen's critics accuse him of being. Allen is responding both to those who have criticized his films, and to his own worst suspicions about himself, by showing us a man who really possesses all of these negative qualities so that we can all see that Allen's previous characters, and Allen himself, are not the monsters some would make them out to be.

Allen himself confirmed this interpretation of *Stardust Memories* when he told Diane Jacobs that Bates is "a very sick, neurotic almost nervous-breakdown film director. I didn't want this guy to be necessarily likable. I wanted him to be surly and upset: not a saint or an angel, but a man with real problems who finds that art doesn't save you (an idea I explored in *Interiors*)" (Jacobs, 1982, p. 147).

Deconstructing Harry begins with Allen's standard credits (white letters on a black background) interspersed with the repetition of a shot of a woman angrily exiting a cab and storming up to a door. The lyrics of the opening song, "Twisted," perfectly match the film's themes in their depiction of an egomaniac who others label crazy but who considers himself a misunderstood genius. The film abruptly cuts to a scene of a cookout in the country in which we see a man named Ken (Richard Benjamin) attempting to have sex with his sister-in-law Leslie (Julia Louis-Dreyfus) as his wife and family call to him to come outside and join the picnic. Even when interrupted by Leslie's blind grandmother, Ken refuses to stop until he's had his orgasm. While mildly humorous, Ken and Leslie's actions are sleazy and pathetic. We soon learn that this scene is from Harry's most recent book and that it is the cause of the woman's anger. Lucy (Judy Davis) was the real-life Leslie, and Harry's use of material from that actual affair in his thinly disguised *roman à clef* has destroyed both her marriage and her relationship with her sister Jane (Amy Irving). Unable to bring herself to commit suicide, she decides to kill Harry, whom she describes as a "black magician" who turns other people's misery into gold.

Reprising a device he used quite effectively in *Husbands and Wives,* another film with a writer at its center, Allen regularly interrupts his narrative in *Harry* with fantasy sequences acting out his stories. Here, Harry is only able to save his life by telling Lucy and showing us one of his early short stories about a young married man who takes a sick friend's identity in order to use the friend's apartment to entertain an Oriental hooker. The man's scheme backfires when Death shows up at the door and tries to take him, thinking he is the friend. We join Harry as he explains to his psychiatrist that his story sufficiently distracted Lucy so that he was able to escape. The psychiatrist points out that Harry's writing, his art, saved his life, but Harry is not pleased by this because, he honestly admits, the life that was saved is in shambles. Harry confesses that he has never grown up, that despite years of therapy and a number of marriages, he is still the same shallow, sex-obsessed egoist he has always been. Even his work, his usual refuge from the pain of reality, has failed him: he is suffering from writer's block. Harry's complaints remind the psychiatrist of another early Block story, one in which an actor (Robin Williams) inexplicably goes out of focus, destroying both his potential for work and his family life. In the end, his family is forced to wear glasses in order to see him. The psychiatrist concludes that Harry "expects the world to adjust to the distortion he's become."

In these early scenes, we are struck by Harry's own lack of focus. Scenes from the purportedly "real world" are disjointed. Dialogue is cut in midsentence and characters' actions are jerky and sometimes repeated. Yet in the fantasy sequences from Harry's writing, these distractions disappear. As Harry confesses to his therapist, the world of fantasy has become more real and comprehensible to him than his life; art has replaced life as the source of all of his meaning. Clearly, like Sandy Bates, Harry is a man going through a nervous breakdown and the film is showing us Harry's life as it appears to him through the contorted haze of his neuroses. It was rumored that Allen's original title for this film was "The Worst Man in the World," and from the film's very beginning, Allen leaves no doubt that Harry is despicable. Unlike other Allen personas, Harry Block is a man whose every utterance is filled with disagreeable and unfunny profanity. We have never heard Woody Allen characters use the word "fuck" in every sentence, or refer to themselves and others as "pricks" and "cunts." While some audience members may giggle at the unaccustomed sound of such language in an Allen film, clearly its use is not intended to be funny. Instead, I would contend, this language is but further evidence of Harry's moral bankruptcy. It is significant that Harry admits repeatedly in the film that his idea of the perfect relationship is an encounter with a prostitute in which sex is exchanged for money with no pretense of emotional involvement or caring. Harry is a man who has cut himself off from all genuine emotion, a man who destroys all his relationships and then complains that he has no one to accompany him to his honoring ceremony at his undergraduate school (a school which earlier expelled him for bad behavior).

When he attempts to convince his ex-wife Joan (Kirstie Alley) to allow him to take his nine-year-old son Hilly (Eric Lloyd) to the ceremony, we learn that Harry discusses penises, Freud, and sex with his son in ways that are more disturbing than humorous, especially given the fact that we know that Allen himself has been accused of child abuse by a previous partner. Also disturbing is Harry's claim that in a world where God is absent, the best men can do is replace faith with the hedonistic pursuit of sexual pleasure. Harry is amorally pleased by his son's decision to name his penis "Dillinger" after someone whom Harry describes as "extremely successful in his area of expertise."

We also find out through another fantasy sequence that Joan was initially Harry's psychiatrist and that his attraction to her was triggered by her apparent willingness to accept him despite all of his "perversions." However, in Harry's fantasy presentation of their marriage, Joan soon sees through Harry, telling him that he isolates himself emotionally from real life by escaping into the fantasy of his art, a realm in which he has complete control. After the birth of their son, Joan rejects Harry in order to pursue her Jewish faith, a move in direct opposition to Harry's own rejection of God for the sake of sex and art. We later learn that it is his half-sister Doris (Caroline Aaron) who is the devout Jew and that the real reason for the breakup of Harry's marriage to Joan was his sexual seduction of one of her patients.

Harry encounters his friend Richard (Bob Balaban), whom he accompanies for medical tests for chest pains. In the waiting room, Harry tries to reassure Richard that modern medical science, as opposed to traditional religious faith, has the tools necessary to defeat death or at least postpone it indefinitely. Given the choice between air conditioning and the Pope, Harry says, he would place his faith in air conditioning every time. Yet, as in Allen's earlier *Hannah and Her Sisters*, medical science is shown to be completely unreliable. Despite being given a clean bill of health by his doctor, Richard dies of a massive heart attack the very next day in the car on the way to Harry's ceremony.

The next scene is a replay of a standard Allen scenario, a final meeting between Allen's older man and a younger former lover who has moved on. The most famous version of this scene takes place at the end of *Annie Hall* when Alvy flies out to California to try to persuade Annie to return to New York and marry him. Throughout his career, Allen has been obsessed with the fantasy of the Pymalion-Galatea relationship, the seasoned older man who becomes a mentor to a young impressionable woman. Inevitably, the woman tires of the relationship, leaving the man feeling abandoned and worthless.

Here, Elizabeth Shue as Fay makes all this explicit by comparing their relationship to that of Henry Higgins and Eliza Dolittle. In his usual attempt to evade responsibility for the consequences of his own actions (in this case an affair which he himself predicted to be doomed from its very beginning), Harry instead demonizes his friend Larry (Billy Crystal) who truly loves Fay and is marrying her the very next day. We later learn that Harry met Fay in an elevator on his way to a rendezvous with Lucy. Harry thus managed to cheat on both his wife and his mistress in the same evening. We see Harry warning Fay not to fall in love with him and even eventually acknowledging that he is incapable of love. When Fay says she already loves him because she loves his writing, Harry correctly points out that it is wrong to confuse one's love for an artist's work with a romantic love of the artist as a person.

Here again is a traditional Allen concern, one most recently explored in his excellent *Bullets Over Broadway* in which David Shayne (John Cusack) constantly asks the women in his life whether they love him as an artist or as a man. This question has particular significance in that we know that David is not really an artist; the gangster Cheech (Chazz Palminteri) is the real author of David's play. That film shares another theme with this one in that Cheech is portrayed as both a great artist and an amoral killer. Indeed, Cheech thinks nothing of murdering a woman simply because she is a bad actress who is ruining his play. *Deconstructing Harry* raises the same issues by presenting Harry as an immoral man who victimizes his family and friends to create material for his fiction.

In his despair over losing Fay, Harry hires a black prostitute named Cookie (Hazelle Goodman), who seems sympathetic to Harry's pretentious expression of his existentialist *angst*. In a parody of his more genuine agonizing in earlier films, Allen has Harry describe the source of his depression with references to Beckett and quantum physics which he knows Cookie will not be able to follow. (Allen has been repeatedly accused of racism for his failure to cast African-Americans in his films. In presenting us with Cookie Williams, a stereotypically unintelligent whore with the proverbial heart of gold, Allen seems to be spitting in the eyes of his critics.) Harry ends up paying Cookie $500 to accompany him to his honoring ceremony while completely forgetting that his friend Richard has rearranged his schedule in order to go with him. In addition, as a result of an offhand joke made by Richard, Harry kidnaps his son Hilly in a scene frighteningly similar to the real-life accusations made against the real Woody Allen by Mia Farrow.

This strange crew proceeds to drive to upstate New York for his ceremony. On the way they stop at an amusement park where Harry gets high from Cookie's marijuana joint and temporarily faces up to his own shortcomings in a fantasy meeting with Ken, one of his fictional alter egos. Ken allows Harry to imagine the scene in which his ex-wife Jane tells Lucy that Harry is leaving her for another woman. Initially thinking that she is the other woman, Lucy tries to confess her affair but is soon stunned to learn that Harry is leaving Jane for Fay, not herself. This situation mimics those found in other Allen films such as *Interiors* and *Hannah and Her Sisters*, yet it does so without the emotional weight or seriousness of those efforts. Harry manages to feel guilt for his misdeeds while simultaneously trivializing the pain he has caused to others. The wonderful actress Judy Davis, who was able to bring her character Sally remarkably to life as a complex and interesting person in *Husbands and Wives*, is here reduced to no more than a comic stereotype. The pain of others is only interesting to Harry as it relates to his own self-image.

Their next stop on the trip down memory lane takes them to the home of Doris, Harry's half-sister, for a discussion of religion and morality. Harry belittles religious faith for creating arbitrary divisions between people which only serve to promote hatred and discrimination. We see Harry's short story on the topic in which he compares a devotion to Judaism to the devotion expressed by fans of the film *Star Wars* while fictionally portraying his father as an ax murderer and a cannibal despite the fact that we earlier learned that Harry's mother died in childbirth delivering him. Doris's husband Burt (Eric Bogosian) accuses Harry of anti–Semitism and suggests that Harry probably even denies the Holocaust. Harry responds that he not only doesn't deny the Holocaust but sees it as a precursor of worse to come. "Records are made to be broken" he ominously warns Burt. Despite all this, another fictional character, Helen (Demi Moore), allows Harry to see that Doris still loves him while pitying him for his incapacity to live with metaphysical ambiguity or find meaning through any form of faith. This discussion recalls the torments of Judah Rosenthal (Martin Landau) in *Crimes and Misdemeanors* as he abandons the faith of his father Sol for a hedonistic view of life which reduces people to objects who may be murdered when they get in one's way. Again, Harry trivializes this serious issue when he allows Cookie to convince him to go on with his honoring ceremony despite the fact that Richard has just died. Harry himself goes out of focus as Cookie talks him down by assuring him that at least he is a better man than Hitler.

In his most elaborate fantasy, Harry goes to Hell where he forgives his father for blaming him for his mother's death. By this point, Harry is no longer pretending that his characters are fictional. He admits openly that they are not thinly disguised versions of himself; "they're me!" In the midst of a number of unfunny Hell jokes, he discovers that Larry is Satan and finds out that he and the Devil have a lot in common; they've screwed all the same women. Harry argues with Larry over which of them is worse. At least Satan is a fallen angel, he knows that there's a real difference between good and evil. Harry argues that he is worse because for him there are only quarks and black holes. Like Jack Warden's physicist in *September*, Harry sees the universe as a meaningless place "randomly haphazard and unimaginably violent." Harry and the Devil drink a toast to evil as the fantasy breaks with Harry's arrest for kidnapping, possession of an unlicensed weapon (the gun he took from Lucy), and Cookie's possession of marijuana.

Like Sandy Bates, Harry finds himself in jail. Here he is visited by a dead Richard who cracks jokes about the afterlife and tells Harry that the only happiness comes from being alive — a message delivered much more convincingly in *Hannah and Her Sisters* when Allen's character Mickey narrowly escapes a suicide attempt only to find meaning and happiness in a movie theater watching *Duck Soup*. Larry and Fay interrupt their wedding to bail Harry out, only to be attacked again for betraying him. Larry correctly points out, "Harry, you put your art into your work. I put it into my life. I can make her happy." Only after a cop threatens to throw Harry back into the jail cell and bugger him himself does Harry give their wedding his blessing, yelling, "I give up! I give up!"

Harry then dreams of an honoring ceremony attended by his fictional characters with music provided by performers wearing Darth Vader helmets. Harry justifies himself as a man who's "too neurotic to function in life but can only function in art." A young woman student explains how much she enjoys deconstructing his work because on the surface it's "a little sad while underneath it's really happy." The dream and the film ends with Harry inspired to write a new novel on this theme. He now makes explicit all of the film's earlier claims: "Notes for a novel: opening possibility. Rifkin led a fragmented, disjointed existence. He had long ago come to this conclusion. All people know the same truth. Our lives consist of how we choose to distort it. Only his writing was calm. His writing which in more ways than one saved his life." The novel Harry is writing is, of course, the film we have just watched.

We last see Harry happily typing away as the credits run and the music swells with a reprise of "Twisted," whose lyrics undermine this supposedly happy ending in their portrayal of a person who maintains a sense of exaggerated self-importance in the face of the universal condemnation of all others.

Thus, *Deconstructing Harry* ends very much as did *Stardust Memories*, with the main character attempting to justify his past bad behavior by arguing that he was not evil, but only floundering. In the end, Harry is still the same shallow, sex-obsessed egoist he has always been and no amount of rationalization about his supposedly great contributions to art can redeem him. Harry's attempts to pre-empt the criticisms of others by eagerly confessing his sins do not minimize his responsibility for his acts nor excuse his destructive immaturity. They only confirm his hypocrisy. In my view, *Deconstructing Harry* is Allen's most depressing film since *Stardust Memories*. Let us all hope he waits another two decades before remaking this story yet again.

– 13 –

CONCLUSION:
The Dialectic of
Hope and Despair

I have argued that there exists a dialectical opposition between what might be called Woody Allen's more pessimistic films and his more optimistic films, a conflict between despair and a hope based on some sort of faith. Allen seems to have a love-hate relationship with God in which his intellectual tendency toward atheism combats his spiritual yearning for some form of salvation. I have also argued that throughout his career Allen has been, and continues to be, one of film's most forceful advocates for an awareness of moral values, and that an essential theme which permeates all of his films is his contention that contemporary American society is rapidly descending into barbarism precisely because of our failure to maintain a sense of individual moral responsibility.

I. Criticisms

Yet Allen has frequently been accused of advocating moral relativism. Those who make such accusations wonder why Allen finds it necessary to introduce so many characters who argue, sometimes quite persuasively, for positivistic or hedonistic ethical views. These critics ask why Allen allows characters such as Rob (*Annie Hall*), Yale (*Manhattan*), Leopold (*A Midsummer's Night Sex Comedy*), Tina (*Broadway Danny Rose*), Frederick (*Hannah and Her Sisters*), Lloyd (*September*), Judah, and Aunt May (*Crimes and Misdemeanors*) to present their arguments in settings that often seem to validate their views. If, as I have suggested, Allen believes these views to be morally repulsive, then why does he privilege them through repetition?

Furthermore, if Allen favors a return to more traditional values, then why doesn't he present more forceful arguments for grounding these values objectively? Indeed, why does Allen return again and again to these issues as though they have yet to be resolved? If Allen were a true advocate of traditional moral positions, wouldn't he wish to convince us that this debate has been unequivocally resolved in favor of those positions?

While these arguments have been made by a number of critics, they are perhaps most elegantly, and concisely, stated by my colleague Mark Roche of the Ohio State University in a letter to me comparing our differing interpretations of *Crimes and Misdemeanors*:

> On the level of Allen's intentions I share your reading, but I think the philosophy you want the film to privilege is ultimately weak. You adopt the position of faith over hedonism and power positivism, but I think the film shows— perhaps against Allen's intentions— that all three of these positions are ultimately decisionistic: they amount to the same thing formally, simply with different content. In other words, though you select the position of Judah's father, you have no serious arguments to persuade Judah of its validity. We both argue that Judah suffers, but whereas I can refer to his transgression of an objective order, you cannot; therefore, the skeptic might suggest to you that Judah in fact suffers only because he is not yet a free-thinker, not yet beyond bourgeois guilt. I see that as a fundamental philosophical weakness in the existential position. I don't see Aunt May as advocating reason as much as skepticism and power. By the way, her position seems to correlate also to a dominant position of contemporary theory— the reduction of all truth claims to power. In contrast, I would argue for a transcendental ground to ethics (along the lines of Kant or Apel): to deny certain basic concepts and categories, it is also necessary to presuppose them; thus their negation is self-contradictory and self-canceling. I think that reason can give us some unassailable grounds for ethics, even as it fails to analyze every issue exhaustively.

While Roche agrees with me that Allen intends to support an existential moral position such as that represented in Levy's closing monologue, he argues that Allen undermines all ethical positions so thoroughly that the film could well be "read as an unwitting endorsement of stagnant nihilism."

I believe that Allen's presentation of these issues stems from his notions of honesty and integrity. Yes, it would be easier and more optimistic to operate as though there existed an objective ground for moral values, one so unshakable as to invalidate all opposing claims. If such a ground did exist, then Allen would have no need for his underlying pessimism, and the villains in his films would be much easier to identify. However, as I read Allen's work, to assume such a metaphysical foundation in the absence of any evidence would be an inexcusable form of bad faith; one would be pretending to oneself that such a basis exists while simultaneously battling despair derived from an awareness that no persuasive arguments support its existence.

Allen feels an obligation to reveal the true nature of our collective ethical dilemma in spite of his passionate desire to believe that answers exist for the most profound metaphysical questions. This is why Allen himself is so critical of the films in which he allows his burning desire for a happy ending to overcome his honest realization of our ontological position, and it explains his own analysis of both *Stardust Memories* (perhaps his most pessimistic film) and *Hannah and Her Sisters* (certainly one of his most optimistic). As was noted earlier, Allen told Tom Shales in 1987 that "the best film I ever did, really was *Stardust Memories*. It was my least popular film. That may automatically mean it was my best film. It was the closest that I came to achieving what I set out to achieve" (Shales, 1987, p. 90). On the other hand, in another interview that same year, Allen criticized *Hannah*, stating that it was "more 'up' and optimistic than I had intended, and consequently was very popular. It's only optimistic in the sections I failed" (Yacowar, 1991, p. 252).

In answer to a question I posed to him (see Appendix), Allen continues this pessimism by asserting that successful romantic relationships are the result of "pure luck," that faith may be more of a "blind spot or a flaw" than a "gift," and that Judah "feels no guilt."

All this does not imply, however, that Allen's critics are right when they accuse him of nihilism. If Allen were truly a nihilist, then he would accept the claims of the many positivists and hedonists he portrays, rather than fighting against them as vigorously as he does. The source of the dialectical opposition in his films, and indeed, the source of much of his greatness as a film artist, lies in his unwillingness to give in to his despair, his need to continue to fight for his values. Allen has not given up his search for answers; nor does he accept the claim that in the absence of persuasive proof, all ethical theories are equally valid. Like a Kierkegaard or a Sartre, Allen commits himself to a specific framework of metaphysical values (e.g., "acceptance, forgiveness, and love") despite his admitted inability to prove their validity.

II. A Sartrean Ethics

This brings us to an additional question. If Allen concedes that he has yet to prove the validity of his views, then what justifies his rejection of bad faith? In other words, what exactly is bad about "bad" faith? A Sartrean answer to this question begins by pointing out that anyone who chooses to act in bad faith holds a position that is inherently inconsistent. Once I realize my true condition as a free being, I cannot deny the responsibility that freedom entails without falling into bad faith. I cannot simultaneously accept my freedom and deny it without being in bad faith. Thus, the condition of being in bad faith directly implies inconsistency. In fact, bad faith could be defined simply as a condition of inconsistency in which one both recognizes and at the same time denies one's own freedom and corresponding responsibility.

Therefore, bad faith is "bad" only because it implies inconsistency. And, as consistency is one of the major conditions for rationality, one can further say that when a person is in bad faith, he is not being rational. Now, Sartre does not claim that anyone has an obligation to be rational. Sartre is a noncognitivist; he does not believe that any objective moral norms exist. However, Sartre does claim that if one wishes to be rational, then one must avoid falling into bad faith, which means that one must accept one's human condition as a free and responsible activity. In his lecture *Existentialism and Humanism*, Sartre himself put it this way:

> One can judge, first — and perhaps this is not a judgment of value, but it is a logical judgment — that in certain cases choice is founded upon an error, and in others upon the truth. One can judge a man by saying that he deceives himself. Since we have defined the situation of man as one of free choice, without excuse and without help, any man who takes refuge behind the excuse of his passions, or by inventing some deterministic doctrine, is a self-deceiver. One may object: "But why should he not choose to deceive himself?" I reply that it is not for me to judge him morally, but I define his self-deception as an error. Here one cannot avoid pronouncing a judgment of truth. The self-deception is evidently a falsehood, because it is a dissimulation of man's complete liberty of commitment. Upon the same level, I say that it is also a self-deception if I choose to declare that certain values are incumbent upon me; I am in contradiction with myself if I will these values and at the same time say that they impose themselves upon me. If anyone says to me, "And what if I wish to deceive myself?" I answer, "There is no reason why you should not, but I declare that you are doing so, and that the attitude of strict consistency itself is that of good faith" [1948, pp. 50–51].

Thus Sartre is simply pointing out the logical implications of any individual's claim to be acting rationally.

Sartre does not claim that one individual could never criticize another for being in bad faith on moral grounds. Nor would Sartre deny himself or anyone else the possibility of morally criticizing others on many other grounds. However, when Sartre criticizes someone on moral grounds, he does so on the basis of his own freely chosen moral values, whose validity springs only from their status as having been freely chosen by Sartre, and not from any objective basis. In other words, if I choose to criticize someone as being morally "wrong" because that person is in bad faith, that judgment will have no objective validity in and of itself, but will be valid relative only to the set of moral values I have created for myself as a free and responsible individual. Yet, regardless of whether I personally choose to view bad faith as morally wrong, I cannot rationally deny the objective validity of the assertion that if one chooses to be rational, one cannot choose simultaneously to be in bad faith.

This fact does not in any way affect one's ability to make moral judgments on the basis of one's own freely chosen moral values. Even though there is an absence of objectively valid moral standards, I can still choose to judge others and myself on the basis of those moral values I have freely created for myself.

In a Sartrean ethics, the individual, as moral agent, does not simply express his personal preferences when he commits himself to a moral judgment. Indeed, in a Sartrean ethics, a distinction must be made between personal preference and moral judgment. It is here that the principle of universalization assumes primary significance: it plays a central role in the grounding of this distinction.

For the ethical cognitivist, the distinction between personal preference and moral judgment is made on the basis of the objective status of the position in question. Thus, for the cognitivist (or naturalist), the decision to prefer vanilla ice cream to chocolate is viewed as the expression of a mere personal preference because no objectively valid basis exists for making such a choice. However, the cognitivist would probably state that the decision to view murder as wrong is the result of a moral judgment because, according to the cognitivist, there does exist an objectively valid moral basis for holding such a position.

On the other hand, the ethical noncognitivist, such as Allen or Sartre, can have no such explanation of the difference between personal preference and moral judgment, because the ethical noncognitivist does not admit the existence of any objectively valid moral norms. Thus, for the noncognitivist, the distinction between personal preference and moral judgment must be predicated upon the different ways in which each is formulated and used rather than upon their supposed claims to objective moral validity.

Moral judgments, for a Sartrean, differ from personal preferences in that they are the result of specific creative acts on the part of the individual, acts to which that individual is willing to commit himself wholly. Such acts of personal invention cannot be reduced to expressions of emotion because emotional attitudes are themselves, for Sartre, the result of choice. A necessary consequence of making such a judgment is that one commits oneself, to the extent that one wishes to be rational, to a moral stand that one must be willing to universalize to cover all cases identical to one's own in their morally relevant aspects.

A personal preference differs from a moral judgment in that such preferences are not open to universalization. When I decide that I prefer vanilla ice cream to chocolate, this decision in no way commits me to a belief that all persons ought to do the same. On the other hand, if I decide that it would be morally wrong for me to steal, then I am committing myself to the belief that it would be equally wrong for anyone else to steal. It is important to emphasize that the normative content of one's judgment does not determine whether that judgment is a moral one. It is the way in which the judgment is made that creates its moral character.

It would be possible for me to formulate my preference for vanilla ice cream in a way that turns it into a moral judgment. Say, for example, that the workers who make the chocolate flavoring for ice cream decided to call for a national boycott of chocolate ice cream in order to pressure their employers to change what they considered to be unfair working conditions. Now, further suppose that I decide, in the absence of any objectively valid moral norms, to create my moral values in a way that commits me to supporting the workers and their boycott. In such a situation, I would be committed, for as long as I hold my position, to avoiding chocolate ice cream on moral grounds. Furthermore, I would also be committed to the belief that everyone ought to avoid chocolate ice cream.

Moral judgments, therefore, are distinguishable from personal preferences in that the former are open to universalization while the latter are not. This does not mean, of course, that all judgments open to universalization are moral judgments, for most descriptive judgments are also open to universalization. What distinguishes moral judgments from descriptive judgments is the latter's added prescriptive character, i.e., the fact that they commend what they also describe.

While I have no definite evidence that Allen accepts this interpretation of his own ethical position, I would contend that it is certainly compatible with the positions presented in his films and that its use can be helpful in clarifying Allen's views and resolving areas of apparent contradiction.

III. An Existential Answer to Allen's Critics

Allen's critics are quite correct, therefore, when they argue that the existentialist cannot justify his ultimate moral principles (which are few in number and from which all his other moral claims are rationally derived) in any objective fashion. Allen cannot prove that his ultimate moral claims are correct to those who do not also choose to accept them. These claims are created individually in the exercise of one's ontological freedom and are indeed, in principle, unjustifiable.

This is why, in discussing the appropriate response to a neo–Nazi march in *Manhattan*, Isaac is quick to reject the claim that "a biting satirical piece is always preferable to physical force." "No," he answers, "physical force is always better with Nazis. It's hard to satirize a guy with shiny boots." Rational disputation is possible in metaphysical areas only when some common assumptions exist on which to base the debate.

The essential difference in Allen's position from those of the cognitivists (such as Roche) is that Allen acknowledges that his ultimate moral principles are unjustifiable, yet he still finds them capable of forming the basis of an intelligible and workable system. The cognitivist, on the other hand, holds to the notion that the very enterprise of ethics is impossible unless there exists a knowable objective ground for such principles— although, from a perspective such as Allen's, it is not discernible how such a grounding might occur.

Thus, when Allen's characters claim to have an obligation to be honest in their dealings with others, they recognize that they cannot ultimately ground that claim in a knowledge of any natural purpose (as an Aristotle would), or indubitable rational intuition (as Kant and Roche do). No, for Allen, these duties are solely grounded in his free creation of them and his willingness to generalize his choice into a theory of universal human morality. Because he chooses to value certain notions of integrity and honor, he constitutes this valuing in a prescriptive manner from which he generates his own claims for the similar obligations of others. In doing so, he acknowledges that his choice to believe in the value of morality is ultimately an unjustifiable Kierkegaardian leap of faith. As Allen stated in his interview with me, the "conflict between despair and hope can only be resolved on an individual basis, not in any general theoretical way. Faith can't be come to by reason — it's a gift, perhaps even a blind spot or flaw, but helpful, like [a] denial mechanism. Reason goes so far and I admire it. Intuition is just reason but accomplished in the leap rather than taking all the steps."

Allen's fundamental criteria for a moral life are accepted on a faith that is incapable of incontestable demonstration. Reason can go only so far; it can provide insights into the implications of our acts on the basis of our underlying moral principles, but it cannot objectively ground those principles. It seems odd that some of Allen's critics, who might be perfectly willing to accept the premise that their belief in God must be ultimately grounded in religious faith rather than on indisputable proofs, are apparently not able to accept the same restrictions on their beliefs in the natural origins of our duties and obligations.

On the other hand, I do recognize that there is a serious, though unstated, thrust to their criticisms of Allen. They obviously believe that the universe would be a more hospitable place in which to operate ethically if there existed one incontrovertible method of ethical reasoning, a method that could conclusively demonstrate that in any conflict of values or ethical principles, one and only one solution is correct.

Allen would agree that our lack of certain knowledge in the ethical realm renders the universe much more frightening. He also would prefer to believe that rationality can solve all such disputes. Unfortunately, however, he has been unable to discover convincing evidence that this is so. For this reason, he believes that it would be bad faith to pretend to ourselves that such a method is grounded objectively when we are aware that it cannot be. The existentialist's disappointment, anguish, and awareness of responsibility are, for Allen, more authentic responses to the failure of the human attempt to ground ethics than are the arguments of those who continue, against all apparent evidence, to claim that we have succeeded.

IV. Joy, Simplicity, and Hope

Thus, returning to Roche's comments concerning *Crimes and Misdemeanors*, it is true that Allen presents us with no compelling arguments to persuade us of the validity of Ben and Sol's position over that of Jack and Judah. The reason for this, I have argued, is that Allen believes it would be a violation of his integrity as an artist if he were to suggest that an objective ground for ethics exists when he has himself been unable to discover such a ground.

And yet, Allen's conscience requires him to argue for adherence to some form of moral structure. Admittedly, the moral code he proposes in his films is open to many criticisms. Allen makes it quite clear that those who choose the path of morality are by no means assured of a happier or a more successful life than those who choose the path of hedonism. Again and again in his films, he shows us characters who choose morality over self-interest only to end up worse off than those who strive solely for material success. To an Aunt May, Isaac Davis, Danny Rose, and Cliff Stern would all appear to be losers; yet, Allen clearly believes, by adhering to standards of personal honor and integrity, they are living much more meaningful lives than those who, like Yale, Lester, and Judah, have traded their souls for material gain and the satisfaction of their senses.

Allen cannot prove that we ought to act morally. Indeed, his despair derives from his recognition that all empirical evidence seems to confirm Lloyd's claim in *September* that the universe is "haphazard and unimaginably violent." And yet, like Soloveitchik's Adam the second, Allen cannot resist the spiritual impulses within himself. On those occasions when he allows himself the indulgence of faith, he chooses to believe in a moral structure that justifies and rewards its attendant sacrifices by instilling a sense of righteousness, which is much more precious than material success. Allen allows Sol to acknowledge that even if he knew with certainty that his faith was false — that the universe was truly hollow — he would still choose to believe rather than betray the only values upon which a meaningful life may be constructed.

There is no way to predict where Allen's internal struggle will finally lead him. Perhaps the character who best symbolizes this struggle is Louis Levy, the philosopher whose faith and strength of will were strong enough to survive the Holocaust and to create an optimistic postwar philosophy. Levy may have been driven by despair to commit suicide midway through *Crimes and Misdemeanors*; yet, at the film's conclusion, he is miraculously resurrected as the spokesperson for a bittersweet moral optimism, which is able to proclaim that "most human beings seem to have the ability to keep trying, and even to find joy, from simple things like the family, their work, and from the hope that future generations might understand more." Perhaps someday Allen will be able to celebrate Levy's faith without also feeling the obligation to share in his despair.

APPENDIX:
QUESTIONS AND ANSWERS
WITH WOODY ALLEN

How This Exchange Came About

In April of 1993, I sent a letter to Woody Allen's publicist, Leslee Dart of P. M. K. Publicists, informing her of my book and asking for an interview with Allen concerning the philosophical themes in his work. A few days later, I received a telephone call from Ms. Dart in which she indicated that Allen had decided to lend his support to my book by answering written questions (and helping me to obtain photos for inclusion). I was told that I could submit as many written questions as I wished and that Allen would choose which questions he wished to answer. The following month, I submitted a list of fifty questions, as well as a first draft of the book.

There then followed a year during which I regularly contacted Ms. Dart's office by phone and mail in order to determine when I might receive answers to my questions. On each occasion, I was told that Allen was extremely busy but that he would be responding within the next few weeks. Finally, in May of 1994, I was lucky enough to speak to Ms. Suzy Berkowitz, who assured me that she would find out the reasons for the long delay. In a few days, she called me back and told me that my list of questions was much too long. She recommended that I submit no more than a half-dozen questions.

Once I had submitted my shortened list, she kept in regular contact with me until, on July 13, 1994, I received a fax from Allen containing his answers (without the questions listed). In the following transcript, I have combined my questions with the appropriate answers. In some cases, Allen consolidated my questions by giving one answer to two questions. I have numbered my questions to make this clearer, and I have corrected minor errors of grammar or punctuation contained in the fax.

The Transcript

LEE: (1) There appear to be a number of tensions within your work. Philosophically, perhaps the greatest tension is between the desire of many of your characters to ground their lives in a set of traditional ethical values while, simultaneously, they sadly acknowledge that no ontological foundation can currently be found to justify such a belief. This tension could be called "the existential dilemma," as it plays a vital role in the work of a variety of so-called existential philosophers, especially the early writings of Jean-Paul Sartre. Do you agree that a concern with this dilemma pervades your work? Do you believe that it is ever possible to resolve this conflict between despair and a hope based on some sort of faith?

(2) In your films, you often oppose the roles of reason and emotion in the living of an authentic life so as to suggest that you favor the honesty of one's emotional intuitions over the constructs of logic. Is this an accurate reading of your views? What are you saying about the proper roles of "sense and sensibility" in constructing meaning for one's life?

ALLEN: [*Combined answer to (1) and (2)*] Conflict between despair and hope can only be resolved on an individual basis, not in any general theoretical way. Faith can't be come to by reason — it's a gift, perhaps even a blind spot or flaw, but helpful, like [a] denial mechanism. Reason goes so far and I admire it. Intuition is just reason but accomplished in the leap rather than taking all the steps.

LEE: (3) There appear to be two endings to *Crimes and Misdemeanors*, the apparently pessimistic exchange between Judah and Cliff, and the more hopeful soliloquy presented by Louis Levy in a voice-over as we watch Ben dance sweetly with his daughter. I contend that the more hopeful interpretation is the correct one, that Judah, despite his protestations to the contrary, continues to be plagued by feelings of guilt, and that Louis Levy's suicide does not eliminate the possibility of constructing a meaningful life based on work and family. Would you agree? By the way, am I correct in thinking that the character of Louis Levy is based on Primo Levi?

ALLEN: You are wrong about Judah; he feels no guilt and the

extremely rare time the events occur to him, his mild uneasiness (which sometimes doesn't come at all) is negligible.

Louis Levy was related to Primo Levi only unconsciously. I wasn't aware of the similarity in name till long after the picture was out and someone pointed it out to me. I'm very aware of Levi's writing and he is probably present on an unconscious level.

LEE: (4) Throughout your films, many relationships are presented as being of the "Pygmalion-Galatea variety," i.e., relationships between a mentor and an apprentice which always end in the emotional suffocation of the apprentice and the abandonment of the mentor. Additionally, in your most recent films, you seem to take a more pessimistic, Sartrean approach which asserts the impossibility of authentic romantic commitment. What are your current views on these issues?

ALLEN: In relation to impossibility of authentic romantic commitment — this is a question of pure luck, the interfacing of two enormous complexities, and the delusion that it can be "worked at" is just that. Efforts by the parties may aid in a small way but have the same relation to the success of a relationship that a writing class has to a real reader.

LEE: (5) From the many references in your work, it is clear that you are quite familiar with the most influential philosophers in the Western tradition. Although you often make fun of them quite cleverly, you take many of their concerns very seriously. Which philosophers have most interested you? With which do you most agree and disagree? I would be particularly interested to read any of your views on Sartre, Heidegger, Buber, Nietzsche, and Kierkegaard.

ALLEN: *Sartre:* Romantic, politically terrible, great fun to read. *Heidegger:* Very brilliant but a phlegmatic bore to read. *Buber:* A very interesting perspective and full of good insight on the relational experience of existence. *Nietzsche:* The Michael Jordan of philosophers, fun, charismatic, dramatic, great all-around game. *Kierkegaard:* Very witty and romantic. The only one who can write and push religion without turning you off and perfect for the Me generation.

LEE: (6) I see similarities between the philosophical themes which concern you in your films and those to be found in the films of Alfred Hitchcock. For example, Hitchcock's *Vertigo* portrays a man obsessed by his attempt to transform a woman into his ideal lover, a theme which pervades your films. Both of you deal with issues of authenticity, commitment, moral responsibility, and gender roles. In *Crimes and Misdemeanors,* you venture into the Hitchcockian genre for the first time. You show your awareness of this by ingeniously using a clip from *Mr. and Mrs. Smith*, Hitchcock's one foray into the comedy genre with which you have so often been identified. In *Manhattan Murder Mystery*, you explicitly deal with Hitchcockian themes reminiscent of those explored in *Rear Window* and *Vertigo*. Do you see any similarities between your concerns and those of Hitchcock?

ALLEN: With the exception of *Strangers on a Train, Notorious,* and *Shadow of a Doubt* I don't think much of Alfred Hitchcock. I totally disagree with Truffaut's idolization and laughable intellectualization of this delightful but totally shallow entertainer. *Rear Window* succeeds in spite of Hitchcock's pathetic direction of it only because the story is so compelling that it's foolproof. Despite great praise by Vincent Canby, Andrew Sarris and dozens of other film critics, I and the friends I watch films with find *Vertigo* a dreadful howler.

Sorry to have taken so long to answer you but I'm sure you realize my life has suffered from overstimulation these past two years.

Good Luck —
Woody

BIBLIOGRAPHY

Allen, Woody. *Getting Even*. New York: Random House, 1971.

———. *Side Effects*. New York: Random House, 1980.

———. *Without Feathers*. New York: Random House, 1975.

Ayer, A. J. *Language, Truth and Logic*. Paperback. New York: Dover, 1952.

Bailey, Peter J. *The Reluctant Film Art of Woody Allen*. Lexington, KY: The University Press of Kentucky, 2001.

Beauvoir, Simone de. *The Ethics of Ambiguity*. Translated by Bernard Frechtman. Secaucus, New Jersey: Citadel, 1976.

———. *The Second Sex*. Translated and edited by H. M. Parshley. New York: Vintage, 1974.

Becker, Ernest. *The Denial of Death*. New York: Free Press, 1973.

———. *Escape from Evil*. New York: Free Press, 1975.

———. *The Structures of Evil*. New York: George Braziller, 1968.

Berlin, Isaiah. *The Hedgehog and the Fox*. New York: Mentor, 1957.

Brode, Douglas. *The Films of Woody Allen: Revised and Updated*. Secaucus, New Jersey: Citadel, 1991.

———. *Woody Allen: His Films and Career*. Secaucus, New Jersey: Citadel, 1985.

Buber, Martin. *I and Thou*. Translated by Walter Kaufmann. New York: Scribner's, 1970.

Camus, Albert. *The Myth of Sisyphus and Other Essays*. Translated by Justin O'Brien. New York: Vintage, 1983.

Cèbe, Gilles. *Woody Allen* (in French). Paris: Editions Henri Veyrier, 1984.

Coursodon, Jean-Pierre. "*Maris et Femmes:* Manhattan Melodrama" (in French). *Positif*, no. 382 (Dec. 1992): 8–12.

Dostoevsky, Fyodor. *The Brothers Karamozov*. Translated by Constance Garnett. New York: Heritage, 1949.

———. *Crime and Punishment*. Translated by Constance Garnett. New York: Random House, 1956.

Edwards, Paul, editor in chief. *The Encyclopedia of Philosophy*. 8 vols. Reprint. New York: Macmillan, 1972.

Gilmore, Richard. "Visions of Meaning: Seeing and Non-seeing in Woody Allen's *Crimes and Misdemeanors*." *Film & Philosophy*, Special Issue on Woody Allen (July 2000): 115–125.

Girgus, Sam B. *The Films of Woody Allen*. New York: Cambridge University Press, 1993.

Goldberg, Nathan. *Passover Haggadah*. New York: Ktav, 1966.

Guerand, Jean-Phillipe. *Woody Allen* (in French). Paris: Editions Rivages, 1989.

Hein, Norvin; Karff, Samuel E.; *et al. Religions of the World*. 3rd edition. New York: St. Martin's Press, Inc., 1993.

Henry, Michael. "'J'espère que c'est à cause de *Tootsie!*' entretien avec Sydney Pollack." *Positif*, no. 382 (Dec. 1992): 13–15.

Hirsch, Foster. *Love, Sex, Death, and the Meaning of Life*. New York: McGraw-Hill, 1981.

Hösle, Vittorio. "The Greatness and Limits of Kant's Practical Philosophy." *Graduate Faculty Philosophy Journal* (New York: Philosophy Dept., New School of Social Research) 13, no. 2 (1990): 133.

_____. *Die Krise der Gegenwart und die Verantwortung der Philosophie: Transzendentalpramatik, Letztbegründung, Ethik*. 2nd Edition. Munich: Beck, 1994.

_____. "Questions Concerning the Grounding of Objective Idealism." *Graduate Faculty Philosophy Journal* 17, nos. 1–2 (1994): 245–287.

_____. "Why do we laugh at and with Woody Allen?" *Film & Philosophy*, Special Issue on Woody Allen (July 2000): 7–50.

Jacobs, Diane. *...but we need the eggs: The Magic of Woody Allen*. New York: St. Martin's Press, 1982.

Jones, Ernest. *Hamlet and Oedipus*. New York: Doubleday/Anchor, 1954.

Kael, Pauline. "Circles and Squares." Edited by Gerald Mast and Marshall Cohen. In *Film Theory and Criticism*, 3d ed. New York: Oxford University Press, 1985.

Kaufmann, Walter, editor. *Existentialism from Dostoevsky to Sartre*. Revised and expanded. New York: Meridian, 1975.

King, Kimball, editor. *Woody Allen: A Casebook*. New York: Routledge, 2001.

Krier, William J. "'Blazoned Days:' Meaning Changes in the Films of Woody Allen." *Film & Philosophy*, Special Issue on Woody Allen (July 2000): 144–153.

Lax, Eric. *On Being Funny: Woody Allen and Comedy*. New York: Charterhouse, 1975. Reprint. New York: Manor, 1977.

_____. *Woody Allen: A Biography*. Paperback. New York: Vintage Books, 1992.

LeBlanc, Ronald. "Deconstructing Dostoevsky: God, Guilt, and Morality in Woody Allen's *Crimes and Misdemeanors*." *Film & Philosophy*, Special Issue on Woody Allen (July 2000): 84–101.

Lee, Sander. "Alfred Hitchcock: Misogynist or Feminist?" *Post Script: Essays in Film and the Humanities* 10, no. 3 (Summer 1991): 38–48.

_____. "The Central Role of Universality in a Sartrean Ethics." *Philosophy and Phenomenological Research* 46, no. 1 (Sept. 1985): 59–72.

_____. "A Critique of Henry Veatch's *Human Rights: Fact or Fancy?*" In *A Quarter Century of Value Inquiry*, edited by Richard T. Hull, 355–372. Value Inquiry Book Series. Amsterdam: Rodopi, 1994.

_____. "The Essence of the Human Experience in David Lynch's *Blue Velvet*." In *Inquiries into Values and Ethical Views: The Inaugural Sessions of the International Society for Value Inquiry*, 569–584. Lewiston, Maine: Edwin Mellen, 1988.

_____. "Existential Themes in the Films of Alfred Hitchcock." In vol. 11 of *Philosophy Research Archives*, edited by Robert Turnbull, 225–244. 1985.

_____. "The Failure of Sex and Love in the Philosophy of Jean-Paul Sartre," In vol. 11 of *Philosophy Research Archives*, edited by Robert Turnbull, 513–520. 1985.

_____. "Philosophical Themes in Hitchcock's *Rear Window.*" *Post Script: Essays in Film and the Humanities*, 7, no. 2 (Winter 1988), 18–28.

_____. "Sartre's Acceptance of the Principle of Universality." In vol. 10 of *Philosophy Research Archives*, edited by Robert Turnbull, 1984.

_____. "'Sense and Sensibility': Sartre's Theory of the Emotions." *The Review of Existential Psychology and Psychiatry* 17, no. 1 (1983): 67–78.

Maltin, Leonard. *Leonard Maltin's TV, Movies, and Video Guide.* New York: Signet, 1990.

Nichols, Mary P. *Reconstructing Woody: Art, Love, and Life in the Films of Woody Allen.* Lanham, MD: Rowman & Littlefield Publishers, Inc., 1998.

_____. "Woody Allen's Search for Virtue for a Liberal Society: The Case of *Mighty Aphrodite.*" *Film & Philosophy*, Special Issue on Woody Allen (July 2000): 57–67.

Nietzsche, Friedrich. *Thus Spake Zarathustra.* Translated by Walter Kaufmann. New York: Penguin, 1978.

Oaklander, Nathan L. *Existentialist Philosophy: An Introduction.* 2nd edition. Upper Saddle River, New Jersey: Prentice Hall, 1986.

Olafson, Frederick. *Persons and Principles: An Ethical Interpretation of Existentialism.* Baltimore: Johns Hopkins University Press, 1967.

Orth, Maureen. "Mia's Story." *Vanity Fair*, Nov. 1992, 214–220, 294–300.

Pamerleau, William C. "Rethinking Raskolnikov: Exploring Contemporary Ethical Horizons In Woody Allen's *Crimes And Misdemeanors.*" *Film & Philosophy*, Special Issue on Woody Allen (July 2000): 102–114.

Percy, Walker. *The Moviegoer.* New York: Avon, 1980.

Plato. *The Republic.* Translated by Desmond Lee. New York: Penguin, 1983.

Pogel, Nancy. *Woody Allen.* Boston: Twayne, 1987.

Rand, Ayn. *The Fountainhead.* New York : New American Library, 1971.

Rilke, Rainer Maria. *New Poems.* Translated by J.B. Leishman. London: Hogarth, 1964.

Roche, Mark. "Justice and the Withdrawal of God in Woody Allen's *Crimes and Misdemeanors.*" *Film & Philosophy*, Special Issue on Woody Allen (July 2000): 68–83.

_____. "Vico's Age of Heroes and Age of Men in John Ford's film *The Man Who Shot Liberty Valance*," *Clio* (Ft. Wayne, Indiana) 23 (Winter 1994): 131–147.

Rosten, Leo. *The Joys of Yiddish.* New York: Pocket, 1970.

Russell, Bruce. "The Philosophical Limits of Film." *Film & Philosophy*, Special Issue on Woody Allen (July 2000): 163–167

Sarris, Andrew. "Notes on the Auteur Theory in 1962." In *Film Theory and Criticism*, edited by Gerald Mast and Marshall Cohen, 527–540. 3d ed. New York: Oxford University Press, 1985.

Sartre, Jean-Paul. *Being and Nothingness.* Translated by Hazel Barnes. New York: Washington Square, 1971.

_____. *The Emotions: Outline of a Theory.* Translated by Bernard Frechtman. New York: Philosophical Library, 1948.

_____. *Existentialism and Humanism.* London: Methuen, 1948.

_____. *Imagination: A Psychological Critique.* Translated by Forrest Williams. Ann Arbor: University of Michigan Press, 1962.

_____. *Nausea*. Translated by Lloyd Alexander. New York: New Directions, 1964.

_____. *No Exit and Three Other Plays*. Translated by Lionel Abel. New York: Vintage, 1989.

_____. *"What Is Literature?" and Other Essays*. Cambridge, Massachusetts: Harvard University Press, 1988.

Shales, Tom. "Woody: The First Fifty Years." *Esquire*, April 1987, 88–95.

Soloveitchik, Joseph B.. *The Lonely Man of Faith*. New York: Doubleday Dell, 1992.

Taylor, Paul W. *Principles of Ethics: An Introduction*. Belmont, California: Wadsworth, 1975.

Vigiotti, Robert. "Woody Allen's Ring of Gyges and the Virtue of Despair." *Film & Philosophy*, Special Issue on Woody Allen (July 2000): 154–162.

Weitz, Morris, editor. *Twentieth-Century Philosophy: The Analytic Tradition*. New York: Free Press, 1966.

Westfall, Joseph. "Listening in/to Woody Allen's *Crimes and Misdemeanors*." *Film & Philosophy*, Special Issue on Woody Allen (July 2000): 126–143.

Wood, Robin. *Hitchcock's Films*. Cranbury, New Jersey: A.S. Barnes, 1977.

Yacowar, Maurice. *Loser Take All: The Comic Art of Woody Allen*. New expanded edition. New York: Frederick Ungar, 1991.

_____. "Text/Subtext in *Everyone Says I Love You*." *Film & Philosophy*, Special Issue on Woody Allen (July 2000): 51–56.

INDEX